Language and society in the German-speaking countries

Language and society in the German-speaking countries

MICHAEL G. CLYNE

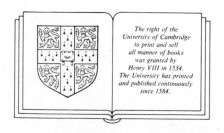

The right of the
University of Cambridge
to print and sell
all manner of books
was granted by
Henry VIII in 1534.
The University has printed
and published continuously
since 1584.

Cambridge University Press

Cambridge

London   New York   New Rochelle

Melbourne   Sydney

Published by the Press Syndicate of the University of Cambridge
The Pitt Building, Trumpington Street, Cambridge CB2 1RP
32 East 57th Street, New York, NY 10022, USA
296 Beaconsfield Parade, Middle Park, Melbourne 3206, Australia

First published 1984

Printed in Great Britain by Pitman Press, Bath

Library of Congress catalogue card number: 83-23981

British Library Cataloguing in Publication Data
Clyne, Michael G.
Language and society in the German – speaking
countries.
1. German language – Sociolinguistic aspects
I. Title
438   PF3112

ISBN 0 521 25759 X hard covers
ISBN 0 521 27697 7 paperback

SE

Contents

Contents

Contents

Tables

Maps

Introduction

This book is intended as an introduction to the sociolinguistic situation in those countries in which German is the national language or one of the national languages. It is an attempt at a synthesis, for the English reader, of a number of existing studies drawn from a variety of sources. Some of the results are reinterpreted, some are complemented by investigations of my own, in order to present a coherent picture. It is hoped that this synthesis may be of some use to students of sociolinguistics and to students and teachers of German. The references in brackets (according to social science conventions) are meant to direct the reader to the source of the information. Translations are given for the benefit of those with limited German, and a glossary of some linguistic terminology employed is intended for germanists and other readers with little training in linguistics. Some of the studies used as a basis employ linguistic methods set in a social context while others apply sociological methods to deal with broader questions of language behaviour, policy and attitudes. In the framework of this monograph, these diverse methods are considered complementary. Due to the enormity of the subject matter under consideration, it has been impossible to deal with every topic for each German-language country. Some areas have been researched much less than others and can be treated only sketchily in this book.

Chapters 1 and 2 focus on German as a national language in the two Germanies, Austria, Switzerland, Liechtenstein and Luxembourg, noting differences in form and function. This treatment precedes the discussion of the social and geographical stratification of German in the Germanies and Austria in Chapter 3 because I am deliberately distinguishing between 'dialect' and 'national variety'. The latter chapter looks at social and educational aspects and implications of dialect use. It should be noted that the use of diverse tools and measures makes comparisons across studies, regions, and (especially) countries in 3.1.1 and 3.2 very difficult. Many of the available sociolinguistic and dialectological studies are very limited in scope and do not by any means capture the full extent of variation. They point rather to general tendencies. Most of the examples in Chapters 1 and 2 are from the lexical and phonological levels since grammatical markers are more significant in distinguishing regional and social varieties than in differentiating national varieties. Of course, any selection of lexemes is arbitrary and cannot be regarded as representative. All German-language countries have problems or dilemmas concerning nationhood or ethnicity (where their people belong or do not belong). In each case, it is a language related or language marked problem.

Chapter 4 discusses communication norms and communication barriers. Some of the topics arise partly from Chapter 3. In Chapter 5, attention is directed to the Anglo-American influence on contemporary German in each of the German-language countries, while Chapter 6 concentrates on pragmatic aspects of communication, especially systems of address. Chapter 7 deals with aspects of language and politics in various German-language countries, approached through contextual language data collection.[1] In Chapter 8, I attempt to bring together some further linguistic manifestations of social change that do not fit into the detailed chapters preceding.

The study of the sociolinguistics of German is a rewarding one, for it offers the opportunity of comparing the same language in action in societies with different historical and cultural traditions or different socioeconomic and political systems. In fact, German is the only European language that has official status in both the capitalist and the socialist bloc.

Generally, the Federal Republic of Germany is referred to as the Federal Republic and the German Democratic Republic as the GDR. However, English stylistics make it difficult to use these terms to designate people from these countries, and the Federal Republic cannot be used adjectively. Therefore, 'East German' and 'West German' are employed to fill the gap.

---

[1] The data were collected up to 1980, and the first draft of the manuscript was completed early in 1981.

To prevent the scope of this book from extending to unmanageable dimensions, I shall exclude from consideration languages other than German minority languages such as Danish and Frisian in the Federal Republic, Sorbian in the GDR, Hungarian, Croatian and Slovenian in Austria. I shall not deal with the other languages of Switzerland – French, Italian, and Rhaeto-Romansh. The discussion of French in Luxembourg in Chapter 1 is restricted to the triglossic situation in that nation and the influence of French on Letzebuergesch and on Luxembourg Standard German. While the German spoken by and to guest workers in the Federal Republic is treated briefly under 4.4, there will be no examination of the first languages of the guest workers as used in German-language countries.

Acknowledgements

My thanks are due to all those who have provided me with information for this monograph, especially Inter Nationes (Bonn) and the Bundeskanzleramt (Vienna), and to Irene Donohoue Clyne, Charles Ferguson, Ferenc Fehér, Anne Pauwels, Pavel Petr, Philip Thomson, Monty Wilkinson, and C.U.P.'s anonymous referees for helpful comments. I am indebted to Leslie Bodi, Norbert Dittmar and Wolfgang Klein who read the manuscript and suggested numerous improvements which have been incorporated into the text. The remaining inadequacies are of my own making. I also thank Sue Campbell and Michael Dargaville for research assistance, Laura Magyary for typing the manuscript, and Jeremy Mynott and Penny Carter for their kind co-operation. I acknowledge with gratitude a 'Special Research Grant' from Monash University in 1980. I am also indebted to Richard Samuel and Joe Hajdu for permission to use and modify their language map.

May 1983   Michael Clyne
                                                             Monash University

Map 1   Places mentioned in the text
      States of:

Federal Republic	Austria
A Schleswig-Holstein	1 Vorarlberg
B Hamburg	2 Tyrol
C Lower Saxony	3 Salzburg
D Bremen	4 Carinthia
E North Rhine-Westphalia	5 Styria
F Hessen	6 Upper Austria
G Rhineland-Palatinate	7 Lower Austria
H Saarland	8 Burgenland
I Baden-Württemberg	9 Vienna
J Bavaria	

Map 2   Dialects and dialect groups
Source: based on Samuel and Hajdu (1969: 13).

1

German as a pluricentric language

1.1 German – a national and international language

German, like English, French, Serbo-Croatian, Spanish, Arabic, Bengali, Chinese, and other languages, is an instance of what Kloss (1978: 66–7) terms a *pluricentric* language, i.e. a language with several national varieties, each with its own norms.

German is the mother tongue of over 94 million people divided among a number of different countries, and has official (or quasi-official) status in six. In each of these it appears in a different form and has different functions. Each nation has its own *standard variety* of German with which its people identify.

None of the national varieties of Standard German has developed into a separate language. Kloss (1978: Ch. 1) gives two criteria for language status: *Abstand* (distance) and *Ausbau* (elaboration). Some languages are guaranteed recognition as such, merely because of their distance from other languages (e.g. Frisian as distinct from Dutch and English). Some, on the other hand, could, historically speaking or in terms of linguistic distance, be regarded as varieties of another language but are independent because they are assigned the same functions as all other (standard) languages, usually to stress political distinctiveness (e.g. Macedonian as distinct from Bulgarian; Moldavian as distinct from Rumanian).

The countries with German as an official (quasi-official) language are:

Federal Republic of Germany (with West Berlin) – 61.3 million users – a highly industrialized, economically successful country with a 'contemporary' capitalist society, linked to the European Community, NATO and the Western Bloc.

1

German Democratic Republic – 16.8 million users – the highly industrialized, most prosperous power of the Eastern Bloc, with a socialist political and social system.

Austria – 7.5 million users – the old centre of Central Europe, which still maintains cultural links with non-German-language countries in both Eastern and Western Europe and enjoys the advantages of active political neutrality (i.e. even-handed politics, rather than non-involvement, see also 7.2.2). It has the only news agency linked to all capitals in east and west. It has undergone a separate development from Protestant North Germany since the Reformation and from the Prussian-dominated 'ethnic' state of Germany (*'Kleindeutschland'*) in the 19th century. 'The Habsburg monarchy was the very antithesis of a national state' (Keller 1978: 474), being neither *'großdeutsch'* (embracing all German-language areas)[1] nor *'kleindeutsch'* (being only German-language-using but embracing only some German-language areas). In 1910, only 23.5 of the 48.8 million citizens of the Austro-Hungarian Empire were native German speakers (Keller 1978: 474). Austria has developed into a highly industrialized welfare state and has derived self-esteem and a new national awareness from its unparalleled recent economic prosperity (low unemployment and relatively low inflation rate).

Switzerland with official national multilingualism (German, French, Italian and, at the regional level, also Rhaeto-Romansh) has its languages distributed on a territorial principle, i.e. most cantons (states/counties) are monolingual, a few are bilingual, and one, Graubünden, is trilingual (in German, Italian, and Rhaeto-Romansh). The 4.2 million German users (about 74% of Swiss citizens) provide us with a classic example of what Ferguson (1959) terms *diglossia* – a language situation in which two different languages or varieties are functionally complementary. In this case Standard German (the 'High' language, hereafter H) fulfils written and formal spoken functions, while the other, a dialect (the 'Low' language, hereafter L), is used for informal ones. But as we shall see, L is intruding into the domains of H. Switzerland has enjoyed long-standing economic prosperity and political neutrality. It practises

---

[1] I am using the term 'German-language areas' in preference to 'German-speaking areas' since some employ both spoken and written German, others only one of these, as we shall see later.

grassroots democracy deriving from the survival of feudal and early capitalist structures into the modern age, something that often appears parochial.

Luxembourg has a population of 330,000 who use Letzebuergesch, German and French in a *triglossic* (i.e. functionally complementary) relationship.[2] Through language planning, i.e. the development of a policy on the use and standardization of languages, the dialect of Luxembourg (*Letzebuergesch* or Luxemburgisch) has been assigned some of the functions of a standard language. In many ways, Luxembourg has maintained many traits of a 19th century German duchy with a small bureaucracy and an inherent conservatism. But it has, for centuries, enjoyed an intermediate position between the French and German spheres of influence and now has a strong attachment to the European Community. It acts as host to its parliament and court and to several of its agencies, and many a Luxembourgian looks forward to the day when his city becomes the capital of a United Western Europe!

Liechtenstein – 15,000 users – is a tiny principality of a predominantly rural character without an airport or a railway station, which is sandwiched between Austria and Switzerland and has assumed the function of a tax haven for many business companies.

In addition, German now enjoys regional official status in some eastern parts of Belgium (150,000 German speakers). In Namibia (once German South West Africa), there are state schools employing German as a medium of instruction, and German dialect-speaking minorities are to be found in Alsace-Lorraine (1.5 million) and South Tyrol (200,000) whose H language is, to an increasing extent, French or Italian respectively. Furthermore, German is spoken as an ethnic minority language in the U.S., Canada, Australia, Brazil, Colombia, and other immigrant countries.

In Western Europe, German is a declining international language, having been largely superseded by English. It still retains much of its importance as a lingua franca in Eastern Europe, e.g. between Poles, Czechs and Hungarians. There are at present over 2 million pupils learning German in the Soviet Union alone (Inter Nationes 1979: 35), and Rumania, Hungary and Czechoslovakia still have sizeable

---

[2] There are, among them, about 62,500 foreign-born, some of whom have great difficulty in adapting to the complex situation.

German-speaking ethnic minorities. In both east and west, German remains a language of research documentation in disciplines as varied as theology, philosophy, music, linguistics, anthropology, chemistry and engineering.

1.2 The status of pluricentricity

The pluricentricity of English and Spanish is now widely recognized; this is much less the case with German. Most publishers, as well as the language research institutes, dictionary committees and international German-teaching institutions are based in either the Federal Republic or the GDR (the most powerful German-speaking countries in west and east respectively), so that 'German German' has predominated in status and as a model for foreigners learning the language. The Austrian government has, in recent years, attempted to redress this situation by establishing 61 Austrian *Lektorate* (native speaker lectureships) at foreign universities (Rittenhauer 1980: 24).

There is a semantic confusion between *deutsch/German* pertaining to Germany, and *deutsch/German* pertaining to the pluricentric language. Moreover, there is a widespread acceptance, by Germans, of the superiority of their variety. For instance, a series of books has appeared in Mannheim, describing the 'Besonderheiten der deutschen Schriftsprache' (special features of written German) in Austria, Switzerland and Luxembourg – and also in the U.S., Canada, Australia, Brazil, and several other countries – based on German-language newspapers there. The emphasis is on the exotic *in comparison with* (*particular*) *West German norms*. However, there is no such book dealing with the *special* features of German Standard German, whether published in one of the Germanies or in Austria, Switzerland or Luxembourg. This may also testify to the 'linguistic cringe' existing in the latter countries. In Austrian and Swiss, as well as in German publications (e.g. Ebner 1969, Kaiser 1969–70, Rohrer 1973, Hutterer 1978, Moser 1979, Schläpfer 1979, Kühn 1980, Mentrup 1980), German Standard German is designated as *binnendeutsch* (internal German), i.e. its centrality is implied. The exception is the *Österreichisches Wörterbuch* (see 1.4.2).

There is widespread confusion among germanists when they consider the German language in Austria and Switzerland. The national standard varieties of these countries are often devalued and assigned according to the historical classification of the base dialects to 'South German regional dialects' (*oberdeutsche Mundarten*) or Bavarian and Alemannic dialects respectively (e.g. by Stroh, Bach, Collinson). As the North German standard is the one with the highest status in the Federal Republic, and the GDR (Moser 1961a: 181), Austrian Standard German and Swiss Standard German are widely regarded, in the Federal Republic, as regional norms rather than national ones on a par with that (those) of the Germanies.

'Richtiges Österreichisch ist anders als richtiges Deutsch' (Correct Austrian is different from correct German), says H. Weigel in *O du mein Österreich* (1968). As Reiffenstein (1973, 1977) has shown, Austrian German comprises a number of sub-systems from local dialect to standard, whose use is governed by the communication situation (see 3.1). The authoritative Mannheim *Duden-Rechtschreibung* (spelling) dictionary lists not only words that are specifically Austrian or Swiss, but also ones that are *regionally* distributed within Germany. The 1974 edition of the authoritative *Duden-Aussprachewörterbuch* (and even the 1969 edition of Siebs' *Deutsche Aussprache*, traditionally the prescriptive handbook of German pronunciation) have made allowances for Austrian and Swiss Standard German. The *Duden-Aussprachewörterbuch* has refrained from listing such pronunciations as specific entries. The policy of GDR linguists varies from that of West German ones on this question. To emphasize the 'cultural independence and separateness' of the two German states, many scholars in the GDR tend to accept that there are four *nationalsprachliche Varianten* of the German language – those of the GDR, the Federal Republic, Austria and Switzerland (e.g. Lerchner 1974 and various books in the *Sprache und Gesellschaft* series). But GDR linguists rarely turn their attention to any but the first two, although the Leipzig edition of the *Duden* records more Austrian Standard items than the West German dictionary (Fenske 1973).

When people from different German-language countries communicate among themselves, they tend to adapt to the 'German' Standard.

1.3 The Germanies

The main division of dialects in German-speaking countries is based on the High German Sound Shift, which began between the 6th and 8th centuries AD in the south of the German-language region, and gradually moved northward. It changed voiceless stops /p/, /t/, /k/ to voiceless fricatives /f/, /s/, /x/ ([ç] or [x]); and affricates /pf/, /ts/ and /kx/, and voiced stops /b/, /d/, /g/ to voiceless stops /p/, /t/, /k/. Dialects (in the far south) which were wholly, or almost wholly affected by the sound shift are termed *oberdeutsch* (Upper German), those (in the centre) partially affected are designated as *mitteldeutsch* (Central German), and those (in the north) unaffected are termed *niederdeutsch* (Low German). (See map 2.) Compare the following pairs of words:

> Low German *p*ad, Upper German *Pf*ad (English path);
> Low German *d*ag, Upper German *T*ag (English day);
> Low German i*k*, Upper German i*ch* (English I);
> Low German bö*k*, Upper German Bu*ch* (English book);
> Low German ski*p*, Upper German Schi*ff* (English ship);
> Low German hei*t*, Upper German hei*ss* (English hot);
> Low German, Central German *K*uh, Swiss German *Ch*ue (English cow);
> Low German *b*äk, Upper German (Bavarian) *P*ach (English brook);
> Low German *d*ör, Upper German *T*ür (English door);
> Low German *g*enuch, Upper German (Bavarian) *k*enug (English enough).

Until the 17th century, Low German had a separate existence as an important literary and commercial language; as the language of the Hanseatic League, it was even used as a lingua franca throughout Northern Europe. There is now no standard Low German language. There is also a division based on original tribal languages – Saxon, Franconian, Alemannic, Bavarian – which lives on in the regional stratification of the German-language area (see map 2).

Of all the German-language countries it is West Germany that encompasses the widest dialectal diversity. Austrian dialects are Bavarian (Upper German) in origin, except for the Alemannic varieties in Vorarlberg. Swiss ones are Alemannic (Upper German), except for a few Bavarian dialects in the Upper Engadine, and Luxembourgian ones are Franconian (Central German). The GDR, however, has both Low German and Central Saxon dialects, and the dialectal basis of the Federal Republic is even more varied – Low, Central and Upper German: Saxon, Franconian, Alemannic and

Bavarian. Moreover, because of the political and cultural fragmentation of the German-speaking regions of Europe, and the specific forms of territorial absolutism replacing the Holy Roman Empire, there was no centre comparable to London and Paris that could lend (or impose) its variety as the standard language. So each region had its own language (see Bach 1956, Moser 1961, Keller 1978) at least until the early 16th century, except that in the late 12th and early 13th centuries, there was a Southern (Upper) German compromise language used mainly in courtly literature.

There were two periods of strong nationalist as well as functional motivation for a uniform standard. The first was the 15th and early 16th centuries, and the contributing factors were: the use of German instead of Latin for legal records (*c*. 1400); the rise of the cities, which attracted people from various regions and extended commerce; the invention of the printing press (1450), making possible publication on a large scale, and especially Luther's translation of the Bible (1522–34), which was intended to be accessible to all German speakers. Although there was a 'compromise language' in the South (*das gemeyne Deutsch*) up to the 16th century, the basis for the merging standard language was East Central German,[3] itself originally a compromise. At the time of the Holy Roman Empire, Germany was not a political entity and could be only culturally and linguistically defined.[4] Linguistic nationalism was directed towards promoting the vernacular as opposed to Latin.

The originally East Central German standard gradually permeated both the northern Low German-speaking regions and the Catholic states, and during the 17th and 18th centuries slowly penetrated into Austria and Switzerland. However, it was in the 19th century that the phonological norms were set for what may be termed 'German Standard German'. By this time Prussia had gained a sphere of influence embracing all German-speaking areas of Europe except Switzerland and those that were part of the Austro-Hungarian Empire – first through a customs union (the Zollverein) and then, in

---

[3] See Map 2.
[4] This situation continued into the 18th and 19th centuries. (Cf. Schiller's *Musenalmanach für 1797: 'Deutschland? Aber wo liegt es?* Ich weiß das Land nicht zu finden, wo das Gelehrte beginnt, hört das Politische auf.' *Germany? But where is it?* I do not know where to find the country. Where the scholarly begins, the political ends.) It was the French revolution that sparked off the movement towards a German nation-state.

1871, through political unification. The model for this unity was *kleindeutsch* (i.e. not including Austria).

The linguistic as well as the political leadership was provided by the north. A myth continuing to the present day is that the 'best' German is spoken in Hanover. Because the north (including Berlin) was originally Low German-speaking, and once used High German as a second language, the High German (Standard German) spoken there tended to accentuate a close relationship between phonemes and graphemes, giving the semblance of 'greater correctness'. With minor modifications, the North German pronunciation became the norm for Standard German pronunciation (*Bühnendeutsch*, stage German) in Austria and Switzerland, as well as throughout Germany, in an agreement concluded between the three countries in 1899. Some of the special features of North German that are now part of the German Standard norms are as follows:

> final /Iç/ in words like: fert*ig*: fertig*t*, fertig*t*e;[5]
> long vowels in words like: *A*rt, St*ä*dte, V*o*gt, Beh*ö*rde, w*e*rden, Pf*e*rd;
> /ç/ in: *Ch*ina, *Ch*emiker.

According to Herrmann-Winter (1979: 141), a number of features of North German phonology have normative status regionally in the northern part of the GDR:

> /e/ for German Standard /ɛ/, as in: erw*äh*nen;
> /f/ for /pf/ in initial position and after /m/, as in: *Pf*laume, Sum*pf*;
> /ŋk/ for /ŋ/, as in: A*ng*st;
> short vowels for long ones, as in: Gl*a*s, Z*u*g.

Today, in spite of a high degree of regionalism in South Germany (see Ch. 3), announcers on the Bayerischer Rundfunk (Munich), the Süddeutscher Rundfunk (Stuttgart), and the Südwestfunk (Baden Baden) adopt the same standards, and sound much the same, as their North German counterparts. (This, however, does not apply to Austrian or Swiss Radio.)

Similarly, in the written language, the *Süddeutsche Zeitung* (pub-

---

[5] Though the infinitive *fertigen* takes the South German pattern. This is a problem of syllable boundary; [ç] is used in syllable-final position, [g] at the start of a syllable.

lished in Munich) follows the same norms as the *Frankfurter Allgemeine Zeitung* (cf. Austrian newspapers, whose language is Austrian Standard). The dominance of the German norms has been aided by the fact that most of the large German-language publishing houses were (and are) situated in Germany. At the level of lexicon and grammar, alternatives to the North German norm may be accepted *regionally*, but not as Standard German. This applies, for instance, to words such as *heuer* (*dieses Jahr*, this year), *Jänner* (*Januar*, January), *Gehweg* (*Bürgersteig*, footpath), and to constructions such as *liegen* (to lie), *stehen* (to stand) and *sitzen* (to sit) with the auxiliary *sein* (cf. German Standard and North German *haben*). Also, the tendency towards graphemic integration (adaptation to German spelling) of lexical transfers ('loanwords') from other languages is greater in the Germanies than in other German-speaking countries. But generally, the one aspect of the German language for which a consensus was reached by the German-speaking countries (at the end of the 19th century) was spelling.

Apart from the *kleindeutsch* model, the *großdeutsch* notion incorporating all German-language regions (including Austria, Switzerland and Luxembourg) under the political and cultural domination of Germany seems to have strongly influenced the German attitude towards national varieties of German in other countries. At the political level, the *großdeutsch* principle has been completely discredited through its barbarous climax under Hitler. In attitudes to language, however, the dominance of Germany is still present (see above, 1.2). However, the uneasy relation between norm and usage makes this whole discussion difficult.

So far we have disregarded the question of whether the Standard German varieties of the Federal Republic and the GDR can still be considered one and the same. This will be the subject of our second chapter.

1.4 Austria

According to Wodak-Leodolter and Dressler (1978: 30), 'Standard High German', as described in Siebs (1969) and the Dudens, is 'not used in everyday speech at all and rarely in schools' in Vienna. The 'highest' variety employed in Austria is what Wodak-Leodolter and Dressler term 'Austrian Standard'. The fact that this overlaps in part with South German regional varieties does not alter the reality that it is *Standard* in Austria. As there is no clear description of Austrian Standard German, its status is often confused through prejudice.

At all levels of language there are marked distinctions between local or regional Austrian dialects and Austrian Standard – both in the capital city and the provinces. Due to its belated overall industrialization, Austria still has a more pronounced class structure than the Germanies, and social class and educational background are indicated through the variety of Austrian German (dialect or standard) used. Vienna is the political and cultural centre and its German exerts an influence on the educated speech of the provincial cities (e.g. Graz, Linz, Salzburg, Innsbruck). This influence is weakest in Vorarlberg, which, linguistically and culturally, has much in common with neighbouring areas of Switzerland, and has been making bids for increased political autonomy.

1.4.1 Phonology

At the phonological level, Austrian Standard is distinguished by the following (German Standard abbreviated to GS in the examples):

> Slightly nasalized diphthong [ɛᵉ] for /aɪ/, as in [krɛᵉde] *Kreide*, diphthongs [ɔᵒ] and [ɔᵒᵉ] as in [frɔᵒ] *Frau* and [frɔᵒᵉde] *Freude*. In all three cases, the diphthongal character is slight and the second element lower than in GS (Wodak-Leodolter and Dressler 1978: 35). [o] corresponds to GS [ɔ] in some diphthongs, e.g. [foːədan] *fordern*.
> Initial [st] corresponds to GS [ʃt] in loanwords, e.g. *St*il, *St*rategie.
> Initial [k] corresponds to GS [ç] in loanwords, e.g. *Ch*emie, *Ch*ina.
> There is a tendency towards voiceless initial [s], as in [sausn] *sausen*.[6]
> There is no glottal stop [ʔ]:[erɪnan] *erinnern*, [tjaːta] *Theater*.[6]
> Stylistic variation takes place between final [ɪk] and [ɪç] in words spelt *-ig*, e.g. [ruːɪk] *ruhig*[6] is Austrian Standard informal register.

---

[6] Also in *regional* South German.

[x] occurs after [r] and some front vowels (cf. [ç] in GS), e.g. [kiəxn], [duəx] or [durx] *Kirche(n)*, *durch*. The sequence [ŋk] is found in words such as [aŋkst] *Angst*, [laŋksam] *langsam* (Wodak-Leodolter and Dressler 1978). Also /e/ is [ə] (not [e]) in numbers such as *vierzehn, fünfzehn*, and some words (e.g. *Kaffee* and *Motor*) are stressed on the final syllable (not the initial one as in GS).

Now that the *Duden-Aussprachewörterbuch* has accepted a broader set of pronunciation options, some characteristically Austrian norms (especially those rules also applied in parts of the Germanies) have been included, something that was not the case prior to 1974. Examples of such Austrian pronunciations are the short vowels in: Behörde, Geburt, Harz, Nische, Städte.

1.4.2 Lexicon

At the lexical level, there is an *Österreichisches Wörterbuch*, published under the auspices of the Austrian Ministry of Education, which covers Austrian Standard, and whose 35th edition (1979) lists certain words as 'als bundesdeutsch empfunden' (felt to be West German). Examples of such words are: *albern* (simple, childish), *Aprikose* (apricot), *Kelter* (wine-press), *krakeelen* (to brawl), *Sahne* (cream), *Sonnabend* (Saturday), *Tüte* (paper bag), *tuten* (to toot). The Austrian equivalents are: *dumm/einfältig, Marille, Weinpresse, schimpfen/streiten, Schlagobers, Samstag, Stanitzel/Papiersackerl, hupen*.

Ebner (1969) has recorded the words whose usage is distinctive in Austrian Standard German. Many of these reflect the separate cultural and political development of Austria. They include words in the following fields:

Food: e.g. *Jause* (afternoon tea, in some regions also morning tea, GS *Kaffee*),[7] *Nachtmahl* (dinner, GS *Abendessen*), *Karfiol* (cauliflower, GS *Blumenkohl*),[8] *Kukuruz* (corn, GS *Mais*),[7] *Palatschinken* (pancake, GS *Pfannkuchen*),[7] *Ribisel* (redcurr-

[7] Transferred from neighbouring languages, e.g. Italian, Slovenian. Purism and integration of lexical transfers were never as marked in Austria as in Germany (Fenske 1973: 160).
[8] Also in Switzerland.

ant, GS *Johannisbeere*),[7] *Schwamm* (mushroom, GS *Pilz*), *Zuckerl* (sweet, GS *Bonbon*); also *Schale* (cup, GS *Tasse*).

The home: e.g. *Kasten* (cupboard, GS *Schrank*), *Polster* (cushion, GS *Kissen*), *Plafond* (ceiling, GS *Decke*), *Rauchfang* (chimney, GS *Schornstein*), *Sessel* (chair, GS *Stuhl*), *Stiege* (stairs, GS *Treppe*).

Institutions: e.g. *Lehrkanzel* (professorial chair, GS *Lehrstuhl*), *Matura* (matriculation examination, GS *Abitur*), *Spital* (hospital, GS *Krankenhaus*),[8] *Turnsaal* (gymnasium, GS *Turnhalle*).

For the months: e.g. *Jänner* (January, GS *Januar*), *Feber* (February, GS *Februar*).

Also *Flugpost* (airmail, GS *Luftpost*), *gewesen* (former, GS *ehemalig*), *ehe* (anyway, GS *ohnehin*), and *zu Fleiß* (on purpose, GS *mit Fleiß*). Another speciality of Austrian Standard is the preposition *auf* used with *vergessen* (cf. GS direct object). Lexical transfers *Affaire* (affair), *Praliné* (chocolate, GS *Praline*) and *Kassa* (ticket-office or cash-register) show less graphemic integration in Austria than they do in the Germanies. Some words are umlauted in Austrian Standard, e.g. (zwölf)grädig ((twelve)grade – adj.), (ein)färbig ((one)colour), Kommissär[8] (commissioner), Missionär[8] (missionary) (Rizzo-Baur 1962: 91–2).

Some morphemes are particularly productive in word formation in Austrian Standard. e.g.:

-ler: Kräut*ler* (greengrocer), Post*ler* (postal employee).

-s-: Aufnahm*s*prüfung (entrance exam, GS Aufnahmeprüfung), Ausnahm*s*fall (exception, GS Ausnahm*e*fall), Gesang*s*buch (songbook, GS Gesan*b*uch), Gepäck*s*träger (porter, GS Gepäckträger).

-∅-: Toilettisch (no *-en*) (dressing table), Visitkarte (no *-en*) (visiting card).

-(e)rl: Hintertür*l* (back door), Schnacker*l* (hiccoughs), Wimmer*l* (pimple) (Rizzo-Baur 1962: 92–8).

Austrian German tends to prefer the weak forms of verbs like *senden* (to send) and *wenden* (to turn) (*sendete, gesendet; wendete, gewendet*).

1.4.3 Grammar

Some words have different genders in Austrian and German Standard, e.g. Austrian: *der* Gehalt (salary) (GS *das*);[9] or are single-gender in Austrian Standard while German Standard offers a choice, e.g. Austrian: *die* Trafik (tobacconist's, GS *der/die*. Much less commonly used in GS), *der* Sakko (jacket, GS *der/das*); or offers a choice of gender, where the German Standard noun can have only one gender, e.g. Austrian: *der/das* Aspik (aspic, GS *der*), *die/das* Ersparnis (saving(s), GS *die*), *der/die* Kunde (client, GS *der*) (Rizzo-Baur 1962: 101), *der/das* Monat (month, GS *der*).

Like regional South German, Austrian German employs the auxiliary *sein* with *liegen*, *sitzen*, and *stehen*.[10] *Kündigen* (to give notice) can take the accusative (instead of the dative).

After a stem ending in *-sch*, the 2nd person singular verb ends in *-t* (German Standard: *-st*): nasch*t* (eat sweets), rutsch*t* (slip), wisch*t* (wipe). Words like *Wagen* (car, waggon) and *Kragen* (collar) take an umlaut plural (GS Ø plural).[8]

Austrian dialects (like many German ones) generally lack a preterite (simple past). Consequently it is sometimes used in Austrian Standard by people wishing to shift to a higher register (stylistic level of language chosen according to 'what is actually taking place, who is taking part, and what part the language is playing' (Halliday 1978: 31)), regardless of its applicability according to German grammatical rules of aspect. For instance, single events in the past are therefore sometimes expressed in the preterite instead of the perfect (Kufner 1961: 88–9). This is further evidence of Austria's 'linguistic cringe', as is the transference of certain words from German Standard as 'prestige forms', e.g. *Mädchen* (Aus. *Mädel*), *nachhause* (Aus. *heim*), *guten Tag* (Aus. *Grüß Gott!*)[11] (Eichhoff 1978: 13). On the other hand, it is with Austrian Standard that middle and upper middle class

---

[9] According to Ebner (1969), Austrian Standard is gradually adopting the German Standard norm here.

[10] In Austrian Standard German, *sitzen* is used with the auxiliary *haben* in the meaning of 'to be imprisoned'.

[11] It has been pointed out to me (Leslie Bodi, personal communication) that the opposition *Guten Tag* vs. *Grüß Gott* may be politically motivated (socialist vs. conservative).

13

Austrians identify (Wodak-Leodolter and Dressler 1978: 31).[12] However, Austrian linguists have not as yet investigated the *attitudes* of different sections of the population to German and Austrian speech as has been done for Dutch and Flemish speech among the Dutch-speaking population of Belgium (Geerts, Nootens, Vandenbroeck 1977; Deprez and de Schutter 1980).

1.5 Switzerland

The position of Standard German in Switzerland can be seen only in relation to that of the 'national dialect' Swiss German (*Schwyzertütsch*) which has, in most aspects of its structure, remained more conservative than Standard German.

Swiss German could be developed into an independent language. One of the reasons why it is not a language (Kloss (1978) terms it an *Ausbaudialekt*) is that it exists only in the form of local and regional varieties. It is, as it were, a pluricentric national dialect. Apart from some recommendations on spelling in Swiss German (Dieth 1938), no standardization has taken place. Communication at the inter-regional level is based on slightly adapting your own regional (rather than local) dialect (e.g. Zürich, Basel, Bern German) to that of your speech partner, often by taking over lexemes and other features from Swiss Standard German. (According to Ris (1979), most rural German-Swiss are now bi- or polydialectal.) Urban dialects are expanding in influence, but there are three main focal points, Zürich, Basel and Bern, so that a uniform national dialect is not likely to develop, despite the publication of grammars and textbooks for the learning of Swiss dialects (Moulton 1962). Wolfsberger (1967) has shown that, due to geographical mobility and the effects of the media, there is some levelling-out of dialects, especially in the direction of the standard language. This is particularly so among the younger and the more geographically mobile.

Within a region or locality, the dialect is spoken as the native language and sole language of informal discourse by all classes and sections of society, i.e. it does not have a sociolectal function (Keller 1973: 149; Ris 1979: 153). This reflects the fact that it is competence in Swiss Standard German and not dialect that identifies people socially (Ris 1979: 48, 57), while dialect indicates their regional (cantonal)

[12] For a discussion of arguments in favour of existence of an Austrian (as distinct from German) literature, see Bodi (1980).

origins, and this diglossia identifies them as Swiss. A uniform national dialect might, among other things, destroy the social unity guaranteed by the local and regional dialect.

1.5.1 Diglossia

Standard German is primarily the written language, as its Swiss name *Schriftdeutsch* suggests. The norms are better defined and more consciously observed in this Swiss variety of Standard German, often regarded as a close 'foreign language' (Boesch 1968), than in dialects (Keller 1973: 144). Thus it is often rather stilted in style. Standard German is employed in the National Parliament (along with French and Italian),[13] in secondary and tertiary education, radio and television, formal church services, the press, worldwide fiction literature (the most important contemporary Swiss exponents of which are Frisch and Dürrenmatt), and non-fiction literature, the latter being regarded by Kloss (1978: 40–6) as a litmus test of whether a dialect has become an *Ausbausprache*. Dialect is used in small cantonal parliaments, early primary education, some fiction literature, and increasingly in radio and TV (for some news broadcasts, women's and children's sessions, interviews and discussions, as well as regional radio programmes), weddings and informal evening church services, secondary and tertiary education (colloquia, working groups, practical classes, non-academic school subjects), the military (less formal situations), advertising, and even some formal speeches (Schwarzenbach 1969, Ris 1979). In other words, dialect is making inroads into *informal* speech in *formal* domains, and even into *formal* speech. As a result, new words are transferred from Standard German and integrated into dialect, e.g. *Raumfahrt* (space travel) becomes *Rûmfôrt*, and *Marktforschung* (market research) becomes *Marktforschig* (e.g. in news broadcasts).

1.5.2 Convergence

Keller (1973) points out that lexical pairing between Standard German and dialect leads to convergence, e.g. dialect *rüere* (to throw) is replaced by *werfe*, or *aanlange* (to touch) by *berüere* on the assumption that each Standard German word must have a dialectal

---

[13] Swiss-German dialect can now also be used (Norbert Dittmar, personal communication).

counterpart. The same process has led to grammatical confusion and simplification, e.g. in the Swiss-German words *zweê*, *zwoo*, *zwäi*, the masculine, feminine and neuter words corresponding to *zwei*. So, although there is a discontinuum (i.e. no intermediate variety) between Standard German and the dialects (Ris 1979), interference from Standard German is experienced in the dialects.

1.5.3 Special features of Swiss Standard German

1.5.3.1 *Phonology* The independent position of Swiss Standard German has been strengthened by Swiss neutrality and the recent German past. But while there are norms for Swiss Standard German, the Swiss generally experience a feeling of inferiority as to their proficiency in it (Boesch 1968: 226). Boesch et al (1957) devised norms for Swiss Standard German aimed at a correct German that still 'sounds Swiss' (Moulton 1962: 137) – ones which differ more markedly from the German Standard norms than do the Austrian ones (see 1.4). (Now out of print.) The Swiss guidelines include a rejection of [Iç] for final *-ig* and the acceptance of double consonants, e.g. [bɛllə] *Bälle*, [gassə] *Gasse*, as well as short vowels in: *A*rzt, *J*agd,[14] *M*agd,[14] Kr*e*bs,[14] *O*bst, V*o*gt, L*i*ter,[14] F*a*brik,[14] N*o*tiz,[14] Städte,[14] Pferd, Geb*u*rt,[14] *dü*ster.[14] (Short vowel forms have been accepted in the 1974 edition of the authoritative *Duden-Aussprachewörterbuch*.) Other Swiss Standard pronunciation features are long vowels in: br*a*chte, Gedächtnis, H*o*chzeit, R*a*che, rächen, R*o*st (cf. [rɔst] grill); a differentiation between close [ə] and open [ɛ], as in: *E*sche/*Wä*sche, w*e*tten/h*ä*tten, H*e*ld/h*ä*lt; primary stress on the initial syllable in lexical transfers from French, e.g. '*Büffet*, '*Filet*, '*Glacé*; and a short open [ɛ] in final position, e.g. Coupl*et*, Budg*et* (Keller 1978: 552). Moulton (1962: 140) points out that Swiss Standard German never uses a glottal stop and (1962: 144) that final consonants may be voiced (e.g. [brav]).

1.5.3.2 *Lexicon and grammar* The Swiss follow the *Duden* as the norm of the written language (Müller-Marzohl 1961: 98). There is also a Swiss *Schülerduden* for late primary and early secondary

---

[14] Also Austrian Standard.

classes which follows the norms of written Swiss Standard German (Schläpher 1979). In his two-volume account of the special features of written Standard German in Switzerland, Kaiser (1969) notes:

words that are specific to the Swiss national variety, e.g. *Nachtessen* (dinner), *aper* (snow-free), *sturm* (confused, dizzy), *wimmen* (pick grapes);

words bearing a meaning different to that in other national varieties, e.g. *Base* (aunt as well as cousin), *Kleid* (man's suit as well as woman's dress), *Steigerung* (auction), *staunen* (ponder as well as be amazed), *abdanken* (bury, give funeral speech as well as abdicate); *wischen* (sweep rather than wipe);

word formation specific to the Swiss national variety, e.g. *Altjahr* (new year's eve), *Freikonzert* (open-air concert), *Pastmilch* (pasteurized milk), *Viehhabe/Viehstand* (farm possessions), *Berufsmann* (tradesman), *radiobekannt* (famous through the radio);

word formation devices employed differently in Swiss Standard German than in other varieties, e.g. no *-s*, as in *Auslandgast* (foreign guest), *Kuckuckuhr* (cuckoo-clock), *Sonntagausgabe* (Sunday edition); morpheme *-s* infixed, as in Land*s*gemeinde (rural municipality), Sport*s*teil (sporting section), Zug*s*verbindung (train connection); morpheme *-en* infixed, as in Mai*en*fahrt (May journey), Farb*en*film (colour film); also Schleg*ete* (brawl), Tanz*ete* (dance, social); Gast*ung* (accommodation of guests), Hirt*ung* (looking after cattle); Pöst*ler* (postal employee), Spört*ler* (sportsman), Übernächt*ler* (overnight lodger); lärm*ig* (noisy);

specifically Swiss gender assignment (in some cases of transference from French, closer to the source language), e.g. *der* Bank (seat), Couch, Semmel (bread roll), Drittel (third), Viertel (quarter), Radio; *der* or *das* Dessert, Grammophon, Taxi; *die* Koffer (suitcase), Photo; *das* Bikini, Efeu (ivy), Tram, Tunnel.

In addition, *Geschwister* (brothers/sisters, siblings) may be singular, and *Architekt* and *-ist* words take *-en* only in the plural. *Ob* is still used for *oberhalb* (above) and *Redacteur* (editor) is integrated as *Redaktor*.

The *ß* has been generally replaced by *ss*.

17

An important aspect of Swiss Standard German is the large component of transfers from another national language, French. The German-language part of Switzerland has never imposed its 'germanness' on anyone else, the way Prussia (Germany) and Austria did on their non-German colonial populations. The German loan-creations and loan-translations employed in the Germanies in place of French transfers (*Anschrift* for *Adresse, Bahnsteig* for *Perron*), have, for the Swiss, an unpleasantly 'un-Swiss' (Prussian?) tone about them (Keller 1973: 143). A few examples of French transfers: *Bahnhofbuffet* (station restaurant), *Glace* (ice cream), *Occasion* (bargain, sale), *präsidieren, Retourbillet* (return ticket), *Velo* (bicycle); *geht dir das?* (does that suit you?, based on: *ça te va?*). Due to the diglossic situation with German in Switzerland, French, though the language of far fewer native speakers, is generally the prestige language and the medium of communication between Swiss-French and Swiss-German speakers.

1.6 Liechtenstein

As far as I am aware, no study of the diglossic situation in Liechtenstein has as yet been undertaken. It is, on the whole, similar to that in the German-speaking parts of Switzerland (Josef Wolf, personal communication). However, Standard German in Liechtenstein has not been codified, although it is used more than Swiss Standard German. Also there is a large degree of uniformity in the Liechtenstein dialect, and the capital, Vaduz, houses the headquarters of many foreign businesses run by Standard German speakers. (In July 1980 there were 1106 Germans and 1994 Austrians living in Liechtenstein on residence permits.) The language of administration is Standard German; it is spoken on all official occasions and in all official places. Standard German is the only language used in parliament and the law courts. Church services are conducted in Standard German, and the only publications in dialect are occasional works of dialect poets (Walter Kranz, Pressechef, personal communication). In schools, the dialect is used as a medium of instruction only in the first weeks of Grade 1 (six-year-olds). Its use is permitted in class where the pupils are experiencing difficulties in comprehension or expression. The reading of dialect texts is discouraged, and it is claimed that facility in dialect reading is increased by the reading of Standard German. The general thrust of mother-tongue instruction is to teach the standard language (*Lehrplan für die Primarschulen im Fürstentum Liechtenstein*, n.d.). Dr Josef Wolf, head of Liechtenstein's Schulamt, finds that 'die Mundart (in letzter Zeit) zu oft verwendet wird' (in recent times the dialect has been used too much). (Personal communication, 20 February 1980.)

1.7 Luxembourg

The population of Luxembourg is trilingual – in French, German, and Letzebuergesch (Luxembourgian), the mother tongue and home language of all the Luxemburgers, which is manifested in Middle-Franconian dialects grouped into a northern, an eastern, a western and a southern division. Letzebuergesch is also spoken in and around Arlon in the Belgian province of Luxembourg. There is also a supraregional Letzebuergesch *koine*, based on the dialect of the Alzette Valley in the south, or on a compromise dialect, and transmitted through the capital, where people from all over Luxembourg have gathered and worked together (Hoffmann 1979: 16). Although it is not given any superior status (Newton 1979: 62) it has become the mother tongue of some sections of the upper and middle classes (F. Hoffmann, personal communication).

The planned development of Letzebuergesch towards a sort of *Ausbausprache* has been going on since (with the removal of its French-speaking territory) Luxembourg became a purely German (Letzebuergesch)-speaking state in 1839, but it was precipitated by German invasions in the two world wars and a reaction against the Germanization policy of the Nazis. It has been less of an issue in recent years. It is the independent status of Letzebuergesch together with trilingualism and triglossia that gives Luxembourg its identity of *national independence*. According to the 1948 Constitution, Luxembourg has no 'official languages'. However, French, German and Letzebuergesch fulfil the functions of national languages (Hoffmann 1979). Letzebuergesch is more standardized than Schwyzertütsch (see 1.5, above), with both a dictionary and a grammar of the 'national dialect', but the orthography is based on that of Standard German.

19

1.7.1 Triglossia

The class structure is expressed through the selection of the H language. The upper and middle classes, and especially the intellectuals, use French as their H, while the lower classes prefer German as theirs, partly because it is the main language of primary education, making it more the written language of the masses, and partly because of its closeness to the vernacular. This is no doubt the reason for German being the principal language of the press. It is the intellectuals who are most likely to *write* Letzebuergesch. The strength of the rural dialects reflects the conservativeness of the people (Hoffmann 1969).

Each 'language' has its own domains of use.

French is the language of the Court, of administration, street and shop signs, and secondary and tertiary education (Luxembourg has a teachers' college, a conservatorium, and an economics college, but university students have to go abroad – mainly to West Germany, Belgium or France). French is also the language of the Luxembourg TV station, but West German and Belgian television have good reception too. French is used for communication with many of the Italian and Portuguese migrant workers (Jakob 1981).

Letzebuergesch and French are both used in parliament.

Standard German is the main language of primary education, of the Luxembourg press, except for some cultural articles and public and private announcements, and of non-fiction literature (making Letzebuergesch an *Ausbaudialekt*, see Kloss 1978: 40–6). There are Luxembourgian editions (in French) of one French and one Belgian newspaper.

Standard German and Letzebuergesch share the domains of church, fiction literature, and primary education (Hoffmann 1979; Verdoodt 1968: IV. Teil). All these languages (and some others) may be heard on Radio Luxembourg, which beams beyond the national boundaries.

The well-defined divisions between the use of French, Standard German and Letzebuergesch even within domains may best be illustrated by the following examples:

> *Education*: the medium of preschools is Letzebuergesch, that of primary education German, while secondary education is conducted in French. But in all classes, Letzebuergesch is used sometimes (Hoffmann 1979: 43–9). All three languages

are taught as subjects at primary and secondary schools. It is the school that makes trilinguals out of a basically monolingual, Letzebuergesch-speaking population.

Correspondence: personal letters tend to be in Standard German (although some intellectuals correspond in Letzebuergesch), but French is the language of local business and official correspondence. The balance between Standard German and French is determined by social distance (degree of intimacy) and class (Hoffmann 1979: 55–65).

Law courts: evidence is given in Letzebuergesch, the counsels speak French (the language of the legal code), and the language of the written verdict is Standard German (Hoffmann 1979).

Parliament: most debates are conducted in Letzebuergesch, documents and draft laws are printed in French, and texts for public distribution are in German (Christophory 1974: 23).

Literature: there are three Luxembourgian literatures, one in each language (Hoffmann 1979: 65–107).

Of all German-speaking countries, Luxembourg is the one where the obligatory point of code-switching into the standard language is highest (Zimmer 1977: 156). Because so many communication needs are fulfilled by Letzebuergesch, and there are two 'High' languages, Standard German is considered even more 'foreign' in Luxembourg than in Switzerland: '. . . das deutsche Wort wird nicht minder als das französische als Fremdling empfunden' (the German word is not felt less foreign than the French one) (Bruch 1953: 95). While Swiss-German transfers new words mainly from Standard German, it is French which is the main basis for renewal in Letzebuergesch.

Because of resentment against Germany, there is a taboo on the use of Standard German for anything relating to national and personal identification, e.g. street signs, letterheads, public notices, tombstones (Hoffman 1979: 59). While Letzebuergesch is the language of solidarity and French that of power and prestige, Standard German is merely a language of convenience.

1.7.2 Special features of Luxembourgian Standard German

There are no special guidelines for the use of Luxembourgian Standard German in Luxembourg, which is basically not a spoken language. German Standard is regarded as the norm and taught in schools, though this norm is not generally adhered to. Language planning efforts and linguistic studies have concentrated on Letzebuergesch, not on Luxembourgian Standard German, as Standard German is the small language community's medium of communication with the neighbouring Federal Republic. In his booklet *Das Luxemburgische im Unterricht* (1969), Hoffmann, one of the best experts on Letzebuergesch, enumerates the *Fehler* (errors) of Luxembourgian children learning through the medium of German at school. His remarks complement Magenau's (1964) analysis of the German of the Luxembourgian press.

The three main special influences on Standard German in Luxembourg are the national dialect, archaisms, and the French language. At the phonological level, this results in a French-type intonation (what Hoffmann (1969: 56) calls 'Schaukelmelodie', rocking melody); lenization (e.g. /t/→[d]; [ʃ] for /ç/; and an absence of aspiration (e.g. [apbau] for [apʰbau]; [mɪttaɪlən] for [mɪtʰtaɪlən]).

In vocabulary, the above-mentioned influences are responsible for the lexical or semantic transference of words not normal in some other national varieties of Standard German and for the use of words employed far more frequently in the Standard German of Luxembourg than that of some other countries covered. This is the case especially in the fields of administration, politics, education, entertainment and commerce, e.g. *Theatercoup* (unexpected event), *Militär* (soldier), *Konferenzler* (conference delegate), *Deputierter* (M.P.), *Dancing* (dance-hall),[15] *Television*, *Coiffeur* (hairdresser), *Spezerei* (grocery), *Camion* (truck), *Camionneur* (truck driver), *Velo* (bicycle),[15] *total*, *klassieren* (classify), *klimatisieren* (aircondition), *Weißkäse* (cottage-cheese, cf. German *Quark*, Austrian *Topfen*), *Athenäum* and *Lyzeum* (types of secondary schools), *beilernen* (to learn something extra). Prepositions cause some confusion.

In word-formation, the dominant 'special feature' is the infixed *-s* morpheme, as in: Nacht*s*tisch (bedside-table), Sonntag*s*nacht (Sunday night), Sport*s*kritik (sports review). Also: *Bett* (bed), *Hemd* (shirt), and nouns ending in *-ment* tend to take an *-e* plural, while *Schlüssel* (key), *Teller* (plate), *Fenster* (window), *Messer* (knife) and *Zettel* (note) are often given an *-n* plural. The analytical comparative

[15] Also Swiss Standard.

with *mehr* is often preferred; discontinuous constituents are sometimes brought closer together (e.g. Du *hättest sollen* am Tage vorher mit ihr fahren, German and Austrian Standards: Du hättest . . . sollen), and Subjunctive II is frequently generalized for indirect speech. Some nouns transferred from French frequently keep their French gender (e.g. *der* Jury, Programm, *die* Pedale, Magenau 1964: 78–9) (Hoffmann 1969, Magenau 1964).

1.8 Some lexical differences

A number of maps in Eichhoff's (1978) *Wortatlas der deutschen Umgangssprachen* demonstrate the importance of the national boundary in the overall distribution of lexical selection, e.g. *Schluckauf* (FRG), *Schlucken* (GDR), *Schnackerl* (Austria), *Gluggsi* or *Higgsi* (Switzerland) (hiccough, Map 5); *das Plastik* (FRG, Austria), *Plast(e)* (GDR), *der Plastik* (Switzerland) (plastic, Map 77); *(Blue)Jeans* (FRG, Switzerland), *Niethose* (GDR),[16] *(Blue)Jean* (Austria) (Map 86).

In addition, there are, of course, dialectal differences within each country. However, for some words and constructions, the older historical-dialectal model applies, i.e. North German (incl. GDR) vs. South German (incl. Austria, Switzerland), e.g. *sein/haben* as auxiliary (Map 125), though *sein* has National Standard status only in Austria and Switzerland; *Gaul, Pferd, Roß* (horse, Map 99). *Fleischhauer* and *Fleischhacker* (butcher) are both recorded in the *Österreichisches Wörterbuch* which, however, designates *Metzger* as 'landschaftlich' (regional). *Fleischhauer* is listed as Austrian and *Fleischhacker* as 'Upper Austrian colloquial' in the Mannheim Duden, which records *Metzger* and *Fleischer* without comment (together with 'North German' *Schlächter*). *Fleischer* appears without comment in the Leipzig *Duden*, which lists *Metzger* as mainly 'South and West German' and *Schlächter* as 'Low German'. The other two designations are not mentioned at all.

1.9 Brief summary

From the above it can be concluded that Austria, Switzerland and

[16] But cf. below, 7.7.

Luxembourg each have their own varieties and norms of Standard German, which differ from the German Standard in phonology, lexicon, morphology and syntax. In the case of Austria and Switzerland, the norms have been defined but not as clearly as those of German Standard. German 'cultural imperialism', semantic muddle, and a 'linguistic cringe' have resulted in attributing an inferior status to the other standard varieties and in creating a confusion between these and dialects. But a new national awareness, especially in Austria, has been reflected in a stronger identification with one's own national variety. In Switzerland and Luxembourg the domains reserved for Standard German are decreasing. While in Luxembourg, most of the language planning efforts have gone into the 'national dialect', it is the Austrian Standard that has been the object of some language planning in Austria (e.g. the dictionary). It must be remembered that Austria's cultural traditions and orientation are vastly different from those of Germany. It is probably to keep up the link between the standard literary language and educated spoken language that Austria has not developed a 'national dialect' in preference to a national variety of the standard language.

The relation between standard, dialect, and 'in-between varieties' in the Germanies and Austria will be compared in Chapter 3. Whereas the use of dialect in these countries is connected not only with regionalism but also with social stratification and/or educational background, class structure appears to be reflected in Switzerland in the levels of the national *standard* variety and in Luxembourg through the relationship between French and German as High languages. Of all the German-language countries, Luxembourg is the one with the highest threshold of code-switching into the standard language. It is the country with the fewest national bonds to Standard German and the greatest discontinuum between dialect and Standard German. The Germanies, of course, lie at the other end of the scale.

1.10 Further reading

There is no single book that covers the pluricentricity question. Kloss (1978) deals with the development of new quasi-languages such as Swiss-German, Letzebuergesch, and Low German. The *Österreichisches Wörterbuch* gives insight into the Austrian conception of

Austrian Standard lexicon,[17] as does Ebner (1969), while Reiffenstein (1977) discusses the status of and variation in Austrian Standard German. Rizzo-Baur (1962) and Kaiser (1969/1970) deal with the Austrian and Swiss Standards respectively. For the sociolinguistic situation in the German-language part of Switzerland, see Ris (1979) and Keller (1973). Hoffmann (1979) is the best account of the Luxembourg situation. The reader will find Eichhoff's (1977–8) word atlas useful.

Althaus, Henne and Wiegand (1980) is recommended as a general handbook of German linguistic questions, containing select bibliographies on all entries.

---

[17] Dressler and Wodak (1982a) have cast doubt on some of the entries, e.g. the labelling of *Tomate* (tomato) as 'bundesdeutsch' when this word has largely replaced *Paradeiser*, which has lost much of its social acceptability in Austria.

2

'East' and 'West' German

2.1 Two German national varieties of Standard German?

The evolution of the national varieties of Standard German described in Chapter 1 took centuries of political and cultural development, sometimes more divergent, sometimes more convergent. It is not much more than three decades since the GDR and the Federal Republic were established and only four years longer since Germany was divided into occupation zones. Since 1949, the two Germanies have not only become separate entities; they also have vastly different social and political systems, opposing political and economic alignments, and have in many ways undergone separate cultural developments. All this has been reflected in the language, while language at the same time has contributed to the differentiations in people's consciousness. In fact, the German language gives unique contrastive insights into the ideologies and approaches of the Eastern and Western Blocs.

A very important factor in the distinctive relationships between language and national identity in the Federal Republic and the GDR is the way in which the two German states see the link with their past. Both have experienced a 'discontinuum' in time as well as in space. However, it was a major concern of the Federal Republic to come to grips with its past or, at least, to be seen to have done so. In the process of *Wiederaufbau* (reconstruction), 'mainstream' West Germans who have, at least in part, accepted the responsibility for the National Socialist past, have developed a shyness towards nationalism and national identification. Certainly, nationalism has been pushed from 'high' culture to the 'low' culture of some groups (e.g. returned soldiers' groups). The GDR has selected some landmarks in high-culture history as its pre-history (e.g. Luther, Dürer, Goethe, Schiller) and, otherwise, within the framework of *(Neu)aufbau* (construction), has distanced itself from the German past, the 'Fascist past', which, according to its political ideology, lives on in the capitalist west. Because of this basic assumption, there are some traditions which can be continued far more in the GDR than in the Federal Republic. Folk-singing is but one example (*Zeit* 1981). Though the Hallstein Doctrine of the Federal Republic claiming sole rights to represent 'the German nation' is a policy of the past, many people in the Federal Republic often still refer to their country as *Deutschland* (see also 7.1). To the GDR, 'Deutschland' no longer exists (*Spiegel* 1978a). The East German state designates itself exclusively as (*die*) *DDR*, (*die*) *Deutsche Demokratische Republik* or *Unsere Republik* (Our Republic), and its citizens as *DDR-Bürger* (GDR-citizens). One of the problems of delineating the German national variety or varieties is the uncertainty of the concept of 'Germany' today – 'Das Kind mit zwei Köpfen' (The two-headed child), as Buch (1978) describes it.

The GDR and the Federal Republic have never agreed on whether the Standard German used in the two countries today constitutes two different national varieties. Up to the mid-60s, West Germans emphasized the emerging differences and warned that these could lead to a communication breakdown between east and west which could damage the 'unity of Germany' (e.g. Moser 1961c: 21). The German of the Federal Republic was treated as the norm, and East German neologisms and style (such as the frequent stringing together of genitive phrases) were criticized (as Hellmann (1978: 17) has shown). On the other hand, up to about 1963, the GDR ignored the whole problem of emerging language differences. Since the mid-60s, research on the topic in the Federal Republic has been more interdisciplinary, with greater emphasis on documentation, and the literature there has tended to play down the differences and stress the common bond which the two Germanies have through the language (Hellman 1978: 19ff),[1] while GDR scholars have highlighted the distinguishing characteristics, giving 'East' and 'West' German a status similar to that of Austrian and Swiss Standard German

[1] Although Moser (1980), in an encyclopaedia article, refers to German in the GDR as a new 'regional variant' of Standard German.

(Lerchner 1974: 265).[2] This is largely due to the political stances we have already mentioned: the Federal Republic prefers to think in terms of a single German nation, the GDR conceives of two nations, a socialist one and a capitalist one, torn apart through class struggle (Schmidt 1972). Discussion of this point became quite intense in the early months of 1981, when the Federal Republic's retiring diplomatic envoy in the GDR, Günter Gaus, suggested it might be necessary to abandon the concept of a single German nation (*Zeit* 1981). Of course, many inhabitants of the GDR are interested in preserving close contact with the Federal Republic as can be seen in the reception of the West German media (see below, 2.3). As Hartung et al (1974: 541) have pointed out, it is impossible 'to name an exact point in time when a speech community (*Sprachgemeinschaft*) ceases to exist' (my translation). But they do claim that there is a separate *Kommunikationsgemeinschaft* (communication community) in each of the Germanies, as well as in Austria and Switzerland.

In 1.8, a few examples were mentioned of lexical items used predominantly in one German-language country. *Schlucken*, *Plast(e)* and *Niethose* (hiccoughs, plastic, blue jeans) were cited for the GDR. None of these words are from the field of politics; *Schlucken* is not a neologism. There are lexical differences which have long existed between the east and the west of the German-language area. The radiation of forms from Berlin in the days of Prussian expansionism affected the west less than the east. With the development of two Germanies the distinctiveness has become more marked and more established. The use of *Niethose* and *Plast(e)* reflect two other tendencies in the GDR: a much greater trend towards purism than in the west, especially the Federal Republic (see 5.3.5); and the Russian influence, which brought 'internationalisms' to the GDR by a different (more devious) route than that which they took to the Federal Republic.

2.1.1 Levels of language affected

The differing views on East and West German national varieties are also due to the criteria employed by East and West Germans to make

---

[2] It was in the mid-60s that products of the GDR started being marked 'made in DDR' (not 'made in Germany') (Kristensson 1977: 127).

their judgment. What they agree on is large-scale lexical differences, particularly in the fields of politics, economics, and social organization and institutions. West German scholars generally argue that the differences are purely lexical in nature (e.g. Schlosser 1981) and belong to the public not the private domain (e.g. Pelster 1981). Hellmann (1973: 141) found that 10.7% of words in several volumes of *Neues Deutschland*, the daily organ of the Sozialistische Einheitspartei (SED) were unfamiliar to his West German student informants. More than half that number were incomprehensible to them, but most of these were proper nouns. Hellman (1973: 150) stresses the psychological factor – some people read something that is unfamiliar to them and decide that they don't *want* to understand it. However, we must not lose sight of the close relationship between language and social context. It is the unfamiliarity with the total context of the Standard German used in the other German state that can lead to breakdowns or restricted efficiency in inter-German communication. What is lacking is a systematic examination of East–West communication in everyday (dialogue) situations. Such a project would be difficult to carry out for practical reasons. Using as his basis West German schoolchildren visiting peers in the GDR, and newspaper texts, Pelster (1981) contends that once institutions specific to east or west are explained, there are no communication difficulties between people from the two Germanies. What has not yet been taken into account is another function of a national variety of a language, namely (national) identification. If people do not identify with their own national variety, they are probably distancing themselves from their political situation.

While the *lexicosemantic* aspects of written 'East' and 'West' German have been investigated extensively, pronunciation differences have not been the subject of a study. As there are no proven specific syntactic or phonological characteristics of Standard 'East German' and 'West German', apart from those in southern or northeastern regional standards, West Germans feel justified in not seeing them as different national varieties. A few isolated examples of possible new developments in the syntax of GDR newspapers are sometimes cited (Moser 1961c: 20 and Becker 1956: 91), e.g. the participial construction influenced by Russian: *Zurückgekehrt erfuhr er die ganze Geschichte* (returned, he learned the whole story; instead of: *Nach seiner Rückkehr* – after his return). However, no distinctive features appear to have stabilized in GDR syntax. English influences on syntax in the Federal Republic are mentioned below, under 5.2.2; but these are not seen as overall changes in grammatical rules of German in the Federal Republic or the GDR. Nor is the frequent occurrence of genitives in what Hellmann (1978: 27) terms the GDR public register ('öffentliche Sprache'), epitomized in the media, and illustrated in the following extracts.

'Die Verordnung orientiert auf die weitere Erhöhung *der* Qualität und Wirksamkeit *der* ambulanten medizinischen sowie arbeitsmedizinischen Betreuung in den Einrichtungen *des* Betriebsgesundheitswesens.' (The regulation gives directions concerning the further increase in quality and effectiveness of out-patients' medical and industrial medical care in institutions of health in the work-place.) (*Neues Deutschland*, East Berlin, **33**, 31; 6 February 1978; p. 2.)

'Heute trifft das Mitglied *des* Politbüros *des* Zentralkomitees *der* MPLA-Partei *der* Arbeit und Premierminister *der* Volksrepublik Angola ein.' (The member of the politburo of the Central Committee of the MPLA-Labour Party and prime minister of the Peoples' Republic of Angola will arrive today.) (*Der Morgen*, East Berlin, **34**, 31; 6 February 1978; p. 1.)

Because of the importance placed on 'participation' in political life in the GDR, i.e. the need for a command of the political institutions and political language, most people – especially the younger ones – develop some competence in the public register and the ability to switch between the public and private registers. For obvious political reasons, no comparison has yet been undertaken between the 'private register' of GDR speech and West German everyday speech.

The GDR notion of different national varieties in the two Germanies is largely conditioned by a *functional pragmatic* approach, stressing vastly changed communication needs in a society based on Marxist-Leninism, and *semantic* criteria, i.e. the *content* that is being expressed in words and sentences which varies in the two Germanies. The 'semantic' argument is often countered in the Federal Republic by the response that differences are mainly in the field of politics and, after all, the right-wing Christlich-soziale Union and the Deutsche Kommunistische Partei (in the Federal Republic) also disagree on the meaning of such words as *Demokratie*. However, the fact is that, in the GDR, the officially designated meanings are part of the shared experience – part of the consciousness – of all members of the speech community, regardless of their degree of commitment to socialist ideology. The crucial question is: Who decides what is a *separate* national variety (when this involves two potential speech communities), and on the basis of what level of language?

There has been much research in both Germanies on this subject. In the Federal Republic, the Institut für deutsche Sprache has established a research centre now based in Mannheim for the documentation of East and West German (including comparative frequency counts based on newspapers and literature), through the initiative of Hugo Moser, one of the pioneers in this field.

A brief glance at East and West German newspapers will reveal a basic difference in the information transmitted. All GDR newspapers display an ideological unity with the state and tend to report on progress in productivity by collectives throughout the country, party news, international conferences, third world liberation movements, and visits by leaders of friendly nations; as well as emphasizing conflict, unemployment, inflation and disease in the west. Even the more conservative newspapers in the Federal Republic carry western news of a negative kind, while small-scale economic developments rarely get a mention. This is one of problems encountered in comparing East and West German newspapers with a view to quantifying linguistic differences, and it is not surprising that such differences in the economic and political fields have been highlighted, as have been the *Freund- und Feindwörter* (friend- and foe-words.)

2.2 Some lexicosemantic differences

The most important lexical and semantic differences between the Standard German of the GDR and that of the Federal Republic are due to the following:

> the creation of new vocabulary to express technological, social, economic and political change, especially in the GDR, and to name new institutions (2.2.1);
>
> the nature of 'outside influence', notably lexical transference from English in the Federal Republic and, to a lesser extent, semantic transference from Russian in the GDR (2.2.2);

31

semantic shift for the reason indicated under 2.2.1 (2.2.3);

the dropping of vocabulary considered obsolete in the GDR, especially words relating to middle-class-capitalist value systems (2.2.4);

language planning, particularly in the GDR, where, under the heading of *Sprachkultur* (4.1, below), it is seen as being justified by the need to equip all citizens with the linguistic wherewithall to participate in the decision-making process (2.2.5).

As Korlén (1973: 146) has pointed out, the potential communication gulf between the Federal Republic and the GDR was increased in the 1950s and 60s by the West German ban on the KPD (Kommunistische Partei Deutschlands), which reduced to a minimum West Germany's confrontation with Marxist ideas. Such a confrontation started with the student revolt of the late 60s and early 70s, whose register was based on a number of traditions (see 7.5).

Many of the new words in widespread use in the GDR are technical terms which express concepts of party and institutional organization, reflect Marxist-Leninist world-views, or depict the situation where people work together in small units, competing against other such units.

Donath (1977) tests the semantic elements constituting central GDR terms such as *operativ* and *sozialistische Arbeitskultur* (socialist work culture) among the staff (administrative as well as production workers) of two factories in the Berlin area. For *operativ*, the production workers and apprentices regarded two meanings, 'in operation' and 'settled speedily and in an unbureaucratic way' (e.g. pertaining to a machine breakdown), as equally central. The master-craftsmen considered the latter to be the primary meaning. Direct responses to spontaneous questions on the meaning of *sozialistische Arbeitskultur* show that, whereas production workers considered the aesthetic appearance of the place of work most central to this concept, leading members of staff considered good physical and technical conditions to be the primary semantic element. However, more indirect reactions point to the centrality of the work safety aspect. All this suggests that many abstract GDR terms are complex symbols representing a generalization of concrete experiences. (This, of course, applies to all abstract terms anywhere.)

2.2.1. Among the many neologisms created since the division of Germany are:

GDR

In the area of economics and politics:

beauflagen – to produce a compulsory quota per factory or other unit

Friedenslager – ('peace camp') the Eastern Bloc (also used ironically , see 7.7)

Funktionseinheit – section, e.g. of hospital or polyclinic

Soldi-Marken – stamps bought by East Germans to raise money for Third World development aid. (Abbreviation for: *Solidaritätsmarken*, 'solidarity stamps'.)

In education:

Elternaktiv – elected representatives of parents of children in a particular class at school. It arranges co-operation between parents, teachers and the official youth organization, Freie Deutsche Jugend (FDJ). Furthermore, it 'supports socialist education in families' (Meyer 1973 IV: 245)

Erweiterte Oberschule (EOS) – ('Extended upper school') – all schools

FEDERAL REPUBLIC

In politics and economics:

Gastarbeiter – guest worker

Kurzarbeiter – worker on short time

Lastenausgleich – equalization of burdens

Mitbestimmung – workers' participation

Radikalenerlaß – barring people with 'extremist' political views from the civil service (see 7.1)

In education:

Gesamthochschule – multidisciplinary tertiary institution, usually including facilities for training both primary and secondary teachers

Gesamtschule – comprehensive school

While the Federal Republic uses *Aktualitäten* or *Wochenschau* for 'newsreel theatre', the corresponding word in the GDR is *Zeitkino*. (Reich 1968, Meyer 1973, Klappenbach and Steinitz 1976.)

33

2.2.2 Some lexical peculiarities of GDR German (e.g. *Überbau*, 'superstructure') have their origins in the Socialist Movement from its German (i.e. pre-Russian) beginnings under Marx and Engels. More, however, have been transferred from Russian and integrated, to a greater or lesser extent, into the German phonological and/or grammatical system, as in the following examples.

> *Apparatschik* – ironical term for functionaries
> *Diversant* – sabotage agent, referring to western military strategies (from Russian *diversija*)
> *Kader* – élite of state organizations and institutions; also: each individual in his/her function within an organization (from Russian *kadry*)
> *Kollektiv* – group of people working together, e.g. *Autorenkollektiv* (authors' collective), *Fußballkollektiv* (football collective), *Gewerkschaftskollektiv* (trades union collective), *Küchenkollektiv* (kitchen collective), *Schülerkollektiv* (pupils' collective), *Wörterbuchkollektiv* (dictionary collective, team)
> *Kombinat* – organizational form in which different branches of industry or stages of production co-operate
> *Agrostadt* – combination of collective farms into a (Soviet-type) agricultural settlement (from Russian *agrogorod*). This is an example of partial transfer.

According to Lehmann (1972), only about 11% of words in the GDR due to Russian influence are lexical transfers. 66% are semantic transfers (i.e. the meaning of an existing German word is changed by analogy with Russian). It is such words that will bear different meanings in the GDR and the Federal Republic (FRG). These include:

> *Akademiker* – GDR: member of the Academy of Sciences
> FRG: member of the academic professions; graduate
> *Aspirant* – GDR: junior academic in training for higher degree
> FRG: candidate (general)
> *Brigade* – GDR: a small collective involved in competition with other small groups for national awards, e.g. *Mähdreschbrigade* (harvest-thresher-brigade), *Maurerbrigade* (bricklayer-brigade), *Schlosserbrigade* (locksmith-brigade), *Traktorenbrigade* (tractor-brigade)

FRG: military brigade
Brigadier – GDR: leader of a *Brigade*
FRG: rank in the army
Neuerer – GDR: initiator of new methods of 'socialist work'
FRG: reformer, (general) innovator
Patenschaft – GDR: social activity through systematic help of
one organization by another
FRG: God-parenthood
Schrittmacher – GDR: worker who is an innovator of tech-
nological progress within the socialist system
FRG: pace-setter (person, athlete or heart machine). (But
these meanings are also current in the GDR.)

The Polish free trades union was generally referred to by West
German daily papers as *Solidarität* and East German ones as
Solidarnošč. In the GDR, the positive term *Solidarität* was used in
references to gifts of aid sent by the GDR to Poland (*Kraft der
Solidarität* – strength of solidarity, *Solidaritätsgüter* – solidarity
goods, *Neues Deutschland*, 23 December 1981; *Strom der Solidarität* –
stream of solidarity, *Neues Deutschland*, 21 December 1981).

Semantic transference from Russian also gave rise to words
unknown in the Federal Republic, as illustrated in the following
examples.

Kulturhaus – workers' educational and social centre, including
a library, classrooms, and a theatre (cf. Russian *dom kultury*)
Plansoll – production target for a particular group and product
within a plan (cf. Russian *planovyj* + noun)

Lexical transference from English in the Federal Republic far
exceeds lexical transference from either Russian or English in the
GDR and, since English is only one of several languages that can be
taken as a third language in GDR schools, English influence on 'West
German' is likely to function as a communication barrier in the
GDR, at least as much as Russian influence on 'East German' does in
the Federal Republic. (Chapter 5 is devoted to Anglo-American
influence on all national varieties of Standard German.)

2.2.3 Sometimes meanings will be specialized or extended according
to the social and political needs of the country or society. So, in the

35

Federal Republic, *Flüchtling*, while used generically for refugees, often means specifically 'a refugee from the east to the west', while in the GDR it means 'a refugee from the west to the east', and a neologism, *Republikflüchtiger* (republic-fugitive), has been created to cover those fleeing from the GDR (*Unsere Republik*) to the Federal Republic. The meaning of *Faschismus* has been extended in the GDR. Such developments can be monitored through the East and West German versions of the *Duden-Rechtschreibung* (spelling) dictionary, published in Mannheim and Leipzig respectively, although the prescriptive nature of the *Duden* has to be taken into account. The following are their respective definitions of *Faschismus*:

antidemokratische nationalistische Staatsauffassung (antidemocratic nationalistic conception of the state) (Mannheim *Duden* 1973: 268).

chauvinistische und offen terroristische Erscheinungsform des Imperialismus in der Epoche der allgemeinen Krise des Kapitalismus (chauvinistic and overtly terrorist manifestation of imperialism in the era of the general crisis of capitalism) (Leipzig *Duden* 1972: 133).

Another example is *Imperialismus*:

Ausdehnungs-, Machterweiterungsdrang der Großmächte (urge of the great powers to expand and extend their powers) (Mannheim *Duden* 1973: 348).

Höchstes und letztes Stadium des Kapitalismus, gekennzeichnet durch die Konzentration von Produktion und Kapital in Monopolen und den Drang zur Neuaufteilung der Welt durch Kriege (highest and final stage of capitalism, characterized by the concentration of production and capital in monopolies and the urge to repartition the world through war) (Leipzig *Duden* 1972: 202).

In the 1950s and early 60s, the Federal Republic designated the GDR as *Mitteldeutschland* (Central Germany; not *Ostdeutschland*, East Germany), in order to keep alive 'hopes' for the return of the former German provinces east of the Oder–Neiße Line, which they referred to as *Ostdeutschland*. Before the Second World War, *Mitteldeutschland* had meant the area between North and South Germany.

Some semantic shifts in the German of the GDR make it possible there to differentiate between a development in the East (with a positive loading) and one in the West (with a negative loading), as part of an east–west socialist–capitalist conflict model – (what Reich (1968) calls *Freund- und Feindwörter*). The following are examples of this.

Agitation (referring to east, positive)

Demagogie (referring to west, negative)

Bündnispolitik – alliance policy (or *Zusammenarbeit* – co-operation) (referring to east, positive)

Koalitionspolitik – coalition policy (referring to west, negative)

Gewinn – collective profit for the whole of society (east)

Profit – profit for an individual or a private company (west)

Wettbewerb – means of increasing productivity through competition between work units to the common good (east)

Konkurrenz – competition between individuals or private companies to increase their profit (west)

(Reich 1968; *SBZ von A bis Z* 1966) (*Gewinn* and *Wettbewerb* are the words of Germanic origin corresponding to *Profit* and *Konkurrenz*.)

2.2.4 Some words have been dropped from the German vocabulary in either the Federal Republic or the GDR. These include, in both Germanies, words reminiscent of the Nazi period, e.g. *entdeutschen* (to de-germanize), *Familienforschung* (racist genealogy), *Wehrmacht* (German armed forces under the Nazis), *Reichsbahn* (*Reich* railways, Federal Republic), *auslandsdeutsch* (ethnic German in other countries, GDR), *Nationalstolz* (national pride, GDR).

However, the GDR unashamedly and paradoxically continues the use of some terms 'inherited' from Nazi Germany, e.g. the name of the GDR railways, *Deutsche Reichsbahn*. Erich Honecker, president of the State Council of the GDR and Secretary-General of the SED's Central Committee, has declared: 'Die *Nationale Volksarmee* der DDR ist die einzige deutsche Armee, die diesen Namen verdient' (The *National People's Army* of the GDR is the only German army deserving this name.) (*Neues Deutschland*, 17 February 1981) – using two favourite Nazi words – *national* and *Volk*. The latter has been rid of its past associations in the GDR and is frequently collocated with *Republik* to denote socialist states. Other examples of deletions in the GDR may be found by comparing the Mannheim and Leipzig *Dudens*. They include words referring to a capitalist social organization, e.g. *Armenrecht* (poor law), *Arbeitgeber* (employer; literally, work giver), *Arbeitslosenfürsorge* (unemployment benefits), *Schulgeld* (school fees), and also *gutbürgerlich* (homely; literally, good bourgeois, as in *gutbürgerliche Küche*), which, to a socialist, contains an unpleasant contradiction in the word formation (good + bourgeois)! Also missing in the Leipzig *Duden* are certain military terms, e.g. *Berufsheer* (professional army), *Kriegsdichtung* (war poetry), and religious expressions such as *Gottesfurcht* (awe of God), *Tischgebet* (grace). In GDR museums, *vor Christus* (BC) and *nach Christus* (AD) have been replaced by *u.z.* (*unsere Zeitrechnung*, our era) and *v.u.Z.* (*vor unserer Zeitrechnung*, before our era). In GDR newspapers, death notices invariably use the generic verb *sterben* (to die) and not the euphemisms for which other German-language countries opt, e.g. *hinscheiden* (to pass on), *verscheiden* (to pass away), *heimgehen* (to go home), *aus dem Leben scheiden* (to pass out of life).

There are some words employed in the early years of the GDR which have now been dropped or replaced, e.g. *Kolchos* (from Russian, collective farm) replaced by *LPG* (Landwirtschaftliche Produktionsgenossenschaft, literally, agricultural production co-operative); *Pjatiletka* (from Russian, five year plan) replaced by *Fünfjahrplan*; *Neubauer* (person who received land in the Land Reform of 1952, literally, new farmer); *Neulehrer* (teacher trained in short programmes after 1945, literally, new teacher): both these terms are now unnecessary.

In addition, certain words are used more frequently in the GDR, e.g. *Errungenschaften* (attainments), *Genosse* (comrade), *Werktätige* (working people); or in the Federal Republic, e.g. *Aktie* (share), *Börse* (stock exchange), *Zinsen* (interest). Some words have a positive connotation in the GDR and a negative one in *many* circles in the Federal Republic: *Genosse* (comrade), *Kommunismus, Revolution, Sozialismus*. On the other hand, the loading of *Demokratie* is positive in both Germanies. The GDR distinguishes between *bürgerliche* and *sozialistische Demokratie* (Reich 1968: 56), *sozialistische Demokratie* being identified with the 'rule of the proletariat' and 'decision for a particular programme'. In the Federal Republic *Demokratie* is representative government with elections in which parties compete (and selection between them), although some minority groups are demanding 'real democracy' in the form of direct participation of all citizens in decision-making. Since the 9th Conference of the Central Committee of the Sozialistische Einheitspartei (May 1973), the main self-definition of the GDR has been '*real existierender Sozialismus*' rather than *sozialistische Demokratie*. But in any case, the different meanings of *Demokratie* have led to the use of *sogenannt* (so-called) or inverted commas with *DDR* in West Germany up to the mid-60s – and its continuation in very right-wing newspapers such as *Die Welt* and *Berliner Morgenpost* owned by Axel Springer.

2.2.5 The question of language policy in the two Germanies is discussed in Chapter 4.

2.3 The GDR's contacts with the Federal Republic and other countries

In spite of the restricted contact between East and West Berliners, due to the wall and the limitations on border-crossing, it is Berlin where the two emerging German national varieties meet.[3]

Both East and West Berlin are international showpieces of their respective political systems, attracting foreigners. West Berlin is generally the point where GDR refugees reach the west. It has become a haven for East German refugee writers, whose works often show a lexical influence from the GDR variety of German. East and West Berliners are able to enjoy one another's electronic media. Lettau (1978: 126) describes television as 'die einzige einigende und entzweiende Zentralinstanz' (the only unifying and dividing authority). It is mainly through watching West Berlin and West German TV that 'DDR-Bürger' become familiar with new concepts and new language developments in the Federal Republic, and the capitalist nations in general. On the whole, GDR television (and radio) have relatively little appeal in the west, but it is likely that GDR German is better understood in West Berlin than in the Federal Republic.

The German newspapers of Czechoslovakia, Hungary and Rumania share with those of the GDR most of the vocabulary used to express the new 'socialist reality'. Roche's (1973) analysis of the German of the Prague *Volkszeitung* demonstrates similarities with Austrian Standard German (with whose speakers Czechs have common historical traditions) and with the Standard German of the

---

[3] In addition, 312,400 West Germans visited the GDR in 1975, and in 1973, 107 million letters were sent from the Federal Republic to the GDR and 108 million received in the Federal Republic from the GDR (Pelster 1981: 141).

GDR (with whom they share the social and political order) as well as some influences from the Federal Republic (through technological and scientific progress). German *Lektoren* (native-speaker lecturers) at universities in East European countries which were previously part of the Austro-Hungarian Empire come from the GDR and would therefore disseminate its variety of German.

2.3.1 National varieties – West German/East German/Austrian: model of a hypothetical situation

Let us return to the question of national varieties by pondering on the relationship between the Standard German of the two Germanies and of Austria. This can be illustrated by venturing into speculation. Let us imagine that Austria had not been reunified in 1955 but had been divided like Germany. We would then have ended up with six German-language political entities (apart from Liechtenstein). East Austrian and West Austrian would then have kept their traditional similarities, as have East German and West German. East German and East Austrian on the one hand, and West Austrian and West German on the other, would have shared newer developments. This hypothetical situation may give support to the notion of emerging national varieties in the Federal Republic and the GDR which, in many ways, have not yet developed as far as the Austrian and Swiss standard varieties.

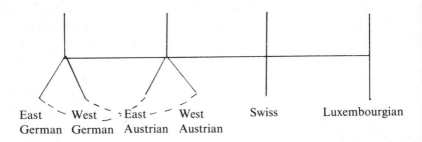

| East | West | East | West | Swiss | Luxembourgian |
| German | German | Austrian | Austrian | | |

If there are 'East' and 'West' German national varieties, as I have argued, they are distinct from each other in a different sense (as regards development, time scale, function, linguistic indices) to their distinction from the Austrian and Swiss ones, as can be seen from the above data and that presented in Chapter 1.

2.4 Brief summary

Because of the short period during which separate national varieties of Standard German could have developed, it is difficult to resolve unequivocally the question of whether 'East' and 'West' German are the same national variety or different ones. Due to international political considerations, the dominant attitude in the GDR is to regard its German as a national variety as distinct from that of the Federal Republic, while West Germans writing on this subject generally do not accept this. However, the public in the Federal Republic tends to be estranged by GDR German. The difference in policy is due to differing relationships to Germany's past, and particularly to whether 'Germany' is still viewed officially as a single nation.

'East' and 'West' German are based on the pre-1945 German national variety of Standard German. Most of the present linguistic differences are lexical – neologisms, lexical and semantic transference from English in the west and semantic transference from Russian in the east; other semantic shifts; dropping of vocabulary considered obsolete in the GDR and/or the Federal Republic. Syntactic and phonological differences are hardly to be found, and this seems to strengthen the 'single national variety' argument. However, this argument can be refuted on semantic and pragmatic grounds. The strong contextual nature of language speaks for two emerging national varieties. Collectively, the language communicates different meanings, different functions to the populations of the GDR and the Federal Republic. Furthermore, to a greater or lesser extent, citizens of the two Germanies identify with their own national variety. If they do not, it is with their own national variety that they choose not to identify, perhaps for reasons of political disillusionment. And yet 'East German' and 'West German' are national varieties in a different sense from the Austrian and Swiss varieties, with their long independent traditions.

The continuum between standard and non-standard varieties in the GDR and the Federal Republic of Germany will be dealt with in Chapter 3.

2.5 Further reading

Probably the most comprehensive account of GDR German, written from a Federal Republic view, is Reich (1968), based on newspapers, official records, and comparisons of East and West German *Dudens*. An interesting collection of articles on the subject is Hellmann (1973), while a double number of *Muttersprache* (Vol. 91, No. 3/4, 1981) has been devoted to the topic. A good summary of the literature and the problems is given by Hellmann (1978). There is no single volume that studies the problem from a GDR point of view, although a number of articles have appeared, especially in the *Zeitschrift für Kommunikationsforschung, Phonetik und allgemeine Sprachwissenschaft* and in *Sprachpflege*. The Russian influence on GDR German is given special treatment in Lehmann (1972).

3

Language and regionalism in the Germanies and Austria

3.1 Standard German and dialect as means of regional identification

Languages are not only means of communication, mediums of cognitive development and instruments of action. Through the variety of languages used, speakers also identify their geographical origins, local loyalty, migration history, and their social background and group membership. Dialects are geographical varieties, while sociolects are social varieties. (Examples of how geographical varieties can at the same time have a social function are given below, under 3.1.1.)

For the historical reasons outlined in Chapter 1, regionalism, and regional identification through language, were and continue to be strong in German-language countries. A speaker's regional identification can occur along a continuum from local dialect via regional dialect, even to be regionally-coloured Standard German. The latter is characterized by secondary (i.e. not the most typical) phonological features and intonation patterns (i.e. 'regional accent') being transferred from dialect (a locally or regionally identified variety) to Standard German and through the choice of lexical items associated with a particular region (Hard 1966: 57). There are certain meanings for which there is no supraregional German Standard German lexeme, e.g. Saturday (southern and western, *Samstag*; northern and eastern, *Sonnabend*), butcher (east central, and some west central, *Fleischer*; southern and central, *Metzger*; northern, *Schlächter*), so that regional identification in speech is unavoidable. Other instances include diminutives, where northern *-chen* suffixes and southern *-lein* suffixes are equally standard.

Dialects themselves, though generally not codified, are autonomous systems with regard to phonology, grammar and lexicon. For instance, some dialects have phonemes that do not exist in others, or in the standard language. Bavarian dialects have /w/, some Low German dialects /γ/. The distribution of phonemes varies between dialects – in Swiss dialects alone, /x/ comes in initial position. Many dialects (especially Upper German ones) lack a preterite (*er kam*) and generalize the perfect (*er ist gekommen*), while some East Central German dialects tend to use the pluperfect (*er war gekommen*) instead. Low German dialects have a uniform case in place of both accusative and dative, while there is systematic confusion between the dative and accusative in Berlin (dialect), and the accusative is generalized in Upper Saxon and Ripuarian (Rhenic). The verb meaning 'to speak' is *redn* in most Austrian and Bavarian dialects, *schwätze* in Swabian, *kalle* in Ripuarian (Rhenic), and *schnacken* in some Low German dialects.

In 1.3, I briefly outlined the dialectal divisions within the German-language area. To an increasing extent, Standard (High) German (based on Central German) has replaced Low German (Low Saxon). For several centuries, many people in Northern Germany (what is now the states of Bremen, Hamburg, Lower Saxony and Schleswig-Holstein in the Federal Republic, and the northern part of the GDR, as well as the north of the former German provinces east of the rivers Oder and Neiße) were bilingual in a Low German dialect and Standard (High) German. In some (mainly rural) areas there are still a large number of bilinguals. Many of them code-switch whole passages from one variety to the other (Stellmacher 1977: 151–63). Through switches, speakers quote what has been said in Low German, express their emotions and reactions or give examples. Low German speakers will also often transfer lexemes or grammatical forms and constructions into their High German (Stellmacher 1977: 164–7) and Standard German lexemes into their Low German (Herrmann-Winter 1974). Because the Low German dialects are so distant from Standard (High) German, they do not form a continuum but are completely discrete systems. However, in the North German *regional* dialects of (High) German, there is a substratum from the Low German dialects influencing the High German of even those who no longer speak a Low German dialect.

In Southern Germany and Austria, the Bavarian, Upper Franconian, and Swabian and other Alemannic dialects are close enough to Standard German to have continued in general use. In the south, and to a lesser extent in Hessen and the Rhineland, dialects are widely employed alongside regionally-coloured Standard German.

A public opinion poll conducted in 1966 by the Institut für Demoskopie in Allensbach (Noelle and Neumann 1967) showed that while 71% of people surveyed in Bavaria and 64% in Baden-Württemberg said they mastered a dialect, this was the case for only 46% of respondents in Northern Germany and West Berlin (including, however, 51% of informants in Hamburg and 67% in Schleswig-Holstein).

Bavarians, (Alemannic-speaking) Badensians and Swabians (Württembergers) are culturally very different from North Germans, and they have all had their separate histories. Bavarians have a lot in common with Austrians (including the main features of their dialects). Bavaria is still known as *Freistaat Bayern* (the Free State of Bavaria). Bavaria and Baden-Württemberg are both more rurally based than most of the other states of the Federal Republic.

Any comparison between the German-language countries must take into account that most of the dialects in Austria are Bavarian in origin, and Bavarian dialects are the most retentive in the Federal Republic. On the other hand, most of the dialects still in use in the GDR are Low German,[1] and Low German dialects are among the less retentive in the Federal Republic. It was the East Central German dialects, the ancestors of the GDR's Upper Saxon varieties, which formed the basis of Standard German. Another point worthy of note is the centrality of Berlin in the GDR, in comparison with the relative insignificance of Bonn in the Federal Republic. However, there is a contrast between the Upper Saxon of many important GDR politicians and the speech of Berliners. Despite Vienna's importance as the political and cultural capital of Austria, many people in the provinces feel that it is remote for geographical reasons.

3.1.1 Variation (see cautionary statement in Introduction)

Within any given area, speakers will select their code(s) from a series of varieties along a continuum from the narrowest local form to something approaching Standard German. To many linguists, only the narrow local forms at the bottom of the continuum are dialect (*Dialekt, Mundart*). They postulate a three-tier categorization which

---

[1] Apart from the Central German dialects of Southern Thüringian.

45

incorporates into a middle category, *Umgangssprache* (colloquial language), any point on the continuum between local dialect and Standard (*Standardsprache, Hochsprache, Einheitssprache, Gemein-Gemeinsprache, Literatursprache*). Hain (1951) shows, in her analysis situation in Hessen, that there are numerous transitional varieties between the two poles. This is confirmed by the research of Schönfeld (1974, 1977), Herrmann-Winter (1974, 1977, 1979) and Dahl (1974) in the northern areas of the GDR, as well as the writings of Engel (1961, 1962) on Swabian and Kufner (1961) on Munich dialect. The continuum has led to disagreement amongst researchers as to the number and nature of the varieties. Schönfeld, and some other GDR scholars, add the categories *hochsprachenahe Umgangssprache* (colloquial language approaching Standard), *mundartnahe Umgangssprache* (colloquial language approaching dialect), and *umgangssprachlich beeinflußte Mundart* (dialect influenced by colloquial language) to the two extremes. This contrasts with the three non-standard varieties described by Engel (see below). In Regensburg, levelling of the town dialect features in the direction of regional standard has led to unsystematic variation (Keller 1976).

As Bausinger (1967: 295) has commented, the multidimensionality of the German language has been obscured by the term *Umgangssprache*. It is ill-defined, with definitions ranging from 'Sprache des Alltags' (everyday language: Wahrig 1968) to 'Hochsprache auf großlandschaftlicher Ebene' (standard language at the level of a large region: Polenz 1954). It can refer to a type of usage or to a (geographical or social) variety. Its norms are not defined (Bichel 1973, 1980). *Umgangssprache* is seen more as what it is not than as what it is. It contrasts with dialect in that it covers geographical varieties beyond the local one. It also contrasts with standard language in that it covers varieties that do not adhere (completely) to the (artificial) norms.

Engel (1961, 1962) in his pioneering study of the phonology, syntax and lexicon of Neuler, a village near Aalen (Württemberg), distinguishes the following three non-standard varieties, based on speaker–hearer relations.

> Bauernsprache[2] (peasant language): *i hoo ən* Mordsd*uu*rscht, aber koe' B*ii*r m*aa*g'e n*e*t.

---

[2] Also termed *Mundart*.

Bürgersprache[3] (townspeople language): *i han* en Mordsd*u*rscht, aber B*ii*r m*a*ag'e n*e*t.

Honoratiorensprache[4] (notables language): *i hab* en Mordsd*u*rscht, aber B*ii*r m*a*g e n*e*t.

Standard German: Ich habe einen großen Durst, aber Bier mag ich nicht. (I am very thirsty but I don't like beer.)

Bauernsprache:[2] 's g*å*t ə b*ä*asr L*uu*ft hae't, aber *e*m Bus isch waarə

Bürgersprache:[3] 's g*å*t ə b*ee*ser W*e*nd heit, aber *e*m Bus isch s war*m*.

Honoratiorendeutsch:[4] 's g*ee*t ə b*ee*ser W*i*nd heit, aber *i*m Bus isch s warm.

Standard German: Es geht ein böser Wind heute, aber im Bus ist es warm. (There is a bad wind today but in the bus it is warm.) (å corresponds approximately to [oː].)

Historically, *Bauernsprache* is the dialect of the village, *Bürgersprache* that of the nearby town of Aalen, and *Honoratiorensprache* the dialect of the state capital, Stuttgart, which has influenced the speech of the whole region. According to Engel, the use of *Bauernsprache* is restricted to the intimate circle (e.g. family sphere, pub). Standard German is associated with foreigners and people from other German-speaking regions. The other two varieties are used in the everyday sphere, and here variety and register selection may overlap. *Bürgersprache* is employed in general interaction in the area around Aalen, while *Honoratiorensprache* is used by and to local dignitaries (doctor, mayor, clergyman, teacher) and to Swabians from other areas. In this respect, dialects are at the same time sociolects. Most speakers have the competence to code-switch between varieties in much the same way as bi- and multilinguals switch between their languages.

In Austria, Tatzreiter (1978) shows that the lexical and phonological differences between neighbouring local Styrian dialects are levelling out in that 'new dialects', which are closer to Austrian Standard German, are being formed. There are also transitional varieties between the old and the new dialects, determined by the speaker's communication networks. The formation of 'new dialects' is common to small communities that are mainly agricultural and ones that are not. A similar tendency is attested by Hutterer (1978:

[3] Also termed *provinzielle Umgangssprache.*
[4] Also termed *württembergische Umgangssprache.*

326), based on the radiation of the Graz town dialect. Surrounding rural dialects are replacing, for example, *Dirndl, Ertag, Pfinztag*, and *i hān* by *Mädel, Dienstag, Donnerstag*, and *i hob* (girl, Tuesday, Thursday, I have) respectively. The latter are the equivalents in the town dialect, which is also becoming the regional dialect (cf. Engel on Swabian, above).

The factors influencing choice of variety are the ones operating in language contact situations (Fishman 1965, Cooper 1969): domain (contextualized sphere of communication, e.g. family, work, school, neighbourhood, church); interlocutor (speech partners will accommodate to each other's speech, as Giles (1977) has shown for bilinguals); role-relationship; type of interaction (public or private, e.g. business transaction, lecture, sermon, carnival, private conversation – this factor being identified by Mattheier (1980) as a key one in the dialect/standard dichotomy); topic (more personal or emotional topics in dialect; politics or occupation in Standard); locale of interaction (e.g. village, town or city; home, street or pub). Code-switching between varieties is undoubtedly not a new phenomenon, but one that had been ignored by dialectologists propagating the myth of a 'uniform local dialect' as Hard (1966: 29) has pointed out. German dialectologists had pioneered the study of linguistic geography – which traditionally involved plotting dots on maps to indicate which item (lexical, phonological, grammatical) was used in the local dialect. Lines called isoglosses separated places using a particular item from ones which did not. On dialect maps and in dialect dictionaries, in fact throughout monolithic traditional dialectological research, no provision was made for variation within the speech of one locality or even of one speaker. This helps explain the sparsity of studies on German urban dialects (Dittmar and Schlieben-Lange 1981, Debus 1962) with their complex sociogeographical stratification and dynamic variation.

Research in many areas of the German-language countries confirms the occurrence of variation, as do the results of a public opinion poll on dialects (Noelle and Neumann 1967). According to this, the domains for which dialects are employed are as shown in Table 1. Domain specialization (dialect for family, Standard for work) is general among dialect speakers in the Federal Republic, most markedly among white collar workers (Ammon 1979: 30). Hain (1951) observed, in her research in Ulfa (Hessen), that the farmer will speak differently to his wife and his farmhand and that young people

Table 1. Percentage of respondents using dialect in three domains (2 states).

	Bavaria	Baden-Württemberg[a]
Family	78	91.9
Friendship	65	80.5
Work	51	60.2

[a] The Baden-Württemberg figures include only people of local origin. They are derived from Heuwagen's (1974) analysis of the 1966 survey.

will use different forms when talking to the elderly and to their own peer-group.

Domain specialization in Bavaria is exemplified in Rein and Scheffelmann-Meyer's (1975) study of Walperskirchen, 30km northeast of Munich.[5] Local dialect is the medium of all everyday communication, including interaction with local officials and shopkeepers, and that of the work domain. It is also the medium of clubs and societies, including youth groups. Standard German is the language of school (except for grade 1) and also of the church (though parish council meetings tend to be conducted in regional dialect). In municipal politics, local dialect is spoken by people functioning as individuals; only in their capacity as office-bearers do they employ Standard or, more usually, regional dialect (*Umgangssprache*), which is considered more proper for formal domains and prepared speech. Standard and regional dialect are the appropriate mediums for general politics in this triglossic community.

Recent studies in the GDR indicate a high degree of situational variation among speakers. Schönfeld (1977) finds that 40% of production workers and 72% of leading employees questioned in a steel works near Berlin and a light globe factory in the city are conscious of switching to a higher register at central work meetings (rationalized as part of socialist work ideology or motivated by the behaviour of others). It should be noted that, in the GDR, all sections of the population are involved in committee work and political discussions. Using non-standard varieties is identified with a 'matey'

---

[5] There are parallel situations in the villages of the Saarland, except that there many people do not speak Standard though they understand it. (Wolfgang Klein, personal communication.)

tone, and it is with a peer group of friends, acquaintances and colleagues that *mundartnahe Umgangssprache* is most used at work. This concurs with investigations conducted by Herrmann-Winter (1979) in the Greifswald area in the north of the GDR where non-standard forms were employed most to friends and colleagues, to some extent to colleagues of lower status but rarely to immediate superiors in the work situation. Both Schönfeld and Herrmann-Winter note a strong reluctance of speakers to use non-standard varieties to children for fear of disadvantaging them at school.

Senft's (1982) study, based on participant observation and inter-views among local workers in a metal factory in Kaiserslautern (West Germany), indicates a high degree of uniformity in both phonology and syntax within the variety spoken by his (35 to 47-year-old) subjects. Listeners responding to tapes of other workers in the factory were able to detect differences in syntactic complexity between the speech of the sectional head and foreman on the one hand and workers on the other. Senft asserts that the listeners had been influenced by the content and discourse development. He finds, on the whole, that the informants rated male voices mainly on linguistic and personal characteristics and female ones on sociopsychological (emotional) factors.

3.1.2 Who speaks dialect?

The Allensbach public opinion poll on dialects (Noelle and Neumann 1967) gives us the breakdown of dialect-using respondents through-out the Federal Republic shown in Table 2. The results of the poll also give us a general profile of dialect, non-Standard speakers in the Federal Republic (Noelle and Neumann 1967, Heuwagen 1974): they have low incomes and low social aspirations, they are working class, live in small rural municipalities, and are South German.

Ammon (1973a) has defined the following as the principal factors determining whether a person is a dialect speaker:

(i)   The communication radius of the speaker
(ii)   The speaker's self-image

Other factors are social contacts and social mobility (Ammon 1973a). These are all connected with occupation, in particular with the division between physical and intellectual work in industrial societies,

Table 2. Percentage of respondents using dialect in three domains by occupational class.

	Domain		
Occupation	Family	Friends	Work
Worker	72	64	46
Agricultural occupations	81	74	67
Professional and white collar employees	55	51	19
Self-employed in trades and commerce, or profession	58	58	36

and also with the power structure (Ammon 1973a). On the basis of his research on Swabian and Franconian speakers, Ammon (1973b) draws the conclusions listed below.

(i)   Socioeconomic status correlates strongly with the selection of language variety (see also the responses to the public opinion poll, above). Unskilled industrial workers are more likely to speak Standard than are agricultural workers. Skilled workers and self-employed tradesmen are more likely to speak it than are unskilled workers. People in non-manual occupations tend to speak Standard more than those in manual occupations. Ammon (1979: 29) constructs the following sociolinguistic hierarchy (with those at the bottom using most dialect and least Standard):

> ↑ Capitalists
> Leading employees
> Self-employed merchants
> Self-employed tradesmen
> Self-employed farmers
> Lower employees
> ↓ Factory workers

Working class people gravitate between dialect and a 'mixture' of dialect and Standard German; the middle class often vacillate between this 'mixture' and Standard German (Ammon 1979: 32–3). It should be noted, however, that Hasselberg (1981) found 26% *middle-class monodialectal* speakers among his 7004 children in Hessian comprehensive schools.

(ii)   Males are more likely to speak Standard than are females, especially women who are not in employment away from home. This appears to contradict conclusions from English-speaking countries (e.g. Mitchell and Delbridge (1965), Australia; Labov (1966), U.S.; Trudgill (1974), Britain), who all report women using standard varieties more than men. But it is among *rural* women that dialect is more prevalent in the Federal Republic. Also, Ammon's results are not duplicated in a Viennese study and they overlap only partially with the findings of research in the GDR (see below).

(iii)   Young people are more likely to speak Standard German than are old people. (This point will be taken up in relation to the 'decline of the dialect', see below, 3.2. For recent developments, see 3.3.)

Mattheier (1980: 27–9) uses public opinion polls to show that, with few exceptions, more women know and employ dialect than do men, but women are also more likely than men to devalue and reject the dialect in areas where it is being abandoned. While women speak more dialect in the family, men use it more in the work and friendship domains. Women have a greater tendency to react to social conventions in their replies to questions on language use (Mattheier 1980: 35–7).

There is evidence that older women are more traditional and dialect-bound in their speech, while middle-aged and younger women will adapt to prestige norms. In most of the areas of South-Western Germany, Vorarlberg (Austria) and Liechtenstein where Graf (1977) studied the use of the subjunctive in dialect, the ratio of Subjunctive I (e.g. *sei*) to Subjunctive II (e.g. *wäre*) was much higher in the speech of older women than in that of older men.[6] In the middle and younger age groups, however, the pattern was reversed. Thus it was the women who conformed to the change, even within their dialect speech. In Senft's (1982) study of the speech of Kaiserslautern metal-factory workers, in which the age group (35–47) *was kept uniform*, no major sex-specific differences were registered in phonology or syntax.

---

[6] There are two subjunctive moods in German. Traditionally Subjunctive I, based in form on the present tense, is used in indirect speech and Subjunctive II, based in form on the past, is employed to denote the hypothetical. However, the latter is also used increasingly for indirect speech.

On the basis of conversation and interviews with 75 speakers in the industrial and business growth centre of Osterholz-Scharmbeck, 20km north of Bremen, Stellmacher (1977) established age, low socioeconomic status and an informal communication situation as factors correlating with dialect usage. But in his data, while the elderly use dialect more than other age groups, the oldest and the youngest groups hold the most positive attitudes towards dialect. Sex and degree of mobility do not stand out as significant factors in dialect usage. However, any differences between Ammon's and Stellmacher's findings could be due to regional factors. In a study of the Regensburg town dialect, Keller (1976) found that the younger generation initiated changes but that there were phonological and lexical instances where the variety of the older and younger generations overlapped but differed from that of the middle generations.

The results of Wodak-Leodolter and Dressler's (1978) research based on interviews in Vienna are of significance for two reasons. Firstly, many other studies on dialects in the Federal Republic and Austria were conducted in rural areas and provincial towns, but Vienna is one of the largest cities in the German-language area (the third largest after Berlin and Hamburg). Secondly, the data could test whether the social function of dialects in Austria is similar to that in the Federal Republic today. It should be noted that Wodak-Leodolter and Dressler focus on phonological aspects. They reach the following conclusions:

(i) Working class people (those with only primary education) tend to use local dialect, occasionally switching to higher varieties. Such switching is commonplace among the lower middle class (those with secondary or technical education), a parallel to the uncertainty and hypercorrection among the lower middle class in New York (Labov 1970). The middle and upper classes in Vienna (those with higher education) generally employ Austrian Standard German or regional dialect.

(ii) Women employ less dialect and more Standard than men. They are more conscious of language and adhere to prestige norms more strongly due to their insecurity. The discrepancy with Ammon's findings is probably due to urban–rural differences as well as to the distinction between housewives and women employed outside the home.

(iii) Young members of the middle class are more likely to speak dialect than are older ones. This is because the taboo on the speaking of dialect has been removed in Austria in recent years (see below, 3.3).

(iv) Intra-individual code-switching occurs significantly in the lower middle class, with its social insecurity, and in 'upwardly mobile' speakers, who have been able to move up the social ladder but have a confused identity. It occurs less in the working class. Wodak-Leodolter and Dressler (1978: 50) claim that this type of language behaviour is 'non-existent' in the middle and upper middle classes. (However, this is perhaps due to the interview situation.) The older generation of the lower middle class, especially women, produce the most hypercorrect forms.

Sound changes in Vienna are currently occurring both 'from above', with the lower middle and working classes and the upwardly mobile adapting to the middle class, and 'from below', with the middle class breaking the taboo on (local) dialect.

Despite the latter new tendency, it can be seen that the point on the continuum from which one's speech is selected in a particular situation is intricately interwoven with the class structure in both Austria and the Federal Republic. In this connection it may be interesting to make comparisons with recent research in the GDR.

Schönfeld (1974) conducted a comprehensive survey of a village near Stendal in the Ostaltmark (in the north of the GDR). The older the speakers there, the more likely they are to use the local Low German. Another factor correlating with use of local dialect is a low level of education. The regional dialect (*mundartnahe Umgangssprache*) is employed by those with no more than 8 years of formal education, the sons and daughters of tradesmen, and rural labourers. It is not usually employed by those whose fathers were members of the intelligentsia or white collar employees. A person who learned to speak in a village is $1\frac{1}{2}$ times as likely to master a dialect than those who migrated from a town or city. While older women use and master dialect more than their male peers, younger and middle-aged women tend more towards the use of, and attitudinal support for, Standard German than younger and middle-aged men. There is a strong attidudinal preference for Standard except among the 16–25 age group, the majority of whom are completely tolerant towards all language varieties. Otherwise, attitudes are occupation-determined. Standard is preferred most by the intelligentsia and housewives who use and prefer Standard and least by seasonal workers.

In a study among 300 production workers and 100 'leaders'[7] in steel works near Berlin and a selection of 72 workers of different status there and at a Berlin light globe factory (Schönfeld 1977), the more socially mobile – the 'leaders' and apprentices – employ more situational variation in speech than do the production workers. Those people directly involved in production are known to speak 'differently' from those not directly working in production. 'Leaders', researchers, and secretaries are identified as Standard (or near-Standard) speakers.

Herrmann-Winter (1977) has investigated the *acceptance* of regional grammatical and lexical forms in and around Greifswald. She tests attitudes towards: plural -*s* (as in *Jungens*), and dative of possession (e.g. *Peter sein Fahrrad*, Peter his bike, for *Peters Fahrrad*, Peter's bike), discontinuous preposition-pronouns (e.g. *Da* kann er nichts *für*, for *Dafür* kann er nichts, he can't help it), *tun* + infinitive (e.g. *tut er glauben*, he does think, for *glaubt er*, he thinks), and diminutives ending in -*ing* (e.g. *Größing*). Workers and 'leaders' in industry, agricultural workers and the intelligentsia accepted more than the median of deviations,[8] while less than the median was accepted by party functionaries, 'leaders' in agriculture, those working in transport and communications, and schoolchildren. Those with the highest qualifications seem to be most tolerant of deviations, though this does not necessarily mean that they would employ them themselves. Those with a trades certificate are least likely to accept the deviations – something that can be compared to the hypercorrection and linguistic insecurity of the lower middle class in capitalist countries such as the U.S. and Austria (see above). The 'leaders' in agriculture would use local dialect in everyday situations and observe Standard norms more in situations where Standard is

---

[7] In the GDR, promising men and women are trained to form an élite (*leitender Kader*) in the state, in industry and agriculture. In some ways, the 'leaders' correspond to executives in the capitalist system.

[8] However, 80% of the workers but none of the intelligentsia accepted *Peter sein Fahrrad* (Peter his bike, Standard German *Peters Fahrrad*).

employed. It is suggested (Herrmann-Winter 1977: 230) that they prefer Standard to regional intermediate varieties in order to 'prove their qualifications'.

In a subsequent study, Herrmann-Winter (1979) has investigated both the speech and the language attitudes of speakers in Greifswald and the surrounding industrial and agricultural areas. Among other things, she elicited colloquial words and expressions, neologisms, technical jargon and grammatical constructions that make up the speakers' everyday repertoire. The most phonological deviations from Standard (i.e. non-obligatory regional features) were recorded among workers in industry and trades, mastercraftsmen and in the over-65 age group, and the fewest among the intelligentsia, those with 12 years of schooling, schoolchildren, and others under the age of 25. The importance of the elicitation situation needs to be stressed, for many of the words and expressions would have been acquired in a formal work situation.

The four studies cited above suggest that social position and function in the work force are by far the most important factors in code selection in the GDR, followed by age. The youngest and the most educated, while tolerant of variation, are unlikely to actually use dialect. People's social background at home and their own training and occupational status co-determine their speech. It may be possible to see this in connection with Konrád and Szélenyi's (1978) claim that the intelligentsia has assumed the role of a dominant class in Eastern Europe, corresponding to that of the capitalists in Western Europe. It is difficult to make direct comparison between research results from the Federal Republic and the GDR since different surveys have been conducted in different ways. Stellmacher (1977), in his study of Low German near Bremen, does not share Herrmann-Winter's (1979) presuppositions about obligatory regional features of Standard German (see above, 1.3). At the lexical level, Herrmann-Winter's acceptability tests cover, as *Umgangssprache*, both colloquial and regional dialect words. However, regional words, *belatschern* (Berlin, to persuade) and *Sabbel* (Low German, chatterbox), turn out to be accepted least and colloquial verbs, *quatschen* (to talk rot) and *mitkriegen* (to get the idea), the most. The relation between Standard German use and social and educational status, between (old) age and dialect speaking, and the importance of the speech situation appear common to the three countries under consideration.

An important breakthrough within the political limitations of interviewing beyond the wall was achieved by a team under the direction of Norbert Dittmar (Schlobinski 1982) who were able to study German in three Berlin districts, Wedding (West), Prenzlauer Berg (East), and Zehlendorf (West). The first two are traditional working class districts, separated by the wall. They have observed that the Berlin dialect has remained more intact in Prenzlauer Berg than in any district of West Berlin and that attitudes are more positive towards dialect in the east. This is due in part to the planned housing policy in the GDR keeping Prenzlauer Berg more homogeneous than its western counterpart. Other factors are complex social networks and the role of Berlin dialect in promoting cultural identity against the threat of the Saxon of the GDR hierarchy. In the west, *Berliner Schnauze*, the local urban vernacular, is still employed as a register for a humorous informal atmosphere and to express a close social relationship within the urban milieu (Schlobinski, forthcoming).

3.2 'The decline of the dialect'

Many linguists have claimed, in recent years, that German dialects are declining or have died. (Spangenberg, 1963; Hard, 1966; Leopold, 1968; and Schönfeld, 1974, have all argued in this direction.) As the theory runs, dialects have been, or are being replaced by a more uniform *Umgangssprache*. The terminology muddle surrounding *Umgangssprache* has already been mentioned (3.1.1). Taking into account the various conclusions on the relation between German varieties, I can only agree with Hasselberg (1981: 33–4) that there is a continuum between Standard and dialect, the only two 'systems', and that dialect begins well before the extreme of the continuum. What the proponents of the 'death of dialect' are probably really saying is that the narrowest dialect cum lowest sociolect, Engel's *Bauernsprache*, is rapidly declining and is being replaced largely by the other dialect varieties, Engel's *Bürgersprache* and *Honoratiorensprache*.

In her examination of the speech of collective farmers in the north of the GDR, Herrmann-Winter (1974) observes the rise of a regional North German compromise variety strongly influenced by GDR Standard norms as well as by the dialects. (This is spoken north of the line Anklam–Demmin–Rostock.) The finding is based on speech samples and conversations. Phonological features of the regional dialect include the diphthongization of /eː/, /oː/ and /yː/ to /eI/, /ou/ and /ØI/; variation between /g/ and /j/; a 'thick' [ɫ]; /s/ → /z/ and /b/→/v/; and /sv/→/sw/, as well as the de-affricatization of /ts/ to /s/. It should be noted that the East Central German forerunner of present-day Standard German was itself a kind of regional compromise dialect. Tatzreiter's study of 'new dialects' in the Steiermark (Styria) has already been mentioned above (3.1.1). So it appears that where local dialects were still spoken, they were yielding to regional dialects.

3.2.1 Reasons for the 'decline'

The above-mentioned development is not surprising. The local dialect is closely connected with closed rural communities, which no longer exist in the Germanies or in most parts of Austria. Many villages have been urbanized and incorporated into towns and cities, which has brought about not only a breaking of isolation but also a mixing of populations. Mattheier (1980) sees this as part of a modernization process which has been continuing since the 16th century, in which cosmopolitan features have gradually spread from town to country. In the most recent period, even large, previously rural areas have become industrialized. Moreover, many villagers commute to work in a nearby industrial town or city every day while maintaining their small farms and their place in the village community. They are called *Industriebauern* (industrial farmers). Some people work in towns and cities during the week and return to their villages for the weekend. (50% of the inhabitants of West German municipalities with populations of less than 500 inhabitants are not engaged in farming.)

One of the studies of this situation, by Hofmann (1963), predates the international sociolinguistic boom. It was based in the village of Nauborn (population 2400), about 3km south of Wetzlar (Hessen). 70% of the inhabitants at the time were *Industriebauern*, commuting daily to Wetzlar, and therefore belonged to two communities (Wetzlar and Nauborn). The total population of Nauborn was divided up according to age, sex, occupation, education and employer (Leitz, optical industry, or Buderus, steel works). Hofmann also took into account voting patterns and affiliation with local and other organizations. The study is restricted to phonological aspects of language, the speech of the *Industriebauern* being compared with that of elderly non-commuters in Nauborn and that of Wetzlar workers. The least deviation from the local dialect is observed in Buderus workers aged 45–59, who constitute a very conservative group. Workers in the optical industry, who are much less conservative, have more contact with the town population and have therefore been influenced more by its speech. They often use compromise forms or vary between alternatives. The children are influenced more by Standard German through schooling than by the town dialect.

A more extensive study of this problem is being undertaken by Besch and Mattheier in the Rhineland. They are investigating the speech of men aged between 21 and 65 in the village of Erp, southwest of Cologne. 70% of the population commute to work in the nearby industrial area, only about 15% are involved in agriculture, and many people from Cologne have moved into the area. Their corpus includes natural conversations, interviews, and responses on language attitudes (Besch 1975, Besch and Mattheier 1977).

Commuting is a factor in the decline of the local dialect also in other German-language countries. It is mentioned, for instance, by Schönfeld (1974: 221) in his study of speech variation in a northern GDR village. Resch (1974) found that 47% of young people, aged 18–30, who commute to Vienna daily or weekly from the village of Gols in the easternmost state of Austria, Burgenland, use the Viennese diphthongs /aI/, /au/ or /ɔy/. Only 30% in this age group retain the phonological system of the local dialect. However, 70% of commuters over 30 have kept the original dialect; 48% of skilled workers show the adaptation (cf. 32% who retain the phonology of local dialect); but only 9% of unskilled workers have changed to Viennese diphthongs. The adaptation to Viennese dialect is strongest among those whose first employment was in Vienna and those from ethnic minorities (Croatian or Hungarian) and occurs more among daily than weekly commuters. Compromise forms are very prevalent among weekly commuters of all ages.

An additional reason for the decline of the local dialect could be the changes in family structure from the stable three-generation extended family to the more mobile nuclear family, which is less self-sufficient.

Generally, the postwar decades have been a period of unprecedented mobility in Europe – often across regional boundaries. Mobility was particularly strong in the early years of the Federal

Republic because of the arrival of refugees from the GDR, 12 million expelled from the former German provinces east of the Oder–Neiße Line (Silesia, Pomerania, East Prussia: see Map 1) and *Volksdeutsche* (ethnic Germans) from Eastern and South-Eastern Europe. Many of them were resettled in rural areas of the Federal Republic, where vastly different dialects were spoken. In 1950, 34.7% of the population of Schleswig-Holstein, 26.6% of Lower Saxony, 20.8% of Bavaria, and 18.2% of Württemberg-Baden were people who had been expelled (Moser 1979: 323). While Pomeranians and East Prussians predominated in Schleswig-Holstein, Silesians in Lower Saxony, and Sudeten Germans in Bavaria and Württemberg-Baden, there were smaller groups from each 'home-region' throughout the Federal Republic (Moser 1979: 330). It was only those expellees who remained at home all day whose language was unaffected by the move – old people and housewives. Those at work tended to adapt towards the regional variety of the area of resettlement. Children became bidialectal, employing their parents' dialect at home and the regional dialect of the area elsewhere (Moser 1979). Today the effects of this great migration have largely worn off, although it may have contributed to a levelling-out of some regionalisms in Standard German. (Moser 1979: 335 gives some examples for Württemberg.) The second generation of those who had been expelled, like that of Eastern European refugees all over the world, has come to terms with the permanence of its new environment. This new attitude increased with the passage of time and the certainty that the eastern provinces will not return to German control. A similar situation developed in Austria, where some *Volksdeutsche* from Central and Eastern Europe, speaking non-Austrian dialects of German, were resettled.

Further reasons for the decline in the use of local dialect or in its gravitation towards regional Standard have been the communications explosion, best exemplified by the universal pastime of television-watching and the sharp rise in the number of people receiving secondary (and post-secondary) education. Both the media and school are Standard German domains and Standard German has become the language of children's primary socialization in many areas.

Schildt (1976) suggests that the development away from dialect is more advanced in the GDR than in the Federal Republic, where dialect is still a 'surrogate for the unmastered Standard language' (Schildt 1976: 199). Schönfeld's (1974, 1977) studies seem to confirm a strong standardization process brought about by schools in the GDR. Parents speak Standard to their children for the sake of their education while school attendance appears to have minimized the use of dialect in the younger generation, as has higher education in general. On the other hand, Schönfeld's (1974) research also indicates that this is accompanied by a less prescriptive attitude on the part of the younger generation.

A factor specific to the GDR is the collectivization of farming. Herrmann-Winter (1979) indicates that less local dialect is spoken on large collective farms than on small ones. Since the large farms have necessitated the employment of specially qualified people, some of whom are from outside the area, there is inevitably a press towards regional dialect or more standard varieties. It is possible that the situation in the north-east was different from that in the north-west even before 1945. Estates were larger in the north-east and the families of large landowners are likely to have spoken Standard among themselves even if they employed Low German to people of lower status (Schönfeld 1974: 219).

3.3 The resurgence of regionalism

The decline of the local dialect and the variation in the use of dialect and standard language as outlined under 3.1 and 3.2 are general phenomena in western highly industrialized societies in both the Capitalist and Socialist Blocs. A counter-phenomenon of similar dimensions is the resurgence of ethnic and regional awareness. Even in nations like Great Britain and France, where centralized control has been well established over many centuries, ethnic and regional minorities are beginning to assert their rights. The 19th century nation-state is declining in importance. There is a 'higher' level at which there is a tendency towards internationalization – the European Community with its directly elected parliament is an example. But at the 'lower' level people want to identify, not so much with a nation-state, but with their own region, or ethnic minority. In Fishman's (1972: 285) terms, there is diversification and massification at the same time. All this is largely a reaction to centralized bureaucracy and over-development. The 'opting out' mentality longs for close human contact, good air and scope for creativity, according to Dahrendorf (1979: esp. 49, 156). A way in which people can express their own existence and individuality, demonstrate solidarity and regain confidence is through an exclusive variety of communication, i.e. through the dialect – though often the regional rather than the local one. This has led to an increase in the use of dialect in the Federal Republic and Austria, and to some extent the GDR, over the past decade.

A comparison between the 1966 and 1980 public opinion polls on dialect use (Allensbach 1981) shows a decline in the percentage of dialect speakers but a rise in the proportion of dialect users among them. While the proportion of people who master a dialect has decreased from 59% to 53%, the number of those who can speak a dialect but never use it has dropped from 29% to 16%. (Among 30–44 year olds from 15% to 8%.) According to the 1980 survey, dialect is used mainly in informal domains and in personalized local activities. At the same time, 83% of respondents preferred to remain living in their home region. Schönfeld and Pape (1981: 187–8), in a survey of recent research on GDR varieties of German, record a dialect resurgence there, with the dialect increasingly acquired not from the parents but from the peer group. Dialect then serves as a marker of solidarity and group identification. Such tendencies have no doubt played a role in the positive attitude towards local dialect among Stellmacher's (1977) younger informants and towards *mundartnahe Umgangssprache* among the younger generation in Schönfeld's (1974) GDR study. They have led to the younger members of the Viennese middle class employing more dialect than their older counterparts (Wodak-Leodolter and Dressler 1978). The 1980 Allensbach survey found that 46% of young people speak dialect at work – for them, the domain boundaries between dialect and Standard are breaking down. In contrast, people over 30 normally employ Standard German at work. Family and friendship remain their main domains of dialect use.

Dialect has, however, found its way into pop songs and into slogans and pamphlets of residents' action groups. Dialects, being 'discriminated varieties', have become languages of protest, part of an emancipatory strategy. Forced monolingualism in the standard language is seen as an ideological instrument of domination.

Teaching, social work, and psychotherapy in dialect have yielded fruitful results. It is in this context that Hoffmann (1981) pleads for an interdisciplinary approach to dialectology.

For many decades, dialect speaking was identified with either conservatives, who resisted change, or with fascists for whom German rural varieties were a 'healthy' part of the *Blut und Boden* (blood and soil) ideology. But in the late 60s and early 70s, dialect speaking was propagated by young educated socialists – whom this is intended to bring closer to the working class. It is, in a way, an index of 'social conscience' or of ideology. The recent resurgence of dialect in the Federal Republic and in Austria is closely connected with the conservation movement which has a young, 'green' and radical profile and is associated with action against nuclear power.[9] The 1980 public opinion poll (Allensbach 1981) shows an increase in dialect use among those with tertiary education. Some of the (regional) dialects are used across national boundaries, e.g. Alemannic (South-West Federal Republic, Switzerland, Alsace), Bavarian (Bavaria, Austria, South Tyrol), and serve as a link between groups in different countries challenging the nation-state and the pollution of the environment.

With the dialect resurgence has come a 'rediscovery' of dialect as a potential medium of literature – whether poetry (e.g. the Viennese – Artmann and Jandl, and the Bernese – Eggimann and Marti) or drama and film (the Bavarians – Fassbinder, Kroetz and Sperr, and the Austrians – Qualtinger and Turrini). Hoffmann (1981) contrasts three types of contemporary dialect poets.

(a)   those 'democratizing' literature by writing poems, intended as social criticism, in the 'language of the masses' (e.g. Andrae, Haid, Kusz)

(b)   those 'liberating' poetry from the standard language and treating dialect like any other language as material for literature (e.g. Bellmann, Bünker, Kruse)

(c)   those who use dialect to extend their potential for language play, thereby developing a new relationship to reality (e.g. the Austrian 'concrete poets' – Achleitner, Artmann, Jandl, Rühm).

---

[9] See below, 7.3.

3.3.1 Austria as a special case

The experiments currently made by Austrian creative writers, producers of pop music, and intellectuals in the interpenetration of stylistic registers and sociolinguistic domains through dialect are probably a cause of the confusion of linguists as to whether dialect use in Austria is actually increasing (Wodak-Leodolter and Dressler 1978), or whether it is giving way to Standard German under a North German influence unparalleled in South Germany (Eichhoff 1978: 13). Reiffenstein (1977) sees Standard increasing at the expense of dialects in a general way, but dialect making inroads into literature and politics – which is probably an appropriate assessment of the situation. According to Reiffenstein, there is no diglossia in Austria as Austrian Standard German and dialects are not employed in complementary distribution. However, there are domains (e.g. law, school, church) which are distinctly the province of Standard German. In the cities, there is no domain which is equally clearly the province of dialect, whether in a local or regional form. There is, at the lexical level, a tendency towards Standard, though non-standard phonological rules are being preserved and even extended.

It must be taken into account that, in most parts of Austria, regional identification through language is at the same time national identification, for a regional dialect is distinctively 'Austrian' as opposed to 'German'. The exceptions are the Alemannic dialects in the western state of Vorarlberg, which is increasingly desirous of expressing its regional peculiarity and is hoping to attain greater autonomy, a tertiary educational institution, and other benefits commensurate with its cultural and geographical distance from 'Austria proper'. The situation in the Austrian provincial towns warrants greater attention from sociolinguists than has hitherto been the case.

3.4 Dialects as *Sprachbarrieren* (language barriers)

In the early 70s, the Federal Republic was overwhelmed by a Bernstein fad (see below, 4.3). Not only linguists, but also educationists, social workers, journalists and radical students were convinced that compensatory language instruction in the middle class's 'elaborated code' of the language would cure West German society of all its ills. Soon the dialect, *as well as* or *rather than* the use of 'restricted' instead of 'elaborated code', was thought to be the cause of permanent inequality.

That Standard German is mastered better by the upper classes than by the working class has been indicated by empirical research for at least Württemberg (Ammon 1972: 95), Bavaria (Rein and Scheffelmann-Meyer 1975), and Hessen (Hasselberg 1976b: 77). The problems at school of monodialectal speakers (using only a non-standard dialect) have been the object of a number of studies and the findings are set out below.

(i) Dialect speakers, even in Bavaria, take four years of schooling before they reach the level of Standard German attained by bidialectals (speaking Standard and dialect) by the time they enter school. Errors were made by dialect speakers in the fourth grade (9-year-olds) of a Bavarian primary school in 11.75% of oral utterances and 16.3% of written ones. 71% of the errors in oral utterances and 40% of those in the written language were due to interference from dialect (Reitmajer 1975).

(ii) Dialect speakers encounter greater difficulties in acquiring literacy skills than do Standard speakers, as has been empirically shown for the Swabian area by Ammon (1975).

(iii) There is interference from the phonology of the dialect in the orthography of Standard German. This has been examined in speakers of Rhine Franconian, Bavarian, Swabian, Alemannic, and Pfälzisch (Ammon 1979: 33).

(iv) Dialect speakers obtain results in German inferior to those of pupils who speak Standard at home. They feel uncertain in class and are reluctant to take part in group discussions (Ammon 1975: 101; Hasselberg 1972, 1976: 103–4). This is because Standard German is *the* language of schooling in the Federal Republic. There are sanctions against speaking dialect in class, or at least teachers initiate the use of Standard 'by their example'. Dialect speakers are also less likely to be admitted into *Gymnasien*, the schools which lead to tertiary education (Moser 1972: 196), although here other factors (class, schooling, etc.) have to be taken into account. Nevertheless, Hasselberg (1981) found that only 20% of *middle class* monodialectal speakers in 26 Hessian comprehensive schools were expected to

65

pass Matriculation (cf. 57% Standard or bilingual middle class speakers). It is clearly not easy to determine causes and effects in the relation between language, class, and social and educational inequality. But this is by no means a problem specific to the German language.

There have been three different responses to these problems:

(a) *The argument for Standard German.* This has been argued very strongly by Ammon (1972, 1973a and b, 1975, 1979), who sees only advantages in adopting the standard language, due to its extensive communication radius, its use in formal domains, and its monopoly on the written form of communication (Ammon 1979: 36). The advantages of the dialect, such as its role in collective and personal identification, he claims (p. 37), could be transferred to the standard language. Argument (a) has been accepted in the GDR, where Standard German is regarded as the language of unity.

(b) *The argument for extending the permitted domains of dialect.* This argument was widely debated in the long educational and political controversy surrounding the guidelines for German in schools proposed in the early 70s by the SPD government of Hessen. The guidelines contained an emphasis on the teaching of communicative competence in whatever variety or varieties of the language the pupil has available to him/her. They attempted to separate the ability to communicate effectively from the exclusive use of Standard German in the school domain. In fact, it was argued (Christ et al 1974) that, through the imposition of Standard German, working class children are either muted or cut off from their home background. Standard German was seen as the sociolect of the middle class and the school as an assimilationist agent which conceals class struggle. These arguments were countered partly by the denial of such conflicts, partly by an appeal against the 'politicization' of language and education, partly by evoking the cultural heritage of Standard German which might be destroyed, and perhaps most effectively by referring to the need to communicate on a wide radius (cf. Christ et al 1974).

(c) *The difference hypothesis.* Labov's (1970) 'difference hypothesis' – that no varieties are inferior, though they may be different – was strongly supported in the Federal Republic by Dittmar (1973) and other sociolinguists. They emphasize the functional differences of Standard German and dialect.

In recent years a series of contrastive analyses (phonological, lexical, grammatical) has been edited by Besch, Löffler and Reich. They contrast Standard German and dialect and have so far treated Alemannic, Bavarian, Hessian, Rhenic, Swabian and Westphalian dialects. Their intention is to equip German primary school teachers with data to enable them to understand transfers in the Standard German of dialect speakers and to use dialects as a basis for teaching Standard German.

Ammon (1979: 35) contends that this approach actually 're-generates the problem' of disadvantaging dialect speakers, since they, but not Standard German speakers, are expected to be bidialectal. There is probably another powerful argument for making all people in strong dialect areas bidialectal, namely that monodialectal speakers of Standard German can be social outcasts in many such areas. Some of the assumptions of the contrastive series (the value of contrasting dialect and a second language, and the homogeneity of each system) are challenged by Mattheier (1980: 132–6). He also argues the need for *content*-based materials for disadvantaged dialect-speaking children (not just for teachers' use).

On the whole, it may be concluded that nowadays, with the decline of the narrow local variety, dialects are not communication barriers but they tend to reflect and exacerbate social barriers.

3.5 Reasons for stigmatized dialect

The question could be put: 'Is there anything inherent in a dialect which gives it a negative stigma?' Hoffmann (1981: 15) has pointed out that in Luxembourg, a country (as we have seen in 1.7) in which a dialect will be used in the same functions by all classes and sections of a local population, the dialect of Nordösling is regarded as comical and stupid. It is spoken in a mining area the population of which is looked down upon by urban and rural Luxembourgians alike. It appears that the status of the majority of the speakers is transferred to the dialect – something that occurs in many regions in different countries.

On the other hand, Fónagy (1963) has found that certain sounds have particular images for listener-informants from diverse language and other backgrounds, e.g. back, more open vowels and diphthongs are unpleasant in contrast to front, more closed vowels. This would suggest that the sounds themselves could be responsible for the stigmatization of a dialect, just as stereotyped attitudes are held for specific languages. This subject would warrant closer investigation.

3.6 Brief summary

In the Germanies and Austria, there is an overlap between dialects and sociolects, so that dialects are both socially stigmatized and instruments of regional pride and collective identification. They are used far more in the south than in the north of the Federal Republic, where they are more stigmatized. There is variation along a continuum between local dialects with a narrow currency via regional dialects to the standard language. Due to improved communication and educational opportunities, urbanization, internal migration and commuter mobility, local dialects have greatly declined in favour of regional ones. Collective farming is an additional factor in the GDR, where the trend away from local dialect is probably most marked.

The decline of the local dialect indicates at least some levelling-out of class differences in all the countries under consideration. However, in all these countries, social status and/or function in the work force as well as age are still the main personal factors determining one's language variety. There is widespread situational variation in the GDR, the Federal Republic and Austria. Domain, topic, role-relationship and emotional state co-determine choice of variety. This is particularly so in the south of the Federal Republic, where dialect and Standard German tend to be in a diglossic relationship.

A regional resurgence, under way in the Federal Republic and Austria, is characterized by more (regional) dialect speaking, especially among the younger generation. This dialect revival is indicative of a lessening of class differences and reflects anti-establishment political ideologies, which have played a role in the use of dialect in contemporary literature.

The disadvantages of dialect speakers in West German schools have led to two radical proposals – the general adoption of Standard German and the withdrawal of Standard German's monopoly in the school domain. Constructive action to alleviate the problems of the pupils include the developing of materials for teachers which will enable them to use dialects as a basis for teaching Standard German.

3.7 Further reading

Hard (1966) is a good introduction to the study of German dialects which incorporates the sociolinguistic perspective, though of course it does not extend as far as the dialect resurgence. (Keller 1961, written from the traditional and structural viewpoints, is the best publication on German dialects for the English reader.) The most up-to-date book focusing on sociolinguistic and pragmatic aspects is Mattheier (1980). *Dialektologie: Ein Handbuch zur deutschen und allgemeinen Dialektforschung* edited by Werner Besch *et al* was about to appear at the time of writing. Some of the numerous studies on the subject are discussed in this chapter. The reader is referred to the series *Sprache und Gesellschaft* (Academic Verlag, Berlin) which reports on GDR studies on sociolinguistics. Ammon (1979) is a good general survey, while Ammon's books (especially 1973) concentrate on the educational implications of variation in German, and Hoffmann (1981) takes up the new functions of dialects.

4

Communication norms and communication barriers

4.1 Language norms and language planning in German

Language planning may be defined as policy formulation and implementation, by official and non-official bodies, on the creation, alphabetization, standardization and use of languages. Neustupný (1968) has differentiated between two types of language planning (treatment): the *policy* approach, which emphasizes questions concerning the language as a totality (e.g. standardization, alphabetization, stratification) and the *cultivation* approach, which is preoccupied with normative questions such as correctness and efficiency of particular forms.

The German language does not possess central language planning authorities like the Académie Française, nor does the parliament of any German-language country pass laws concerning standard forms, as is the case in Norway (Haugen 1966). During the National Socialist régime, the Reichspresseamt (Reich Press Office) did possess and exercise planning powers, e.g. on 13 December 1937, it 'abolished' the word *Völkerbund* (League of Nations) and on 11 September 1939, it declared that *tapfer* (brave) could be collocated only with *deutsch*! (Berning 1964: 163–4).

There has been a 'purist' movement with a long tradition in Germany which has concerned itself with *Sprachpflege*, i.e. the cultivation approach. In the Federal Republic, the main body of 'purists', the Gesellschaft für deutsche Sprache (the Society for the German Language) has experienced a decline, due to general permissiveness in society and to the structural linguists' emphasis on tolerance (*de*scriptive, not *pre*scriptive). By its own admission, the Gesellschaft für deutsche Sprache has relaxed its policy on 'foreign words' (*Der Sprachdienst* 11, 1967; 718), but it is still somewhat preoccupied with the defence of traditional norms in the interests of 'clear and effective communication'. The society now has 300–400 individual members and an ageing membership. It offers advice on 'correct' German through its periodical, *Der Sprachdienst*, and its inquiry office, which receives about 600 written and 200 telephone queries on language use per year. It also publishes a journal *Muttersprache* with articles on contemporary German.

In Austria, the conservative camp publicly manifested itself from 1950 until June 1978, through a fortnightly half-hour radio programme,[1] 'Achtung, Sprachpolizei' (Attention, Language Police!), which kept thousands of listeners on guard against violations of the 'norms'. The programme stimulated listeners' questions and had the effect of correcting some tendencies, such as the dropping of the genitive -*s* in some public notices (Hornung 1968). Over the years, however, the audiences decreased as the concept of the programme became outmoded,[2] and there is now no programme of its kind on Austrian radio or television. In the past decade, in keeping with reformist tendencies in the political and social life of Austria, the major language cultivation organization has been not the ultra-conservative Verein Muttersprache (Mother Tongue Society), but the Österreichische Gesellschaft für Sprachpflege und Rechtschreiberneuerung (Austrian Society for Language Cultivation and Spelling Reform), which has advocated deviations from norms where appropriate to efficient communication (see also below, 8.1).

The Deutschschweizerische Verein, founded in 1904, exists for the purpose of promoting 'besseres und reines Deutsch' (better and pure German). To this end, it runs a bi-monthly, *Sprachspiegel*, and issues guidelines for business, proof-readers, and others. It has succeeded in having a language advice bureau established. No such body exists in Luxembourg although its population, like the German-Swiss, use German principally as a written language.

The most highly developed language planning agencies are those in the GDR (see above, Ch. 2). The notion of *Sprachkultur*, devised by

---

[1] From 1971 to 1978, 15 minutes.
[2] 'Im Laufe der Jahre hat sich das Konzept von der Gestaltung der Sendung her überlebt' (over the years the concept has become outdated in respect to the shaping of the programme) (letter from Gundomar Eibegger, Landesintendant des Studios Wien, 18 April 1980).

the Prague school of linguists, an endeavour to cultivate and perfect a language, has been taken over by GDR linguists since the 1960s and extended to emphasize the sociolinguistic and pragmatic perspective – adapting the language to the demands of contemporary living, appropriate to the given situation. The most effective instrument of cultivation is the Leipzig *Duden*, which lists those words and meanings that are acceptable to state and party. The journal *Sprachpflege*, founded in 1952 and originally intended as a guide to proof-readers, popularizes language policy. It contains both programmatic articles on aspects of applied linguistics and language planning, and advice on 'appropriate' (rather than 'correct') German. Its editorial board is assisted by the Duden editorial board and by the Institut für Sprachpflege und Wortforschung (Department of Language Cultivation and Lexical Research) at the University of Jena.

An important role in 'cultivation' is played by dictionaries, grammars and handbooks. Decisions for such authoritative reference books as *Duden-Rechtschreibung* (Mannheim) for lexicon and spelling, *Duden-Grammatik* (Mannheim) for grammar, *Duden-Aussprachewörterbuch* for pronunciation, and Wahrig's *Deutsches Wörterbuch* and latterly the six-volume *Duden* for lexicon and meanings are made by the staff of private enterprise firms and by committees of academics.[3] Though the Dudens have become increasingly flexible in recent editions, they are still conservatively directed somewhat more towards norm than towards usage. They are less normative than the dictionary of the Académie Française or the Oxford Dictionary. The use of monolingual dictionaries in the wider (non-academic) community is probably not as developed as in English-language countries, perhaps because most spelling rules are not as difficult in German as in English. (Additional reasons may be that the authoritative *Duden-Rechtschreibung* only indicates meanings for certain lexical transfers and 'internationalisms' and that Grimm's *Deutches Wörterbuch*, the publication which spanned a century, has 16 volumes and is hardly within the reach of the average native speaker.) On the other hand, English does not have an

---

[3] A committee of the Ständige Konferenz der Kultusminister (Council of state education ministers) in West Germany has made recommendations on spelling conventions since 1956.

authoritative reference grammar corresponding to the Duden.[4] The Mannheim Dudens are sold and used in Austria, Switzerland and Luxembourg (with the reservations expressed above in 1.4). At the 'policy' level, the non-use of dialects in certain domains (e.g. public administration, education in the Federal Republic) is a piece of unwritten planning, with certain sanctions imposed (e.g. discrimination, ostracization, school failure; cf. 3.4). At the 'cultivation' level, on the other hand, a number of non-standard rules are on the way to acceptance. These include the treatment of *brauchen* (to need) as a modal verb (i.e. without *zu*) (Grebe 1968: 39), the substitution of the present indicative for Subjunctive I in indirect speech *daß*-clauses, and the use of *trotz* (despite) with the dative as an alternative to the genitive (Süsskind 1968: 195). Of these, the first two have received recognition in the *Duden-Grammatik*, and the third only limited acknowledgement (1959: 833–5). There is also a growing tendency, in speech, to employ *weil* (because) as a co-ordinating (not subordinating) conjunction, e.g. *weil ich hab' ihn nicht gern* (Standard: *weil ich . . . habe*) (personal communication, Norbert Dittmar and Wolfgang Klein). This has previously been more common in Austria than in the Germanies.

Here we can record differences between written and spoken Standard German. For instance, in his study of the subjunctive in the comprehensive corpus of spoken Standard German collected by the now defunct Freiburg branch of the Institut für deutsche Sprache, Bausch (1979) notes the relatively rare occurrence of Subjunctive I, and that largely in the public domains. He regards its use as interference from the written language (p. 214). In Bausch's corpus only 0.73% of finite verbs are in Subjunctive I as opposed to 5.99% in Subjunctive II. In Jäger's (1972) corpus, the corresponding percentages are 2.79 and 3.95 respectively. However, Subjunctive I is still in active use in upper German dialects, as Graf (1977) has shown. In many, especially Swabian, Alemannic, Baden and Vorarlberg dialects, it predominates over Subjunctive II. (Cf. also 3.1.2.) In spoken Swiss Standard German (e.g. on the radio), too, Subjunctive II is very rarely used as a replacement for Subjunctive I (Rohrer 1973).

---

[4] The comparative use of dictionaries and other language reference books in different language communities needs to be studied empirically among people of matching socioeconomic backgrounds.

Gloy (1974: 239–71) has listed five criteria (or justifications) for norms: structural (systematic, e.g. *als* has to be contrasted with *wie*); historical (tradition dictates the norm); moral quality of varieties (what people are 'doing' to the language by using lexical transfers, or by creating new words, e.g. in the GDR); comprehensibility; and actual use. He sees language norms partly as *social control* (Gloy 1978: 132). In fact, the norms are often an instrument for maintaining the power structure. Many of the arguments in favour of orthographical reform in German gravitate around this.

4.1.1 The spelling reform issue

Since the Second World War, there has been widespread discussion of a possible spelling reform in German. At the centre of this discussion is the capitalization of nouns, which is complicated by a 'grey area' of nouns which are part of idiomatic expressions, and the use of adjectival nouns. This has led to anomalies such as the following:

mit *B*ezug auf/in *b*ezug auf (with reference to); *a*uto*f*ahren (to drive); *R*ad *f*ahren (to cycle) (Moser 1968).

In 1954, a West German committee drafted the 'Stuttgarter Empfehlungen' (Stuttgart Recommendations). They were modified by the Arbeitskreis für Rechtschreibregelungen (Working Party on Spelling Rules) of the Ständige Konferenz der Kultusminister, as the 'Wiesbadener Empfehlungen' (1958). These recommendations, which form the basis of spelling reform proposals in German-language countries today, are set out below.

(a)   Moderate minisculization (*gemäßigte Kleinschreibung*), i.e. lower-case in all words *except* the first word in a sentence, proper nouns (including names for God), pronouns of addresses (*Sie* and its derivatives; *Du/Ihr* and their derivatives in letters, appeals and declarations), and certain scientific and technical abbreviations (e.g. H_2O).

(b)   The restriction of *comma* use to cases where the sentence rhythm and grammatical structure correspond (at present, syntax is the sole criterion).

(c)   The graphemic integration of lexical transfers from other languages, including those of Greek origin (e.g. *Theater* → *Teater*, *Rhythmus* → *Ritmus*).

(d)   The separation of compounds that are, strictly speaking, verb and adverb, e.g. *auto fahren, rad fahren*.

The recommendations were accepted 14:3 by the Federal Republic's commission. In the Federal Republic, the supporters of spelling reform have included writers, academics, schoolteachers, the Duden editorial board, SPD and FDP (liberal) politicians, and trade unionists, while opposition has come mainly from the ranks of some publishers and politicians of the right-wing Christian Democrat and Christian Social parties.

The Wiesbadener Empfehlungen were accepted also by the GDR's commission, but the Austrian commission deadlocked 10:10 in 1961, and in the following year, a committee comprising representatives of Austrian writers, university lecturers in German and two *Sprachvereine* (language societies) opposed spelling reform, while the Niederösterreichisches Institut für Lehrerfortbildung (Lower Austrian Institute for Teacher In-Service Education) supported it. In 1963, the Swiss orthographical commission voted 31:1 against the proposals, which did not differ significantly from those accepted by the Schweizerische Lehrerschaft (Swiss Teachers' Federation) in 1950–1. (It should be noted that Switzerland is the only German-language country to have replaced *ß* by *ss*.)

The Swiss commission was rather biased, being composed of publishers, printing company proprietors, conservative academics and certain authors (Nerius and Scharnhorst 1977: 187–8). It found the proposed rules for punctuation too vague and the recommended graphemic integration of transfers distasteful. The commission's main objection, however, was to the relaxation of capitalization, which had developed with the structure of German and was, they held, indispensable to effective communication. 50 instances of ambiguity introduced by the proposed changes were cited – some of them highly emotive, e.g. *Jene schweizer, die den deutschen Boden verkaufen, . . .* can be interpreted as *Jene Schweizer, die den deutschen Boden verkaufen, . . .* (Those Swiss who are selling German land. . . .) OR *Jene Schweizer, die den Deutschen Boden verkaufen, . . .* (Those Swiss who are selling land to the Germans . . .) (Studer 1963). By 1968, the Swiss *Nationalrat* (National Parliament) and a number of cantonal parliaments were discussing spelling reform, and some of the directors of education had recommended it (Bruderer 1973: 87).

Neither of the Germanies was prepared to threaten the unity of the German-language area by 'going it alone'. Wherever the proposals were discussed, the relationship to literary tradition, technological costs, and problems of transition were seen as the main obstacles. Following the example of other languages was often cited as a motive for spelling reform (German being the only remaining European language with capitalization of all nouns). But by far the most powerful argument has been the educational one.

According to an article in *Die Zeit* (23 February 1973) cited by Zoller (1974: 93), three-quarters of all children who are kept down at school are not promoted because of their spelling, and 30% of all spelling errors are in capitalization. At primary school, there are twice as many failures in spelling as in arithmetic, and dictation is the main cause of non-promotion to secondary school. Spelling reform became an important issue in the educational debate which raged in the Federal Republic in the early 1970s. It was claimed that the present spelling rules (especially the capitalization rules) discriminate against working class children, who have had less exposure to written German in the home than middle class children. A relaxation of spelling requirements was one of the guidelines proposed for German in the schools of Hessen (Christ 1974: 103; cf. above, 3.4).

On the other hand, a survey among 1244 schoolchildren (Pomm, Mewes and Schüttler 1974) suggested that there were no significant class differences in the distribution of pupils' spelling errors. A reform as proposed in the Wiesbadener Empfehlungen would diminish the orthographical errors of *Hauptschüler* (those going to dead-end schools) by 70% and those of pupils in the final year of the *Gymnasium* (the school leading to university) by 93% (Pomm, Mewes and Schüttler 1974: 75). In any case, the social sanctions of 'bad spelling' – non-admission into continuation schools and certain professions, mockery, rating as 'unintelligent' (Augst 1974, Zoller 1974), were increasingly recognized. So was the wastage of teachers' and pupils' time in schools due to the emphasis on capitalization (Bauer 1973: 109), corresponding to that placed on the spelling of words in English-language countries.

In 1973, pressures for orthographical reform in the Federal Republic probably reached their climax. In that year, there were numerous citizens' action groups campaigning for change, e.g.

aktion kleinschreibung; verein für rechtschreibvereinfachung (society for orthographical simplification). There was also an ultra-right-wing Bund für deutsche Schrift (Association for German Script), an organization with relatively little support, advocating the maintenance of capitalization of nouns as well as a return to the distinctively German gothic script. A combined conference of the Gewerkschaft Erziehung und Wissenschaft (teachers' union), PEN, and the Schriftstellerverband (authors' union) in 1973 supported spelling reform, as did a petition signed by 50 cultural personalities. The conference of secondary and tertiary German teachers (Germanistentag) in Trier in the same year emphatically advocated the need for *Kleinschreibung*, and declared itself opposed to using spelling marks as a criterion for promotion to a higher school grade and in favour of a boycott on marking spelling errors, which some teachers actually carried out.

In 1973, public opinion polls found that 51% of West Germans were in favour of moderate minusculization and 32% against it, while 54% of Swiss were in favour of its immediate introduction, 25% of a gradual introduction, and only 17% against. Of the Germans, men favoured spelling reform more than did women, and young people more than the old (Zoller 1974: 116).

At the instigation of the Bund für vereinfachte Rechtschreibung (Association for Simplified Spelling), a new conference on spelling reform was held in Zürich. In Switzerland there were still powerful conservative forces holding back reform (Nerius and Scharnhorst 1977: 191). New spelling conferences in Austria and the GDR in 1973 set in motion research on the implementation of orthographical reform in both countries.

A new *Zeitschrift für germanistische Linguistik* (Journal of German Linguistics) was established in 1973: all its articles were to be printed in moderate minusculization. The magazine of the IG Druck und Papier (Printers' Union) also went over to *gemäßigte Kleinschreibung*. To an increasing extent, poetry was written in the new orthography;[5] so were private and business letters. But the education ministers could not be moved into reforms. In the pendulum swing to the right in matters social, educational and political in the subsequent years, the spelling debate gradually subsided. The issue is still discussed, but

---

[5] Some poets (e.g. members of the George circle) and philologists (e.g. Jakob Grimm) have turned to minusculization in past eras.

in more closed circles (Mentrup 1979). An international conference on German orthography took place in Vienna in 1979. At that conference, the Gesellschaft für deutsche Sprache proposed a 'purified majusculization' in which rules are more clearly defined (Augst 1980). There are committees in the Federal Republic working on proposals for *gemäßigte Kleinschreibung* and modified capitalization and one in the GDR promoting the Wiesbadener Empfehlungen, but each country appears to be waiting for unanimity. Meanwhile, schoolchildren are still penalized as a result of the unnecessary imposition of capitalization – and the *Zeitschrift für germanistische Linguistik* now publishes articles with capitalized nouns! However, the situation in Austria was liberalized in 1974 by a declaration to schools from the Ministry of Education requesting tolerance in areas of orthographical uncertainty, especially in primary schools (Augst 1980).

4.2 Communication barriers

In Chapter 5, I shall outline how the spelling of lexical transfers can function as a communication barrier in West German society (5.7). The role of dialect (and the town–country dichotomy) and orthography in general in perpetuating class distinctions has already been considered (3.4; 4.1.1 respectively). Sex-specific language barriers will be discussed under 8.5. An important part in this process is played by the media, especially in the Federal Republic, largely through the implementation of the widespread use of lexical and semantic transfers and of *Fachsprache* (technical language).

Another important aspect of the problem is that the complexity of German syntactic rules for embedding offers potential for considerable syntactic differences between more 'learned' and more 'ordinary' registers. (In English, such differences are manifested mainly at the lexical level.) This applies to both participial and dependent clauses.

Compare the following:

> Die *über drei Jahre durchgeführte* Untersuchung (the investigation conducted over three years); Die Untersuchung, die drei Jahre dauert (the investigation which takes (will take) three years).

The former construction, in which the second sentence is embedded into the noun phrase, is more characteristic of the 'learned' register, as is the next example:

> . . . daß diese Veröffentlichung, die erst jetzt, wo die Ergebnisse schon ohnehin bekannt *sind, erschienen ist,* . . . (. . . that the publication only appeared now that the results are known anyway . . .).

In more ordinary register, the *erschienen ist* would follow *erst jetzt* directly, and the sentence would most likely be split.

German academic register is also marked by the following:

(a) Agentless passives, and impersonal and reflexive constructions (Polenz 1981, Panther 1981), e.g. Als allgemeiner Begriff *empfiehlt sich* . . . (as general concept. . . . *recommends itself*).

(b) Hedged performatives using modals *kann, muß* and *darf* and passive infinitives (Panther 1981), e.g. Wir können allgemeine Übereinstimmung *voraussagen* (we can *predict* general agreement). Ein Kreis von Entscheidungen ist *zu kennzeichnen* als Aggression (a group of decisions is *to be characterized* as aggression).

(c) A large number of nominalizations and compound nouns (Polenz 1963).

4.2.1 Media

There are few English-speaking countries where the distinction between high-quality national dailies and mass-circulation newspapers is as marked as it is in the Federal Republic. This is manifested in the layout, content, sentence lengths, syntactic structures and lexical choices. The extreme examples are undoubtedly the *Frankfurter Allgemeine* (daily circulation, Monday to Friday, 355,900; Saturday 426,700),[6] and the *Bild-Zeitung* (daily circulation, 5,853,000).[7] In *Bild*, headlines and pictures play an important part, while the print and columns are quite even in the *Frankfurter Allgemeine*, which lacks illustrations on the front page. According to Eggers (1969: 15), the typical sentence in the *Frankfurter Allgemeine*

---

[6] 1979 figures kindly provided by the publishers.
[7] 1980 figures kindly provided by the publishers.

has 13 words, while *Bild*'s typical sentence is 5 words long. Braun (1979: 38) found that only 13% of the sentences in *Bild* comprised 21 words or more, as compared with 34.6% in the *Westdeutsche Allgemeine Zeitung* (a regional newspaper) and 46.3% in the *Frank-furter Allgemeine*. In Mittelberg's (1967: 244–5) corpus of 12 topically-selected articles from each 1964 issue, 19.5% of *Bild* sentences and 40% of sentences in the *Frankfurter Allgemeine* had subordinate clauses. If we count only logically dependent clauses (i.e. not subordinate clauses used as independent sentences), the *Frankfur-ter Allgemeine* has 250% more subordination than *Bild*. On the other hand, exclamations, requests/demands and rhetorical questions abound in *Bild* (Mittelberg 1967: 195), and the subjunctive (Mit-telberg 1967: 293) and other more complicated formations are avoided. Syntax and lexicon are kept to the comprehension level of the less discerning reader. Because of the predominance of co-ordination and the limited space afforded to political news, the *Bild* reader is told what to believe, without very much evidence being given. *Bild* is the newspaper of the masses who read it on public transport. Since Axel Springer, the proprietor of *Bild* (and of many other West German newspapers), gives his readers an ultra-conservative view of the world, German syntax plays a part in the manipulation of newspaper readers.[8] On the other hand, the *Frankfurter Allgemeine* (also a conservative newspaper) employs a lexicon (including lexical and semantic transfers and technical terms) and a syntax (with participial constructions and multiple embeddings) which only the linguistically most able and the highly motivated can cope with.

In-between the *Frankfurter Allgemeine* and *Bild* are the other two national dailies, the *Süddeutsche Zeitung* (liberal) and *Die Welt* (ultra-conservative; another Springer publication), and the many regional dailies, most of which belong to a small number of media chains and derive their news from common sources. Examples of regional dailies are the *Stuttgarter Zeitung*, the *Neue Ruhr Zeitung* and the *Frankfurter Rundschau* (which is a left-wing liberal news-paper, with a small circulation also in other regions).

A similar situation obtains in Austria, although the two extremes do not have equivalents. Table 3 is based on six articles on the same

---

[8] On the manipulation of readers by the West German press in general, as exemplified by reports of parliamentary debates, see Hoppenkamps (1977).

Table 3. Some syntactic characteristics of a number of Austrian newspapers (12 April 1978).

	Simple sentences %	Succession of simple sentences, linked with comma %	Complex sentences %
Wiener Morgen Kurier (fairly conservative)	36.5	23.0	40.3
Arbeiterzeitung (socialist)	29.5	15.9	54.5
Salzburger Nachrichten (liberal)	39.0	7.8	53.1
Die Presse (liberal)	34.0	9.5	56.3
Neue Kronen-Zeitung (right-wing)	60.9	7.3	31.7

topic, one in each of five Austrian newspapers, on 12 April 1978. (The Austrian government daily, *Wiener Zeitung*, which features official announcements of all kinds, is not included.) The comparison covers three types of sentences: simple sentence; a succession of simple sentences, linked with a comma; complex sentence, comprising a simple sentence and one or more subordinate clauses.

In the GDR, many newspapers are the official organs of political parties (which are all subservient to the Sozialistische Einheitspartei Deutschlands – the government party). Often the same article, word for word, appears in several, or all of the daily newspapers. However, an analysis of eight news reports on the same topic, one in each of five East Berlin dailies, yielded the comparison shown in Table 4. *Neues Deutschland* is the official organ of the Sozialistische Einheitspartei Deutschlands; *Neue Zeit* of the Liberal-Demokratische Partei Deutschlands; *National-Zeitung* of the National-Demokratische Partei Deutschlands; and *Der Morgen* of the Christlich-Demokrat-ische Union. (All parties are subordinated to the SED.) *BZ Am Abend* is the GDR's nearest equivalent to the *Bild-Zeitung*. While *BZ Am Abend* does not differ from the other newspapers as to the proportion of complex sentences, *Der Morgen* appears to employ fewer simple

Table 4. Some syntactic characteristics of a number of GDR newspapers (16 February 1978).

	Simple sentences %	Succession of simple sentences, linked with comma %	Complex sentences %
BZ Am Abend	61.9	8.4	29.5
Neue Zeit	64.7	7.0	28.1
National-Zeitung	68.0	10.6	21.3
Neues Deutschland	62.7	3.1	34.0
Der Morgen	50.0	7.1	42.8

and a larger number of complex sentences than the other dailies. In addition, in the articles studied, *Der Morgen* uses by far the highest number and percentage of participial constructions (*Schachtelsätze*) and *BZ Am Abend* the lowest. *Der Morgen*, as the newspaper of the Christlich-Demokratische Union, perhaps tries to avoid syntactic simplification which could be associated with centralized control and foreign (either Russian or American) influence.

While there have been numerous examinations of language and the media in the Federal Republic, this topic needs to be taken up more in Austria and Switzerland. Investigations of GDR newspaper German tend to give much emphasis to *Neues Deutschland*, and we know relatively little about the language of television, radio, and the other daily newspapers in the GDR.

Böhm *et al* (1972) found that the syntactic complexity of West and East German radio news broadcasts was greater than that of urban everyday speech. This is particularly so in news about conferences, treaties, visits and debates, while the coverage of accidents, crime and weather is syntactically simpler. The average sentence length varied from 12.4 words on the Südwestfunk (Baden Baden) to 16.1 on the Norddeutscher Rundfunk (Hamburg). Cloze tests based on news broadcasts demonstrated the comprehension difficulties of (15-year-old) German pupils from working class backgrounds who were attending *Hauptschulen*, in comparison with middle class informants and those attending continuation schools. They could understand the sensational parts but not the political sections (Böhm *et al* 1972: 168). No doubt knowledge of, and/or interest in the content must also have played a part. In about 50% of the news items, information and opinions are combined in a way that is confusing to the uncritical hearer (p. 170). Among the sources of comprehension problems in radio and TV news broadcasts are lexical transfers from English and other languages, and complex syntax. Even the separation of prefixes from verbs can be very taxing on the temporary memory where there are several phrases or embedded clauses (as is demonstrated by Yngve's (1960) hypothesis).

There is considerable situational variability in syntactic usage. In her study of the passive, based on a large corpus of spoken Standard German collected by the Institut für deutsche Sprache (old Freiburg branch), Schoenthal (1976) found passive constructions far more prevalent in the public domains (6% of utterances) than in private discourse (0.9%). They also occurred less in reportages (e.g. sport) than, say, in non-topical interviews or reports (e.g. of the visit of a foreign celebrity). Similarly, the average length of German sentences was higher in the public sphere (15.2 words) than in private domains (12 words).

4.2.2 *Fachsprache*

The use of *Fachsprache* (technical language) has been attributed, by Ammon (1973a: 76–81), to the division of labour between and within industries. Schönfeld and Donath (1978) conclude that, within factories in the GDR, technical terms can cause a communication barrier. They cite an incident (p. 23) where workers could not name a machine that was disturbing them. They show that occupation, educational level (general and job training), years of service, the nature of employment, and the reading of professional and trade literature are criteria for the mastery of *Fachsprache*. In the factories they studied, the foremen were best able to understand and use *Fachsprache*. Abbreviations, which may be seen as part of *Fachsprache*, also make for in-group communication that may exclude those outside the group. Much *Fachsprache*, especially from the fields of politics and economics, has found its way into the everyday speech of individuals and groups in all German-speaking countries as well as into the mass media. This is a way in which all but

83

people with a wide general knowledge and diverse interests can suffer some communication breakdown (Mentrup 1978). There are also problems in communication between 'experts' and lay people (Lippert 1978 and other papers in Mentrup 1978). Such problems are, of course, not restricted to German-language countries, but at the syntactic level, register differences (see above, 4.2) tend to exacerbate them.

4.3 Restricted and elaborated code

The early thesis of Basil Bernstein (1962), the English educational sociologist – that middle class children employ a more complex syntax and a more differentiated and less context-bound lexicon ('elaborated code') and working class children a 'restricted code' – was widely and fanatically acclaimed in the Federal Republic in the late 60s and early 70s. Propagated by Oevermann, who conducted investigations in Germany (Oevermann 1970) which paralleled (though did not always agree with the results of) Bernstein's London research, the thesis became part of the debate on educational reform that was current at the time. It was argued that if children are conditioned, by family class factors, to use a 'restricted code', i.e. restricted strategies of verbal planning, they think in a restricted way and their cognitive development is impeded. Compensatory language instruction as from preschool level was seen by many Germans as the answer to what came to be known as *Sprachbarrieren* and, more generally, to social inequalities in various spheres of life.

Journalists, educationists, social workers, and industrial chaplains, among others, took up the 'deficit hypothesis' without being aware that it had already been severely challenged, not only by Labov (e.g. 1969) and other proponents of the 'difference hypothesis', but also by members of Bernstein's own school (e.g. Coulthard 1969, Robinson 1965). The notion of the two 'codes', their link with class(es), and the compensatory language programmes had all been found wanting, and Bernstein himself had progressed beyond the much-quoted and widely accepted theory. There were Germans such as Kleinschmidt (1972) who tried to replicate Bernstein's research, and concluded that the connection between 'restricted code' and working class children and between 'elaborated code' and middle class children could not be upheld. Kleinschmidt found that it was the level of authoritativeness in the family that was crucial in determining the 'elaborateness' of speech.

Klein and Wunderlich (1971), Dittmar (1973) and Steger (1971) introduced Labov's work to the German-reading public. In the meantime, some Marxist ideological supporters of the deficit hypothesis realized that compensatory language instruction, even if it were effective, could not lead to a one-class society, let alone a 'dictatorship of the proletariat'. It could, at best, bring some more members of the working class into the middle class!

Subsequently, three major studies in the Federal Republic – Klann (1975), Neuland (1975) and Jäger (1978) – found class differences in samples of children's speech, but not the ones described by Bernstein and his followers. Neuland's corpus of 32,000 words is derived from descriptions of five pictures and the retelling of three stories by 40 preschool children, whose age, sex and socioeconomic status are taken into account. Intelligence and creativity tests ensured that the middle and lower class children were comparable. Lower class children used more nouns and prepositions, middle class children pronouns, verbs, articles, numerals and interjections. The class predominance of nouns and pronouns was actually the reverse of that in Bernstein and Oevermann. Lower class children did tend to employ more imperatives and interrogatives while statement sentences and relative clauses were more common among the middle class informants. But there appears to be a common repertoire of sentence patterns, with no differences in the incidence of subordination. More importantly, there were particular words which were class-specific, e.g. *sich einigen* (to agree), *Einladung* (invitation), *Eigentum* (property): middle class; colloquial words *Butters* (for *Butterbrote*, sandwiches), *Buxe* (for *Hose*, trousers), *Polente* (for *Polizei*, police): lower class. The middle class children employed more specific lexemes, such as *Gummistiefel* (gum boots) and *Strickjacke* (cardigan), whereas more general ones predominated among the lower class, e.g. *Arbeitszeug* (work stuff), *Geburtstagssachen* (birthday things). Due to their divergent social experiences, the two groups associated different items with the words *Arbeiter* (worker) and *Polizei* (police). From Neuland's work it can be concluded that any deficit (rather than difference) is only a later phenomenon caused by the middle-class-oriented school situation.

Klann's conclusions are based on 56 4th grade (*c.* 9-year-old) pupils retelling two stories to an unfamiliar adult. Klann's detailed comparisons indicate great difficulty in establishing class-specific language styles. Not only do class and sex differences sometimes polarize tendencies in the use of syntactic rules in different directions, but parental language support and the child's intelligence have a differing impact on the syntax in the two socioeconomic groups. However, Klann is able to conclude that the middle class children produced speech that was, in fact, less complex and more 'ornamental' than that of the lower class children. The latter's speech was, on the whole, structurally and cognitively more complex in their attempts to relate those parts of the stories relevant to them. Complex embedding was more common in the lower class, while middle class children tended more towards simple embedding. While the working class pupils kept to the original text, the middle class informants simplified its syntax. However, pro-forms (e.g. pronouns) were to be found most in the speech of the lower class children. Klann calls for research into class-specific speech to be directed towards a pragmatic approach – verbal planning strategies within the framework of a theory of action which can be substantiated by social psychology.

Jäger's (1978) 160 ten-year-olds and 80 fourteen-year-olds (matched for class and sex) related a cartoon entitled 'Warum weint die Giraffe?' (Why is the giraffe crying?) to a member of their peer group they themselves had selected. The lower class children tended to comment less than the middle class children and were less able to pass on concepts to others. They had more difficulty in structuring the plot, their formulations were more involved, and their language contained more deviations from the norms. The middle class children's texts were longer, more abstract, and more plastic.

Jäger (1972) ironically described compensatory language instruction as a 'Bürgerliches Trauerspiel' (bourgeois tragedy). The theoretical basis of the programmes and the social situation prevented them from achieving social mobility, according to Jäger. In fact, middle class children alone were benefiting from them. Fear of the teacher was causing lower class children to use 'restricted code'. Bernstein (1970) himself repudiated the way in which he had been interpreted, in an article entitled 'Der Unfug mit dem kompensatorischen Sprachunterricht' (The nonsense about compensatory language instruction), published in a German progressive education journal.

As a result of the ensuing disappointment, sociolinguistics, which for several years had been generally identified with the Bernstein 'codes', fell into disrepute in the Federal Republic, but recovered its status largely through empirical studies of variation and guest worker German. Apart from the shaky theoretical foundations of the deficit hypothesis, Britain can hardly be regarded as a model for the relationship between language and class in the Federal Republic, which has a rather different class structure. By 1972 the debate in the Federal Republic had added the dimension of dialects to the perception of communication barriers (e.g. Ammon 1972). In spite of the cooling down of the heat of the educational reform debate in recent years, the problems of working class monodialectal speakers in the education system are still under discussion, as I have shown (3.4).

4.4 Guest worker German and German foreigner talk

The greatest communication barrier of all is that experienced by the 1.9 million guest workers[9] and their families in the Federal Republic (together totalling 4.6 million) and by similar individuals and groups in Austria, Switzerland and Luxembourg. Those in the Federal Republic come mostly from Turkey, Yugoslavia, Italy, Greece or Spain. They tend to lead a marginal existence due to the policy assumptions that they are only *temporary* members of the West German work force and that the Federal Republic is not an immigration country. In 1978, two-thirds of the guest workers then in the Federal Republic had been there for six years or more, and one quarter had lived there for over ten years (Rieck and Senft 1978: 90). The guest workers have brought many of their dependants to the Federal Republic. There are now about a million 'foreign' children in West Germany, many of whom were born there. In addition, Stölting (1978: 99) estimated about a million 'potential migrants' among children waiting in the guest workers' home countries.

Some ethnic groups tend to concentrate in certain cities or regions (e.g. Turks in West Berlin, Yugoslavs in Stuttgart, Greeks in Munich). Many companies prefer to employ only guest workers of a particular nationality. This may result in large school populations of ethnic minority children in particular districts, e.g. some primary

---

[9] To an increasing extent, *Migrant, Immigrant, Arbeitsmigrant* and *ausländischer Arbeiter* are used in the German literature in preference to the more popular but less appropriate *Gastarbeiter*.

schools in the West Berlin suburb of Kreuzberg draw over 50% of their enrolment from children of Turkish background. According to Stölting (1978: 100), 'an average of *c*. 60% of the foreign school-children do not get the final certificate of the Hauptschule which is required for admission to vocational training'. A concern, in recent years, for the problems of guest workers has highlighted the unsatisfactory nature of schooling arrangements, regardless of whether the children are likely to return to the country of origin or, as is more probable, to stay in the Federal Republic. The two main models currently followed are: (i) 'national classes' for up to two years as a preparation for joining ordinary German classes (general model); (ii) 'national classes' in primary and non-continuation schools (in Bavaria since 1973, in North-Rhine Westphalia since 1976), with an optional transfer to German classes (in North-Rhine Westphalia compulsory after Grade 6). Bilingual classes of type (ii) are on the increase and particularly prevalent in Bavaria. A variation on these models are 'international' preparatory classes consisting of different groups of 'foreigners' (Stölting 1978). But the 'general model' is still very widespread after children have attended pre-paratory classes. Where numbers warrant this, special classes are formed for foreign pupils, using German as the medium of instruction (Stölting 1978, Gutfleisch and Rieck 1981).

Increased preoccupation with migrant problems has been accompanied by a snowballing of research into the German spoken by guest workers. 'Migrant worker German' shows striking uniformity, regardless of the speaker's base language. The speech of those guest workers whose German has not developed beyond a very restricted stage (i.e. the basilect) is marked by the deletion of articles, prepositions, subject-pronouns, copula and auxiliaries; the over-generalization of a particular verbal form (either infinitive or stem), a tendency towards the deletion of bound morphemes, co-ordination (not subordination), and the generalized use of *du*, and of *nix* for *nicht*, *nichts*, *nie* and *kein*. But of course there is considerable variation. At the second cut-off point on the continuum (the mesolect), there are indications of the generalization of *die* as a definite article, as well as the extended use of *müssen* as an auxiliary (perhaps a reflection of their status!) (Heidelberger For-schungsprojekt 1975, 1976, 1978, Dittmar 1979, Gilbert and Orlović 1975, Meisel 1975, Clyne 1968b). Lattey and Müller (1976) suggest that many guest workers use a stable, rigid, formulaic variety in the work place and a more innovative interlanguage in expanded *communication situations.

Through interviews and participant observation, the Heidelberger Forschungsprojekt (1975, 1976, Dittmar 1978, Klein and Dittmar 1979) ranked Italian and Spanish adult learners according to their German proficiency and postulated an order for the acquisition of grammatical rules, e.g. '(preposition +) subject and nominal complex' is an early rule, as is 'simple verb'. Then follow 'simple verb modified by modal', then 'simple and copulative verb modified by modal or auxiliary' and finally 'simple and copulative verb modified by modal and auxiliary' (Dittmar 1978: 139). Meisel and his project team in Hamburg are studying the acquisition of German by Italians, Spaniards and Portuguese through a longitudinal study, following their cross-sectional research (Clahsen, Meisel and Pienemann 1983). Often the basilectal features of the migrants' German gradually give way to first-language interference as the functions of the first and second languages become more similar. Stölting (1980) has shown that, among Yugoslav children in Essen, German has largely become the dominant language, which is the source of interference in the first language. However, the situation varies between ethnic groups, language maintenance and problems of German acquisition being much greater among the Turks.

The Heidelberger Forschungsprojekt (1976: 308–28) has isolated factors which appear to correlate with a higher level of syntax: (in order of importance) contact with Germans in leisure (applies mainly to those married to German speakers); age on arrival; contact with Germans at work; qualifications in home country; years of schooling; period of residence in Germany. Three factors of lesser significance were sex, base language and living conditions (the latter being closely connected with 'contact with Germans in leisure'). A study by Bodemann and Ostow (1975) on communication between guest workers and Germans in the domains of work, the law and administration contributes the following points to the discussion:

(1) The *Weisen* (wise people) – guest workers selected by the company to act as interpreters – control communication, 'monopolize' both the German language and advancement in the factory, and assist in the exploitation of fellow-countrymen.

This demonstrates the hierarchical significance of competence in German and the role of German as an instrument of exclusion.

(2) The court interpreter controls communication between Germans and foreigners.

(3) The employment of a homogeneous group of guest workers (i.e. of one nationality) by a company reduces the power of 'Weisen' and facilitates an improvement both in conditions and in communications.

(4) *Du* is used by German work superiors to guest workers as a symbol of power. The reciprocal *du*, usually reserved to express solidarity (see 6.4), is employed in this very asymmetrical situation, presumably because of the guest workers' marginality.

The appropriateness of the term 'pidgin' for guest worker German has been the subject of controversy (e.g. Heidelberger Forschungsprojekt 1975: 26–35, Meisel 1975, Clyne 1968b, 1977a, Fox 1977, Gilbert 1978). Generally, those employing the term do so in line with the notion (Whinnom 1971) of a pidgin being a code used for restricted communication between people of more than two different mother tongues, e.g. German, Italian, Serbo-Croatian, Turkish, Greek, as well as through linguistic comparisons with well-defined pidgins. The marginal and subordinate situation of foreigners in a country in which they are not *supposed* to integrate has parallels with that of plantation workers, although it is necessary to keep industrial and plantation pidgins separate. The relationship to the target-language-speaking community is one of the points on which the use of the term 'pidgin' for guest worker German is challenged (e.g. by Meisel 1975). Meisel argues that the migrants' amount of contact with German entails a continued language learning process rather than the opportunity for an independent pidgin to stabilize. But the vast majority of guest workers have very little access to the dominant group and do not attend German classes, and they are frequently addressed in foreigner talk (see below). Another matter of disagreement is how stable a pidgin needs to be (Meisel 1975, Gilbert 1978, Heidelberger Forschungsprojekt 1975, Clyne 1977a). Like any language or variety, guest worker German is marked by variation. In an early publication, the Heidelberger Forschungsprojekt (1975) postulates four stages along a continuum in the migrants' development of German:

P1   Deficient knowledge of German, better comprehension than production.

P2   Contact with Germans and other guest workers, but they are not part of the main communication network and the subjects' German is insufficient for their communication needs.

P3   Relatively stable; pidgin is integrated with their social and communicative needs; no motivation for further language acquisition.

P4   Completely integrated; speech gravitates towards regional dialect.

Most of the subjects fall into categories P2 and P3. Schumann (1978) describes a pidginization process in a similar second-language acquisition situation in the U.S. Some misgivings about the term 'pidgin' (e.g. Stölting 1975: 56) are associated with a feeling that the scientific preoccupation with this language variety may detract from the social and political needs of migrant workers. Gilbert (1978) has devised the term 'industrial immigrant talk' to avoid the issue of the existence of a pidgin.

One argument favouring the notion of a guest worker pidgin is the widespread use, by Germans *to* guest workers, of 'foreigner talk', marked by linguistic indices similar to those of guest worker German (Clyne 1968, Meisel 1975). Even though the Bloomfieldian (1933: 473) principle of foreigners and native speakers imitating one another is now generally not acceptable, there is widespread evidence of foreigners' language competence influencing the way they are addressed (e.g. Clyne 1977b, Snow, van Eeden and Muysken 1981, Mühlhäusler 1981). Also, the use of foreigner talk reduces (or eliminates) the foreigners' access to the target language.

No extensive studies have yet been undertaken on these problems in other German-language countries. In German Switzerland and Luxembourg, the situation is complicated by di- and triglossia respectively. However, investigations (e.g. by Snow, Van Eeden and Muysken; R. Appel; Hyltenstam; Hammarberg; and Viberg) of similar phenomena have taken place in the Netherlands and Sweden.

4.5 A note on language in institutions

There is now a very extensive literature on language in institutions in German-language countries, covering classroom interaction (e.g. Goeppert 1977, Ehlich and Rehbein 1977), doctor–patient interaction (e.g. Bliesener 1980), psychotherapy (e.g. Sluga 1977, Flader 1978, Klann 1978, Trömel-Plötz 1978b, Wodak-Leodolter 1980), court (e.g. Leodolter 1975, Hoffmann 1980) and restaurants (e.g. Ehlich and Rehbein 1972).

All these studies constitute in some measure research on communication barriers. For instance, summarizing courtroom studies in Vienna, Dressler and Wodak (1982b) contrast the security of the middle class defendants who use a single linguistic style with the insecurity of the working and lower middle classes manifested in style shifts. However, most studies contribute particularly to knowledge on the nature of interaction and the roles of language. It has not been possible, within this monograph, to assess – perhaps through comparisons with similar studies in English-language countries – the specifically German character of institutional interaction.

4.6 Brief summary

German is not a language with strong centralized planning agencies, with the exception of the GDR *Duden*. The role of conservative 'language societies' has declined over the years, and the general attitude towards norms is tolerant.

There is a social polarization of the German language due to variations in syntactic complexity, the use and integration of English transfers, and the use of technical language. The media (especially in the Federal Republic) play a role in exacerbating such barriers, and some people there and in Austria are denied access to objective information because of the sociolect used by most high-quality media.

Many people (especially schoolchildren) are discriminated against because of their inability to follow the confusing rules of capitalization. Attempts at achieving orthographical reform have highlighted a problem of pluricentric languages – maintaining unity despite differing vested interests in different countries. Demands for orthographical reform have waned as has the educational debate with which they were associated. A major part of this was the West German response to Bernstein's deficit hypothesis, which has been found to be somewhat misguided.

Examples of communication barriers may be found in the study of language in institutions. The greatest communication barriers, however, arc those experienced by the guest workers, due to their social marginality. The German spoken by many guest workers has features and functions in common with pidgins. Foreigner talk employed by Germans to guest workers restricts the input of Standard German.

4.7 Further reading

The spelling reform issue is summarized in Augst (1974) and Mentrup (1978). GDR Sprachkultur is treated from a number of viewpoints in Ising (1977) and normative issues are discussed conservatively in the periodicals *Sprachdienst* (Federal Republic) and *Sprachpflege* (GDR). There is a flourishing German literature on *Fachsprache* in general. Ehlich and Rehbein (1980) is a good summary of research on language in institutions. The papers in Mentrup (1978) are of special interest in the German context. The main results of the two large projects on guest worker German may be found in Klein and Dittmar (1979) and Clahsen, Meisel and Pienemann (1983).

5

Recent Anglo-American influence

5.1 Anglo-American influence in a general context

A language can undergo renewal and enrichment through neologisms, semantic shift (especially extension of meanings), and transference from other languages. Transference of items and elements is the result of culture contact. Virtually all languages have had periods of large-scale language contact. Manifestations of this in the history of the German language have been the Latin influence on Old High German and 16th century German, as well as the French influence on Middle High German and 18th century German. There have been epochs of nationalistic purism (Nüssler 1979). One such period was the 17th century, when writers who saw themselves as language planners grouped themselves into *Sprachgesellschaften* (language societies), one of whose tasks was to develop a German free of foreign (especially Romance) elements. Another was the time of the National Socialist dictatorship in Germany (including Austria), when words of 'non-Germanic' origin were replaced by 'pure Germanic' lexemes.

The present period of openness to internationalization and foreign influence in the Germanies may be seen partly as a reaction to the National Socialist era. Moreover, it is a consequence of postwar political and cultural developments. By the end of the Second World War, the German language had lost most of its international status to English in the west (as had French) and much of its position in the east to Russian. To an increasing extent, political alignments concentrated around what were to become the two 'super-powers', the United States and the Soviet Union. They were the super-powers in a technological and scientific as well as a political sense, and they provided German-language countries with new concepts as well as the new vocabulary of politics, economics, technology and many other fields. English influence in the west and Russian influence in the east reflect an 'internationalization' and facilitate the ready translatability of concepts and texts from language to language. They have contributed to the efficiency of press agencies and simultaneous translation. In the Federal Republic, the period of intense language contact was initiated by the presence of American and British occupation troops over most of its territory since four years before its foundation in 1949.[1] Parts of Austria, too, were occupied by armies from English-language countries until 1955.

In the western German-language countries, English influence on the German language is symptomatic of the internationalization of many domains. Close economic, political and/or strategic alliances like NATO, the European Community and the European Free Trade Association; scientific, technological and cultural co-operation; the mass media; multinational corporations; and supranational tendencies in the arts, student politics, terrorism, the pop and drug scenes, and pornography are all examples of these. More people from more different language backgrounds are communicating than ever before (except perhaps in wartime), and, in Western Europe, their lingua franca tends to be English.

This has resulted in the replacement of national languages by English in some domains within one country (e.g. computer science and air travel in most Western European countries, academic publishing in the Netherlands and Scandinavia), between nations with related languages (e.g. as a conference language in Scandinavia, Hughes 1972), and, to a growing extent, sometimes even between the ethnic groups of one nation (e.g. in Belgium). Naturally 'specialized' vocabulary (*Fachwortschatz*) is then transferred from English into the vernaculars throughout Western Europe and beyond. (This has been discussed beyond German, e.g. by Fishman, Cooper and Conrad 1977; Zandvoort 1964 for Dutch, Filipović 1974 for Serbo-Croatian.)

In almost all the schools of the Federal Republic and Austria, English is now the first foreign language,[2] a situation also common to

---

[1] It is interesting to note, however, that French had little or no influence on the German of the French-occupied areas.

[2] Except in the Saarland and some areas of Baden-Württemberg bordering on France, where it is French.

95

the Netherlands and the Scandinavian countries (where it is introduced in the primary school). Young children from, say, the Federal Republic, Sweden and the Netherlands will converse with each other in English when they meet on holidays. The majority of students entering universities and colleges of advanced education in the Federal Republic will have taken nine years of English at school.

Exposure to English is greater in the Netherlands, Belgium and Scandinavia than in the German-language countries, due at least in part to the predominance, in the former, of sub-titled, rather than dubbed English films on their television channels, which are seen even by children who cannot read their first language!

I will not attempt to distinguish here between American and British influence, but in most cases it is American culture that has been the source of English transference into German in the postwar period. In some cases it is impossible to differentiate between new developments due to English influence and those that have other causes. The lifespan of different transfers varies, as would be revealed by diachronic studies if they had been undertaken. English influence on contemporary German has not been examined extensively in Switzerland and Luxembourg. The remarks on these countries are therefore superficial, as are those on comic language, a promising area for future research. There is a need for macrosociolinguistic studies on the use of functions of (spoken and written) English in the German-language countries, both internally and in communication with people from other countries.

5.2 Types of transference

There are a great many examples of elements and rules transferred from English into German and these include not only lexical but also semantic and syntactic transfers.

5.2.1 Lexical and semantic transfers

By far the most common type of transference from English has been at the *lexical* level – words such as *Beat, Cockpit, Marketing*, and *Team*, which have been taken over from English in form and meaning. This includes nouns (e.g. *der Appeal, Blue Jeans, das*

Comeback), verbs (e.g. *babysitten, jobben, killen*), adjectives/adverbs (e.g. *fit, high, live*) and interjections (*bye bye, hi!*).

There are also *semantic* transfers, where the meaning of English words is transferred to existing German ones with which they share some phonic correspondence, partial semantic correspondence, or both. Instances include the following:

'loan-translations' (each part translated), such as: *Beiprodukt* (by-product), *Datenverarbeitung* (data processing), *Drogenszene* (drug scene), and *Gehirnwäsche* (brain-washing);

'loan-renditions' (one part transferred, one *based* on English), such as: *Autodienststation* (service station; literally, car service station); *Titelgeschichte* (cover story; literally, title story); *Untertreibung* (understatement; cf. *Übertreibung*, overstatement);

'loan-meanings' (transference of meaning), such as: *feuern* (to fire from job, original German meaning: to fire, shoot), *sehen* (to see, visit, original German meaning: to see with one's eyes);

'loan-idioms' (morpheme-for-morpheme transference of idiom), such as: *das Beste aus etwas machen* (to make the best of something), *Geben und Nehmen* (give and take), *grünes Licht geben* (to give the green light).

(Carstensen 1965, Carstensen and Galinsky 1967; terminology based on Betz 1949.)

Some semantic transfers were originally lexical transfers from English or French, whose meaning or domain has been extended as a result of further language contact, e.g. *starten* (from the domain of sport and motoring to a more general usage), *realisieren* (from a transitive verb, 'to realize' a wish or ambition, to an intransitive one, 'to grasp', 'to understand') *resignieren* (from 'to resign oneself to one's fate', to 'resign from a job'). Sometimes older transfers are revitalized through English influence, e.g. *Allergie* (allergy, extended beyond the medical field), *Generation* (as in '*dritte Automobilgeneration*' – third generation of cars) (Carstensen 1979b). On the basis of Galinsky's (1980) comparative analysis of English and German dictionary entries, the time lag for the reception of semantic transfers from English is longer than that for lexical transfers.

5.2.2 Syntactic transfers

According to Carstensen (1965: 80), the transference of English syntactic rules has led to the transitivization of verbs in environments where this was unusual for German, e.g. 'Ich fliege Lufthansa' (I fly Lufthansa; ich fliege *mit der* Lufthansa), '4000 Tote befürchtet' (headline – 4000 feared dead) (Carstensen 1965: 80). Some grammatical categories have become convertible in advertisements based on an English model, e.g. '*Moore* dich gesund' (*Moore* yourself well; proper noun→verb) (Carstensen and Galinsky 1967: 19). Besides, English influence has prompted the early placement of the genitive in phrases like 'Hamburgs Bürgermeister' (Hamburg's mayor; for *Der Bürgermeister von Hamburg*), as well as the loose addition of the age designation in newspaper articles, e.g. 'Johann Müller, *51*, wurde gestern zum Bürgermeister gewählt.' (Johann Müller, *51*, was elected mayor yesterday. Previous norm: Der *51-jährige* Johann Müller . . .)

5.2.3 'Pseudo-transfers'

Some new lexemes, which resemble English but do not exist in the language, have been created in Germany, often involving the compounding of English morphemes, e.g. *Dressman* (male mannequin), *Herren-Slip* (fashionable word for *Unterhose*, underpants), *Showmaster* (quizmaster). These are known as *Scheinentlehnungen* ('pseudo-transfers') (Carstensen 1980b).

5.3 Domains of English transference

5.3.1 Federal Republic of Germany

The main domains of English transference are:

> sport, e.g. *Clinch, Comeback, Handicap, Rally, Sprint, Basketball*;
> Technology and Information Science, e.g. *Computer,*[3] *Know-how, Pipeline, Plastik*;
> Travel and Tourism, e.g. *Charter, checken, Countdown, Hosteß, Jet, Service, Ticket*;

---

[3] *Computer* is the word employed by the general public, while people in the relevant professions tend to use *Rechner*.

Advertising, e.g. *Bestseller, Image, Look, Trend*;
Journalism, e.g. *Facts, Front-page, Back-page, Layout*;
Economics, e.g. *Boss, floaten* (to float a currency), *Full-time-Job, Manager, Publicity, PR, Splitting* (income splitting), *Supermarkt*;
Politics, e.g. *Establishment, Hearing, Sit-in*;
Armed Forces, e.g. *By-pass, crashen, Control-box, Debriefing, Jeep, taxien*;
Cosmetics, e.g. *After-Shave, Beauty-box, Hair tint, Make-up, Spray*;
Entertainment (especially pop-music), e.g. *Evergreens, Happening, Hitparade, Quiz, Sex, Show, Song*;
Medicine, e.g. *By-pass, Clearance, Tranquillizer, Stress* (in general everyday use).
(Carstensen 1965, Carstensen and Galinsky 1967; Leopold 1968; Moser 1964, Fink 1970.)

Some domains are relatively unrepresented, e.g. the law, obviously because there is very little German–English contact in this field due to the differences in the legal systems prevailing in the German- and most of the English-language countries.

In comics, which are widely read by West German (and also Austrian, Swiss and Luxembourgian) children, many of the sounds are represented by transfers from an (American) English original or from (American) English 'comic language' in general. Comics are, after all, an American cultural influence. Frequently there is a conversion of grammatical category, based on English, e.g. from verb to interjection: *Beiß!* (bite!), *Brumm!* (growl!), *Hup!* (toot!, beep!), *Quietsch!* (squeak!), *Schluck!* (gulp!), *Kreisch kreisch!* (screech screech!), *Schnaub!* (gulp!), *Klirr!* (clatter!, rattle!), *Krächz krächz!* (splurt! – of computer/machine). Another sound representation is the actual transfer, more or less integrated into the German phonotactic (and graphotactic) system (see below, 5.6): *Boing! Dring!* (Ring! – of telephone), *Juuppa!* (Yippee!), *Klick klick!* (click – of gun), *Kratsch!* (Crash!), *Päng!* (Bang!), *Rubbel!* (Rub!), *Schnip!* (Snip!), *Schnorch!* (Snort!). *Bing bong!* appears to be a contamination between English *Ding dong!* and German *Bimm bamm!* Many of these sound representations have not only found their way into a children's register in German but are employed generally for onomatopoeia.

5.3.2 Austria

The situation in Austria differs historically from that of the Federal Republic insofar as Austria never had a period of indigenous intense purism, but also in that the influence of both French and the languages of some of the neighbouring countries far exceeded that of English up to the Second World War. In Germany the German–English language contact was greater. Viereck *et al* (1975: 216), comparing the extent of English transfers in daily newspapers, find that in Austrian newspapers 'anglicisms' appear in the text rather than in advertising while the reverse trend is evident in the Munich-based *Süddeutsche Zeitung*. The percentage of English transfers in the sports section is far higher in the supraregional Viennese paper *Die Presse* and (especially) the Graz regional daily *Kleine Zeitung*, than in the *Süddeutsche*. Viereck *et al* explain the discrepancy by the replacement of older English transfers (including many of those in the field of sport) by German neologisms in 19th century Germany, a development which did not have a parallel in Austria. However, on the whole, the transference of English items into Austrian Standard German is very similar to the situation in the Federal Republic.

5.3.3 Switzerland

There are three factors that make the situation in Switzerland different from that of the two countries treated above: the diglossia (see above, 1.5), the long-standing extensive French influence on both Swiss Standard German and Swiss-German dialects, and the role and language policies of Swiss business companies. The Swiss tend to react against puristic neologisms, which are identified with Germany.

The domains of transference (e.g. entertainment, business, fashion, sport, technology) and many of the examples are the same as in the Federal Republic (Charleston 1959). There are some additional transfers, such as *Dancing* (dance, dance-hall) and *Parking* (parking area). While West German multinational companies tend to propagate the use of German, the Swiss ones (perhaps because of the multilingualism of the Swiss nation) are far more prepared to use English as their language (Clyne 1977c). This strengthens the influence of American and British multinationals on the German language in Switzerland. There are also English lexical transfers that are widely used in Swiss-German dialects (some of them products of an earlier period of language contact), e.g. *Glôn* (and *Klaun*, clown), and *tüchste* (to shoot, meaning to play soccer) (Dalcher 1966: 15–7), as well as words that have been integrated into dialects in a manner different from that employed in Swiss Standard German, e.g. Pipe*linie*, Grep*frucht* (grapefruit), Kchi*nd*näper (kidnapper) (Dalcher 1965: 19).

Some lexical transfers from English are replacing ones from French that were general in Swiss Standard German well into the postwar period,[4] e.g. in entertainment: *Dinner* (for *Dîner*), *Show* (for *Revue*), *Song* (for *Chanson*, sometimes with a change of meaning to cover the new musical style), *Star* (for *Vedette*); in economics: *Boom* (for *Hausse*), *Boss* (for *Chef*); in travel: *Ticket* (for *Billet*); general: *Baby* (for *Bébé*) (Dalcher 1966: 18). Often it is unclear whether a transfer is of English or French origin (Charleston 1959: 272).

5.3.4 Luxembourg

As we have seen (1.7.2), Luxembourg Standard German draws heavily on French for its lexical and idiomatic renewal and as a basis for semantic shift. Consequently many of the English transfers used in Luxembourg (Magenau 1964) may have come via French, e.g. *Dancing* (dance-hall), *Folklore*, *Match*, *Meeting*, *Weekend*. However, the presence of European Community officials and the European Parliament, a large number of international banks and Europe's only state commercial radio station, broadcasting American English in word and song, has greatly increased Luxembourg's immediate exposure to English. This has contributed to the transference of English lexemes, especially in the domains of economics, politics, and entertainment.

5.3.5 GDR

Many of the words transferred from English in the GDR are those used also in the Federal Republic and Austria. However, they occur far less frequently in the GDR, and some of them have a more

---

[4] To a much lesser extent, the competition between old French and new English transfers exists in the West German press (Burger 1979).

restricted meaning. Not only is cultural contact with the English-language countries more limited, but within the framework of the GDR's official language policy (*Sprachkultur*, see 4.1), the use of 'foreign words' is not approved of. Some GDR linguists are regularly arguing against their use, and debating which lexical transfers can be regarded as necessary and which ones cannot be justified (Faulseit 1965, 1971; Ludwig 1977). Such matters are discussed at party conferences. The main argument against transfers is that they are not universally comprehensible and they are a means of 'showing off' (Faulseit 1965, 1971).

In his comprehensive account of English transfers in GDR newspapers, Kristensson (1977) shows that they tend to express:

> concepts referring to capitalism or western politics, or life in a Western Bloc country, e.g.
> > *Royal Navy, Barkeeper, Boß, College, Drugstore, Lobby, Trend, Trust; Paratrooper, Ranger;*
> international concepts, e.g.
> > (in tourism): *Camping, Hotel;* (in publishing): *Edition, Offset;*
> the automation and rationalization of production, e.g.
> > *Computer, Container, Training, Dispatcher* (via Russian, meaning: person responsible for keeping abreast with the state of production in an industry);
> new inventions in electronics, e.g.
> > *Bassreflexboxe* (bass-reflex box), *Stereo;*
> new developments in fashion and cosmetics, originating from the west, e.g.
> > *Dreß, Jersey; Shorts, Tweed; Make-up, Spray;*
> new western developments in pop-music, e.g.
> > *Beat, Diskjockey, Disko, Evergreens, Hits;*
> sports concepts, e.g.
> > *Basketball, Clinch, Coach, Fighter, Hat-trick, Knockout, Referee* (Ludwig 1977).

The transfer, *Meeting*, which came in via Russian, is limited to the political sphere. A very common transfer which is restricted to the GDR is *Broiler* for West German *Brathähnchen*, Austrian *Brathendl*. Other GDR transfers not used in the west are *Dispatcher* (see above) and the compounds *Goldbroilergaststätte* (golden roast chicken restaurant) and *Vitaminbar* (café serving fruit, vegetables, salad and fruit drinks). The use of some English lexical transfers must also be seen as part of language planning in the framework of the conflict model mentioned in 2.2.3. They contain a connotation of moralistic disapproval and are intended to stress the decadence and undesirability of living conditions in the west, e.g. *US-Horrorkunst, High Society, Slumlord; Image, Show-Demokratie, Slogan, Trick; Big-Business, Go-Go-Girl, Manager, Motel-Wohnsitz* (Motel-residence); *Pop-Industrie, Westbeat, Beat- und Pop-Liebhaber* (beat- and pop-fan) (Kristensson 1977). Some words, e.g. *managen,* have both a general colloquial meaning (to manage something) and one specifically referring to capitalist systems (to launch someone in a career) (Koller 1978: 319–20).

5.4 Media of transmission

5.4.1 Institutions

The main institutions promoting the spread of English transfers into German are the press, radio and TV, advertising agencies and dictionaries.

Carstensen (1965: 22–5; 1971) has demonstrated the importance of the weekly news-magazine *Der Spiegel* (modelled on *Time* and *News-Week*) in the introduction of new lexical, semantic and syntactic transfers from English into the German language. *Der Spiegel* is widely read, by people who regard themselves as liberals, discerning readers, with an above-average education (Grimminger 1972). Some of the transfers in any given issue of *Der Spiegel* are nonce forms; others have found their way into general German usage. It has been asserted that *Der Spiegel* is 'tonangebend für die Sprachregelung von drei Vierteln der deutschen Presse und für wesentliche Teile des deutschen Funks' (sets the tone for the language policy of three-quarters of the German press and substantial sections of German radio and TV) (*Deutsche Tagespost,* Würzburg 1962; cited in Carstensen (1965: 24), my translation). While this may be a little overstated, and applies to the creative register of *Der Spiegel* and not simply to transfers, it contains a large element of truth. Many transfers have come from *Der Spiegel* via weekly and regional daily newspapers or illustrated magazines such as *Stern* and *Brigitte* into the language as a whole. Another very influential intermediary of

English influence is the weekly *Die Zeit*, also a popular newspaper for more educated people, for those who understand and use English lexical transfers.[5] Mass circulation news-pictorials like *Bild-Zeitung* also make extensive use of 'anglicisms'. The need for instant translation on the part of news-agencies makes for frequent semantic and lexical, and sometimes syntactic transference in West German newspapers, as well as in news broadcasts and telecasts.

In other German-language countries, newspapers also disseminate lexical and other transfers from English, as Viereck *et al*'s (1975) study based on the Austrian papers, *Die Presse* and *Kleine Zeitung*, has shown. It should also be mentioned that both *Der Spiegel* and *Die Zeit* are read in Switzerland and Austria. In the last quarter of 1979, 48,449 copies of *Der Spiegel* and 6631 of *Die Zeit* were sold each week in Switzerland, as were 28,793 copies of *Der Spiegel* and 6298 of *Die Zeit* in Austria.[6]

The electronic media are also important in the transmission of transfers from English. American pop music is presented on the West German radio stations as well as the American Forces Network, broadcasting from within the Federal Republic. Many young West German (and Austrian) children are able to reproduce the hits even before they know the meanings of most of the words! Many lexical transfers are disseminated through radio and television news and documentaries (Clyne 1973: 177, Viereck *et al* 1975). About 97% of West German households now watch television (Noelle-Neumann 1977: 277). In 1979 about 54% saw the TV news daily and 25% several times a week (Noelle and Neumann 1974) and the percentage is likely to have increased since.

Carstensen (1965: 25–7) describes advertising as an area where the number of English transfers is especially high (though many of them are part of the special language of economics: Römer 1968: 128). But Carstensen also points out that many of the English-sounding words and brand-names have originated on German desks (see also 5.2.3 above). More than half of advertising in the Federal Republic is in the

---

[5] In an empirical study on the use and comprehension of English transfers (Clyne 1973: 167; see below, 5.4.2), *Die Zeit* was the most widely read newspaper among the younger, more educated group, those with the most English, who used and understood the most transfers.

[6] I thank the two publishers for this information.

press (personal communications, Hannelore Kröter, Gesellschaft Werbeagenturen).

When in doubt as to the meaning or acceptability of transfers, people will generally consult a monolingual dictionary. This applies particularly to the more educated sections of the population (three quarters of the more educated informants, compared with a quarter of the less educated, in Clyne 1973: 166). The most widely used and most authoritative dictionary in the western German-language countries, *Duden-Rechtschreibung* (Mannheim edition) contains lexical transfers together with their pronunciation and meanings. More copies are sold of the *Duden-Fremdwörterbuch* (Dictionary of Foreign Words, which covers more lexical transfers than the *Rechtschreibung*) than of any other *Duden* dictionary with the exception of *Rechtschreibung* (personal communication, Dr Paul Grebe). This speaks for the interest that German-language users have in 'loanwords'. The reception of English transfers in the *Duden* is conservative, though by no means purist. The same may be said for the extensive *Deutsches Wörterbuch* edited by Gerhard Wahrig (1st edition, 1968). The most complete inventory of English transfers to date was that by Neske and Neske (1972). Carstensen and his colleagues at Paderborn are currently working on a comprehensive dictionary of anglicisms in German.

5.4.1.1 *Institutional policy* In response to a series of questions concerning their attitudes to, and criteria for the use of 'loanwords' (Clyne 1973), West German newspapers and magazines indicated that there were no guidelines and that every journalist could make his/her own decision as to lexical selection. Such a choice is qualified by a restriction to words that are generally understood (e.g. in *Stern*, *Bild-Zeitung*) and a tendency towards a *pseudo-moderne Sprache* (pseudo-modern language) through the use of anglicisms (e.g. in *Bild-Zeitung*). Similar answers were given by those working in the electronic media, who also claimed 'die Verständlichkeit für jeden Zuschauer' (Zuhörer) (comprehensibility for all viewers (listeners)) as their main goal (e.g. Norddeutscher Rundfunk). Only words that have become 'Bestandteil der allgemeinen Umgangssprache' (part of everyday language) are used, except for technical language (*Fachsprache*), names and quotations. Decisions as to which transfers are part of the language are made in an ad hoc way by consulting reference books (*Duden* on lexicon, Siebs on pronunciation of transfers) (e.g. for Süddeutscher Rundfunk).

Advertising agencies similarly asserted that they used only words that were part of 'language usage', e.g.:

Die Werbung selbst fühlt sich nicht berufen, englische Wörter in die deutsche Sprache einzuführen . . . Doch weil dann mit der Werbung solche Begriffe oft eine große Publikation erfahren, wirkt es dann so, als sei es die Werbung, die diese Begriffe eingeführt hätte, oder einführen will (LINTAS Werbeagentur Hamburg). (Advertising does not see itself called to introduce English words into the German language. Yet since concepts then receive great publicity through advertising, it seems as if advertising had introduced or wants to introduce these concepts.)

There are contradictions to this in reality, with some transfers regarded by advertisers as 'part of German' not being identified by speakers as words they (or others) would use in their German (Clyne 1973: 174). The use of English brand-names is seen as promoting international communication or safeguarding copyright. The advertising agencies did not seek to promote a particular image for a product by the use of transfers, but at least one of them (Deutsche Bundesbahn, Werbe- und Auskunftsamt: German Railways, Advertising and Information Office) regarded young people and the managerial sector as the main target groups when English transfers were employed.

The editorial staff of the *Duden* (Mannheim) works with a large corpus derived from books and periodicals (but not spoken language). However, decisions on the inclusion of items are made through discussions among its members. In Wahrig, much leeway is left to the individual contributor, though semantic transfers in translated works and lexical transfers used only in advertising are excluded (personal communication, Professor Gerhard Wahrig, 10 January 1973).

The above comments apply to a large degree also to Austria and Switzerland, despite the different conditions described in 1.3 and 1.4.

5.4.2 People

Tests conducted in Stuttgart on twenty students aged 20–31 with a knowledge of English and twenty people aged over 35 with very little or no knowledge of the language (Clyne 1973) suggest that it is the younger and the more educated people who are agents of transmission of English transfers. Informants were questioned about a corpus of 51 contemporary lexical and semantic transfers derived from texts (other than advertising) in newspapers and periodicals (*Die Zeit, Die Welt, Stuttgarter Zeitung, Süddeutsche Zeitung, Stern*). They were asked for the meanings of the words and expressions, whether they themselves would use them, whether they had heard or read them, and if they would not use them, who would. The younger, more educated group knew most of the transfers and, on the whole, used them most. Older and less educated people often had difficulty in understanding the transfers, let alone using them. They generally expected younger people with a knowledge of English to employ the transfers. The age of the informants and of their children is a determining factor in the knowledge of transfers. In normal conversation, those speakers who frequently transfer from English will tend to vary this according to interlocutor, employing transfers less to older people and/or those who do not know any English.

Viereck *et al* (1975) asked 193 Austrian informants, distributed according to age, sex, education and knowledge of English, for definitions of 32 transfers drawn from newspapers. They found that age and knowledge of English were less important as criteria for the knowledge of anglicisms than were education and exposure to newspapers and TV. Men knew more of the transfers than did women.

In a more extensive study, Viereck (1980b) tested the use and comprehension of 42 transfers taken from *Die Presse, Kleine Zeitung* and the *Süddeutsche Zeitung*, selected – from 17 areas of the newspapers (e.g. politics, radio/TV, Sunday supplement). The 297 informants, all from Styria, were sampled according to the Austrian census. Age, sex, education, knowledge of English, and media consumption were taken into account. Through questionnaires, passive and active comprehension and use were assessed. Passive knowledge was greatest for transfers in the subject areas of travel/holidays, radio/TV and jobs; active knowledge in travel/holidays, general advertising and radio/TV. Transfers were used by the informants most in the fields of radio/TV, general advertising and travel/holidays. Men used and understood more transfers than did women. The main variables correlating with use and knowledge of transfers are: English proficiency, level of education and age (or rather youth).

Lexical transfers also often occur in the everyday register of people whose *Fachsprache* (special language) at work contains a large incidence of transference and in that of young people preoccupied with the pop scene. However, on the basis of research undertaken by Pechtold, Dobaj (1980) found that Austrian salespeople had a fairly low command of the meaning of English transfers used widely in their own special fields. This applied most to those in the radio/TV field (52.5% active command) and least to those in the photography trade (65.5%), the other fields being clothing and cosmetics. Again men scored higher than women.

There is a sparsity of empirical studies on the use of English transfers in everyday speech in the GDR, but it is likely that they occur most within networks of people who read specialized literature in the English language, of those with western contacts or sympathies, and of those who watch most West German television. Schönfeld and Donath (1978) surveyed foremen, workers and apprentices in two factories in the GDR on the knowledge and comprehension of 79 lexical transfers, not exclusively ones from English. Foremen had the best command of these items. Among workers, level of education influenced the knowledge of the transfers, as did (to a lesser extent) political education. Many of the words are employed in the fields of politics and economics. For apprentices, too, the main factor was educational level, followed by party function, consumption of mass media, and the reading of trade journals.

5.5 Reasons for transference

At the beginning of this chapter, I outlined the social, political and scientific developments that have led to the large-scale transferences from English into German. There is a puristic attitude which holds that some or most transfers are unnecessary. This attitude is now uncommon in the Federal Republic, Austria and Switzerland but officially supported in the GDR (see above, 5.3.5). It disregards the contribution made by language contact to language change all over the world since the start of history. In fact, all transfers are necessary – either for semantic, stylistic or sociolinguistic reasons; otherwise they would not be employed.

Galinsky (Carstensen and Galinsky 1967: 71) lists the following stylistic functions of (lexical) transference from American English:

providing 'American color', establishing precision, offering intentional disguise, brevity, vividness, tone (e.g. sneering parody), and variation of expression. This applies to all German-language countries, including the GDR.

Transfers can fill gaps in lexical fields, even by taking on meanings that those words do not convey in the source languages (see below, 5.6). Sometimes, too, transfers are part of an 'in-group' language or are intended to give the user status or prestige. They are the basis of in-group bilingual puns and jokes – a kind of 'linguistic one-upmanship' – at least in the Federal Republic of Germany and in Austria. They are to be found in graffiti on walls and on school and university desks.

5.6 Integration of transfers

Lexical transfers can be integrated, to a greater or lesser extent, into the grammatical, phonological and graphemic systems of the German language. The degree of this integration, together with the stability of the transfers, reflects whether transfers are considered peripheral or central elements of the recipient language. The GDR linguist, Heller (1966), has shown that German speakers will regard some 'loanwords' (e.g. *Flöte* flute, *Gummi* rubber, *Sport*) as far more integrated into (and less foreign to) the language than some less used lexemes of German origin (e.g. *Flechse* sinew, *tosen* to rage, roar, *gastieren* to appear as a guest – which uses the same bound morpheme *-ieren* as many transfers).

Lexical transfers can be placed on a continuum according to their degree of integration. At the bottom of the continuum (zero integration), we would find, for example, the verb in Moser's (1964) quotation from a member of the West German Army: 'Ein Tief *moves heran*' (a low (pressure zone) is moving close), where the lexeme is transferred, complete with English grammatical morpheme (an integrated transfer would be **muft*). Transfers that are combined with German morphemes (e.g. *super*klug, superclever; *Smart*heit, smartness; *Fix*er; *Rival*in, female rival) can be considered more integrated than those that are not (e.g. *Fairness, Fairneß; Filmstar*, not Filmstar*in*), with fluctuating or double forms (e.g. *campen/camping*) occupying an intermediate position. The use of the hyphen between a German and a transferred morpheme is often an indication of a lower degree of integration (e.g. *Trial-Fahren*, test driving; *Mai-Meeting*; cf. *Haarspray*, hairspray; *Musikbox*). There is variation between higher and lower degrees of (phonological) integration: [dʒæːz]/[dʒes]/[jats] 'jazz';[7] [dʒɔp]/[tʃɔp] or [jɔp] 'job'; ['kʌmbæk], [kʌm'bæk][8] 'comeback'. We can attribute this variation to the speaker's and hearer's knowledge of the source language, their educational background, the communication situation, and the interlocutor's attitude to transfers (see 5.4.2; 5.5). Some speakers vacillate between the variants, depending on the formality of the situation and the knowledge of English of the speech partner. At the graphemic level, variation also occurs, e.g. *Hostess/Hosteß*; *Stop/Stopp*; *Cosmetik/Kosmetik* (Carstensen 1965: 34). Semantically, lexical transfers are integrated by changing the structure of the appropriate German lexical field. Transfers frequently occupy a broader or narrower range of meanings than in English. For instance, *Bestseller* (used in English only for books) is extended to refer to home appliances or ladies' clothing in German, while *Ticket* is usually restricted to air tickets, and *Job* is specialized to mean an additional or part-time position or non-career employment. Semantic transfers (e.g. *realisieren*; *kontrollieren* – meaning 'beherrschen', to control; *lieben* – meaning 'gern mögen, to love) could also be regarded as highly integrated lexical transfers, where an attempt is made to eliminate any formal marker of 'foreignness'.

In the course of time, some transfers become more integrated. Words originally spelt with a *c* are written with a *k*, e.g. *K*lub, *K*ode, *K*olumnist, but not *K*omputer!

Transferred nouns need to be given a gender. This is determined by factors such as: nearest semantic equivalent (e.g. *der* Job < *der* Beruf, *die* Couch < *die* Liege, *das* Girl < *das* Mädchen), morphological factors, especially suffix analogy (e.g. der Entertain*er* because German nouns ending in -*er* are generally masculine), natural gender, number of syllables – monosyllabic nouns being usually masculine (Arndt 1970, Carstensen 1980c, Gregor 1983). Sometimes there are several semantic equivalents, or there are a number of competing determinants of gender allocation. Hence some nouns can have two or three genders, e.g.:

---

[7] Sometimes [jats] is restricted to signify older, classical jazz.
[8] Such compounds tend to shift the stress to the second syllables or morpheme.

der/das Countdown, Poster, Spiritual, Spray;
die/das Dinner-Jacket, Folklore, Trademark;
der/die Couch, Glamour, Lobby, Speech;
der/die/das Dreß, Gospel, Juice.

The indefinite article *ein*, which is used for both *der* and *das* nouns, creates some uncertainty as to the gender of many transfers and leads to the vacillation between masculine and neuter (Carstensen 1980c).

On the other hand, different genders can distinguish several meanings of a transfer, e.g. *der* Single (bachelor), *die* Single (single record), *das* Single (singles match in tennis). A change in gender away from the link with the semantic equivalent of the word in the source language may signal greater integration. This may have been the case with *Team*, whose gender was given as feminine (cf. *die* Mannschaft) in the 1952 *Duden* and in Mackensen's *Deutsches Wörterbuch* (1952) but neuter in the 1954 *Duden* and in subsequent dictionaries. On the other hand, Carstensen (1980c) and Viereck (1980b) both find that older transfers are best known and are therefore the ones used most with an English pronunciation. An alternative explanation is proposed by Gregor (1983: 168), namely that *die Team* was an earlier irregular gender assignment since *Mannschaft* at the time had a different meaning and could not act as a model while *das Team* was based on *Spielerpaar* (pair of players) or *Gespann* (team).

Some adjectives (e.g. *fair*) tend to be inflected; others (e.g. *supersonic*, *up-to-date*) are not. Transferred verbs are generally assigned to the weak conjugation (e.g. *gemanaget*). Some verbs (e.g. *babysitten*) are employed only in the infinitive form. This may be related to problems in separating the prefix from the rest of the verb and the formation of the past (*ich babysittete? ich sat baby? ich sittete baby?*). Similar difficulties of separation occur in some verbs of German origin (e.g. *bausparen*, to invest in a building society).

5.6.1 Variation in integration between national varieties

Some nouns have been assigned to different genders in different varieties of Standard German, e.g.:

die Cottage (Federal Republic) – *das* Cottage (Austria) – *der* or
die Cottage (Switzerland);

die Couch (Federal Republic; Austria) – *der* or *die* Couch (Switzerland);

der or *das* Dreß (Federal Republic; Switzerland) – *der* Dreß (Austria);

das Match (Federal Republic; Austria) – *der* Match (Switzerland);

der or *das* Service (Federal Republic) – *das* Service (Austria).

Also, while *Box* is used in the Federal Republic, *Boxe* appears in many compounds in the GDR (e.g. the electronics terms Baßreflex*boxe*, Kompakt*boxe*, Nachbau*boxe*, Ton*boxe*) (Kristensson 1977: 131).

5.6.2 Dictionaries and integration

Both *Duden-Rechtschreibung* and *Duden-Aussprachewörterbuch* (Dictionary of Pronunciation) tend to choose a phonologically integrated form (e.g. [buŋgaloː]), or else give two variants (e.g. [pusl, pʌzl], [jats, dʒæs]), while Wahrig tends towards more unintegrated forms. The phonologically least integrated forms as well as the highly integrated ones are to be found in Neske and Neske. Carstensen (1980c) has shown that the gender allocation of transfers in dictionaries does not always correspond to variations in usage.

5.6.3 Social aspects of integration

In the Stuttgart study (Clyne 1973), it was found that the forms that are more highly integrated (e.g. [putslə] *Puzzle*, [ʃaːtə] *Charter*, [jats] *Jazz*, [(t)ʃɔp] *Job*) were employed by the older and less educated, or at least non-English-speaking people, while the younger, more educated and/or English-speaking informants either used unintegrated forms exclusively or fluctuated between higher and lower integration (depending on interlocutor and situation). But Fink's (1980: 179–80) research indicates that even 3- to 6-year-old preschool children use unintegrated forms of some transfers (*Jeans, T-Shirt*).

5.7 Transference and communication barriers

All twenty of our Stuttgart students (Clyne 1973, see above, 5.4.2) understood at least 41 out of 51 lexical and semantic transfers and 'pseudo-transfers' occurring frequently in the German press. However, none of the twenty other informants (aged over 35, with little or no English) understood more than 41. Eight failed to understand 20–29 of the words, three missed 30–39, and two 40–49. The older subjects, in fact, had a negative attitude towards English transfers. Several of the over-35s did not recognize words presented to them in writing, e.g. *Charter, Image, Manager*, which were later read by them as [kaːtə] [Imaːgə], and [manaːgə]. However, they recognized and were able to give the meaning of the words when they were pronounced by the field worker. In other words, they would probably not have understood these words in the press although they had learned them through television. On the other hand, they knew only highly integrated regional forms for words like *Puzzle* [putslə] and *Spray* [ʃprəi]. It seems that the widespread use of unintegrated transfers from English by the media (the result of international understanding) has contributed to internal communication barriers between young and old, English- and non-English-speaking Germans (Austrians or Swiss), more educated and less educated people. Transfers have developed into sociolectal markers.

This is supported by Fink (1975) who tested (in context) 30 transfers recurring in advertising with 195 informants in South-East Westphalia. While students, graduates and schoolchildren shared a fairly high degree of comprehension (55–65%), relatively few workers (28%), farmers (29%) and housewives (33%), and generally people over 35 understood the transfers.

Transfers also play a part in exacerbating communication barriers between age groups and between social groups in Austria (Viereck 1980b; see above, 5.3.2). Viereck *et al* (1975: 222–3) also found that women knew less transfers in the fields of politics and economics than their male counterparts – another potential communication barrier.

Koller (1978: 318) suggests that many of the English transfers used in GDR newspapers are not generally understood by the readers. This would not be surprising, since the context to which the transfers refer is unknown to most GDR readers. Schönfeld and Donath (1978: 45) found, in the GDR, that foremen often wrongly assumed that workers and apprentices understood the lexical transfers they themselves knew.

Transference may be seen as one of a number of areas of education-based communication barriers in the German-language countries (cf. 4.2, above).

5.8 Brief summary

The Anglo-American influence on German may be attributed to internationalization, inter-cultural contact, and the widespread learning of English as a second language. This applies particularly to the Federal Republic. In Austria, there has been less traditional contact with English-language countries; on the other hand, there has been little or no indigenous purism. While this is also true in Switzerland (whose multinational companies have not enforced the use of German), English transfers in Swiss Standard German are competing against earlier ones from French. In Luxembourg, much English transference has come via French; English has influenced the German of the GDR to a lesser extent, due to that country's relative isolation from the Western Bloc and to official disapproval of 'foreign words', as they are not understood by all GDR speakers. Some of the English transfers in the GDR have come via Russian.

The English influence on German has come in the form of lexical, semantic and syntactic transfers. The degree of integration varies, and there are also pseudo-transfers coined in the Federal Republic. The main domains of use of lexical transfers are sport, technology and information science, travel and tourism, advertising, journalism, economics, politics, armed forces and entertainment – new developments originating from the U.S. and Britain. In the GDR, the transfers are often used in a derogatory sense as part of a conflict model.

The English transfers are transmitted by the press, electronic media, advertising agencies and dictionaries, although these institutions only admit to registering or employing words that are already widely used. The characteristics found to mark people who use transfers most have been youth and education (Federal Republic), education and exposure to newspapers and TV (Austria), work function, education, party function, mass media and trade journal communication and probably western contacts (GDR). There is evidence of lexical transfers, especially in their written form, causing communication barriers.

5.9 Further reading

The most complete book on the subject is still Carstensen (1965) which, however, has been updated by countless articles and treatments of specific issues. A recent collection of papers reflecting the present state of research in the Federal Republic and Austria is Viereck (1980a). Kristensson (1977) is the most substantial study of English influence on the German of the GDR, while Gregor (1983) is devoted to the gender assignment of nouns transferred from English. For a comprehensive summary of research in the general field, see Galinsky (1977).

6

Communication patterns

This is an area in which relatively little research has so far been undertaken. The following remarks are necessarily cursory and impressionistic, due to the paucity of data.

6.1 Discourse structures

The specific way in which discourse is organized in a language is at least partly influenced by cultural attitudes concerning time and space. A study of later-year secondary school assignments in various subjects from the Federal Republic of Germany and Australia, with teachers' or examiners' comments on them, and of German- and English-language essay-writing manuals (Clyne 1980) suggests that essay-writing plays a far less central role in the German education systems than in those of English-language countries, where essays are a major medium of assessment *across the curriculum*. In German-language countries they are largely language exercises and the formal rules are of lesser significance than in English-language countries. In German-language countries *content* is paramount in expository discourse. Digressions from a linear structure are tolerated much more in German-language countries, as are repetitions. The less linear and less formal structure of German (academic) discourse is also evidenced in books and articles in fields such as linguistics and sociology (Clyne 1981). There one finds digressions, and digressions from digressions – which entail recapitulation and repetitions to stress the *main* line of argument. Reviewers from English-language countries sometimes comment adversely on such discourse structures while those from German-language countries will usually refrain from any criticism of this kind. A contrastive study of academic discourse by English and German speakers is currently being undertaken by the author.

Meetings of German-speaking organizations (clubs, societies, committees) traditionally tend to run in a somewhat more informal way than their English-speaking counterparts (Clyne and Manton 1979) although there is considerable variation due to innovations in recent decades in some institutions. Again, linearity is less important. (The rule that only one motion be before the chair at a time is followed less in German organizations.) English discourse, especially in meetings, allows for a more flexible *tempo*, e.g. hurrying up business by moving 'that the motion now be put', or delaying it by deferring it to a sub-committee. But in both languages the 'turns' taken (Schegloff, Jefferson and Sacks 1974) are relatively short, as compared with, say, those in Turkish, which has long monologues and few interjections (Barkowski, Harnisch and Kumm 1976). Morain (1979) draws attention to the greater tolerance of 'open space' (e.g. open office doors, allowing guests to move furniture about at a party) in the U.S. than in the Federal Republic of Germany.

German (especially North German) society attaches great importance to *oral expression* as a mark of education, while in Britain and Australia (except in certain middle and upper class groups), but not necessarily in North America, the emphasis is far more on written expression. On the other hand, in West German university seminars in the humanities and social sciences, students have tended to demonstrate their general knowledge and expertise in public exhibitions of eloquence using the academic register referred to in 4.2. However, there are indications that this has changed in the generation following the post-1968 student movement (e.g. Greiner 1982).

6.2 Communication routines

Coulmas (1979) has argued that the pragmatic conditions for the appropriate usage and communicative function of routine formulae relate to cognitive systems of beliefs, preferences, norms and values. He demonstrates that a proper analysis needs to be reached by a contrastive approach.

In a comparison between German and English, I have distinguished (Clyne 1979) between the following formulae.

(i)   A formula existing in one system and not in the other, e.g. there is no equivalent of *Guten Appetit* (literally, good appetite) in English, as the routine marking the beginning of a meal.

(ii)   Formulae of completely different (or opposite) structures used for a speech act in the two languages, e.g. *Excuse me* in English-speaking countries and *Auf Wiedersehen* in the Germanies for leave-taking at a restaurant meal table; Eng. Is this seat *taken?*, Ger. Ist dieser Platz noch *frei?* (literally, Is this seat still free?).

(iii)   Formulae of corresponding structures employed to realize different speech acts, e.g. *How are you?/Wie geht es?* can be a *greeting* in English, but is an *inquiry* about a person's well-being in German.

(iv)   Formulae of corresponding structures employed to realize speech acts with the opposite intention, e.g. *He's on the phone* is a negative response and (*He's*) *speaking* an affirmative one to a telephone request to speak to Professor Miller. German (*Er ist*) *am Apparat* (literally, (He is) on the phone), however, is an affirmative reply and *Er spricht* (literally, He is speaking) a negative one.

Responses of 60 adult immigrants from each of three language backgrounds (Italian, Greek, German) to eleven communication rules were compared with those of 60 Anglo-Australians (Clyne 1979). The German speakers attached more importance than the English speakers to standardized routines marking the beginning or the end of an interaction: greetings (conversation openers), markers of the start of a meal (such as *Guten Appetit*, which does not even have an English equivalent), and 'goodbye' routines (e.g. when leaving a shop or restaurant table). German speakers were more likely than Greek or Italian speakers to regard a farewell greeting as mandatory when leaving a shop. German speakers were also more likely to fill in another form when they did not receive their medical benefits rebate, and far more inclined to write or call in to the office than the English speakers, who tended to use the telephone.

However, there are few standardized routines to continue the conversation. Comments on the weather are generally considered trite, stupid or inappropriate by German speakers, while many other 'next step' formulae acceptable in English would be considered too personal. It is difficult to *develop* a conversation with an unknown person – unless, of course, you can establish some common ground or identify yourself. For this reason, some 'casual' German discourse appears to comprise merely a skeletal schema, such as:

Opener:	Reply:
Gruß Gott or *Guten Tag!*	*Gruß Gott* or *Guten Tag!*
Ist hier noch frei?	*Ja, bitte!*
(*Guten Appetit*)	(*Danke, gleichfalls*)
Auf Wiedersehen!	*Auf Wiedersehen!*

As patterned small talk seems to be less usual in the Germanies than, say, in English-speaking countries, Germans travelling abroad often misunderstand small talk to be the initiation of a 'close friendship'.

6.2.1 Some national specifics in communication rules

6.2.1.1 *Federal Republic of Germany* House and Kasper (1981) conclude that Germans communicate with a greater degree of directness than do English speakers. They had 24 informal everyday situations – complaints and requests – acted out by two pairs of native speakers, one English and one German pair. House and Kasper establish eight levels of directness for each of the speech acts. For *complaints* there is a heavy concentration on level 6 (the third most direct level) among the Germans (e.g. *Du hättest meine Bluse nicht ohne meine Erlaubnis nehmen sollen!* You shouldn't have taken my blouse without asking my permission. Or: *Du hast meine ganze Bluse ruiniert!* You have ruined my blouse). The English speakers show a spread from level 3 (e.g. Terrible, this stain won't come off!) to 6, while the least direct level (Odd, my blouse was perfectly clean last night), was far more frequent among the English than the German informants. For the *requests*, level 6 was by far the most frequent among the Germans (e.g. *Du solltest das Fenster zumachen!* You should close the window). The English, on the other hand, concentrate around level 3 (e.g. You can close the window). The most indirect level, 1 (It's very cold in here) is considered far more by the English than the German speakers.

House and Kasper also categorize modality markers which downgrade or upgrade the impact of the utterances in both languages, e.g.:

> downgraders: please, kind of, just, I guess, [ɛː], and their German equivalents: *ja, mal, eben, wohl, denn*;

upgraders: absolutely, well, I'm sure, you must understand, and their German equivalents.

Downgraders are used by the English informants $1\frac{1}{2}$ times as often as by the German subjects in the same situations (2.7 times as much for the complaints). There is an overall tendency for the German speakers to use upgraders 4.6 times as often as the English speakers, who hardly employ them at all with requests. The role of intonation needs to be considered in this area. It is difficult to isolate cultural from individual characteristics in the discourse situations tested; but since national stereotypes and inter-cultural communication breakdown are based on differences in communication rules, any progress in quantifying them is of great importance. It is unfortunate that House and Kasper do not reveal the regional origins of their subjects.

Schlieben-Lange and Weydt (1978) contend that, in West Germany, questions are asked and decisions are made in a small group first, whereas in the U.S., discussions and questions are more likely to take place immediately in the entire group.

Schenker (1978) concludes, on the basis of interviews on linguistic etiquette with 500 people in the city of Trier and the nearby village of Maxweiler, that less privileged people are more conservative in their communication rules (e.g. titles, who greets whom first, pronouns of address). Villagers, women, older people and members of the lower class use and value transmitted norms more than townspeople, men, the younger generation and the middle class respectively. The exception is in the use of *du*, which the villagers of Maxweiler prefer because their dialect does not have a *Sie* form.

6.2.1.2 *Austria* Neustupný (1978: 101–3) has coined the term *Sprechbund* (speech area)[1] for societies that have similar systems of non-grammatical (communication) rules. In many respects, Austrians communicate in a way more similar to Czechs, Slovenians, Hungarians and Northern Italians than to Germans (especially North Germans). Many communication routines date back to the Monarchy, the period when all these cultures were part of a polyethnic empire; some are of far more recent vintage. An Austrian novelist remarked that present-day Vienna has many clocks, all

---

[1] After Becker (1948) – *Sprachbund*.

showing different times. This is certainly reflected in pragmatic aspects of language.

Titles are employed more widely than in other German-language countries and still transferred to the wife of the person concerned (e.g. *Frau Professor, Frau Hofrat*).[2] Honorific formulae considered archaic or expressing distance in the Germanies (e.g. *Mit vorzüglicher Hochachtung* – with excellent respect, rather than *Hochachtungsvoll* – respectfully) are still used in letters. In order to be polite, round-about routines involving a slow discourse rhythm are preferred, especially where a request is being made. The expression *Aber bitte* (Mind you!) is used outside honorifics to draw the hearer's attention to a particular point.

Austria is one of the areas of Europe where, to achieve your goals in communication, you need to 'overstate' your case. Understatement in rhetorical or ironical usage, as is practised in Britain and Scandinavia, and to a much lesser extent in the Netherlands and parts of North Germany, is ineffective or misunderstood in Austria. This is particularly the case in requests, advice, warnings and promises. House and Kasper's downgraders (1981; see above, 6.2.1.1) often accompany overstatement due to Austrian politeness rules.

Some differences between Austrian and West German communication routines may be exemplified in telephone booth notices warning would-be vandals:

> Dieses Telefon kann Leben retten. *Zerstört es nicht!* (This telephone can save lives. *Do not destroy it!*) (Austrian)
> *Schützt dieses Telefon!* Es kann Leben retten. *(Protect this telephone!* It can save lives.) (West German)

The Austrian version overstates, in a pessimistic way.

In a study of responses to communication rules in Australia (Clyne 1979: 29–30), German immigrants had more difficulty in understanding and responding to (Australian) irony than did Austrian immigrants. In fact, Austrians have a more creative and lighthearted and less prescriptive approach to language than Germans. This is reflected not only in Wittgenstein and other philosophers, but also in contemporary Austrian literature (e.g. Jandl,

---

[2] *Hofrat*: a high rank in the Civil Service.

Handke), which tends to play with language more freely than German literature.

6.2.1.3 *Luxembourg* Luxembourgian communication routines are based on egalitarianism, a preference for order, discipline and tradition, but a lack of respect for authority, leading to directness. Closeness to the land is reflected in symbolism in everyday speech and proverbs (Hoffmann 1969). This is in spite of the industrialization of large parts of Luxembourg and the fact that 78,000 of its people live in the capital. Understatement and black humour occur frequently in written and spoken discourse.

6.2.2 Regional differences

Schlieben-Lange and Weydt (1978) have made some observations on regional differences in communication rules within the Federal Republic. For instance, they contrast Swabian and Rhenic reactions to compliments – the Rheinlander accepts a compliment, the Swabian plays down the cause of the praise. Another routine that they describe is the Rhenic greeting which consists of the addressee's name articulated with greeting intonation. The utterance *Da können wir mal sehen* (We'll just see) in response to a request has a dilatory function in the Rhineland and Bavaria, but is a promise in Württemberg. Schlieben-Lange and Weydt refer to questions that, in South-Western Germany, represent both a quasi-monologue and the acceptance of a formal obligation to take turns. Such questions are misinterpreted by Northerners as rude, since they give the impression of a reproach in a situation where thanks or some other speech act of acknowledgement would be usual in their own repertoire. Similarly, the utterance *I mag hald net* (I just don't want to) or *Halt so* (That's how it is) in Bavaria fulfils the formal obligation to take turns. In most other regions, a detailed reason would be necessary for the sake of politeness.

Apart from such potential for communication breakdown, there are differences in the degree of verbality between regions of West Germany. Swabians, Westphalians and Schleswig-Holsteiners are generally known for their non-verbality in comparison with Rhinelanders, Berliners and Bavarians. I have also observed different types of proxemic behaviour between different regions, especially for sitting in public places, such as trains and restaurants. Swabians (particularly Stuttgarters) and Schleswig-Holsteiners employ more distant proxemic rules than Rhinelanders and Bavarians, something they tend to be conscious of. The Swabian satirical writer 'Thaddäus Troll' (1970: 114) tells of a country innkeeper's daughter saying to her father: 'Was machet mer bloß, Vadder, do kommet femf Schduagerder, ond mir hent bloß vier Disch!' (Whatever shall we do, father, there are five Stuttgarters coming, and we've only got four tables.) On the other hand, Bavarians are noted for their *Gemütlichkeit* (an atmosphere of jovial togetherness). In suburban trains around Stuttgart (*Nahverkehrszüge*), people will at first 'monopolize' a double seat, with no-one sitting opposite. When the train becomes crowded, new passengers will occupy seats diagonally opposite the others. The same applies generally in the area north of Hamburg, but in Bavaria and the Rhineland, passengers tend to sit next to and/or opposite each other. More distant proxemic patterns are associated with less conversation. Such differences as the above could be explained by recourse to the social and religious history of Germany.

6.3 Attitudes to language, and some consequences

Germans, but not Austrians (see above, 6.2.1), tend to take a more prescriptive attitude to language than do English speakers. This limits the use of verbal humour and verbal irony in everyday discourse. The kind of 'ping-pong pun game' that is played by many English speakers is not known to, or understood by most German speakers. Verbal humour and verbal irony are, at best, the province of creative writers (including journalists of such periodicals as *Der Spiegel* and *Die Zeit*) and cabarettists. It has been observed, in an empirical study, that irony based on understatement is used and understood much less by German speakers than by English speakers (Clyne 1979). House and Kasper's (1981) research indicates that Germans overstate while English people understate (see 6.2.1 above).

German children do not have as rich a tradition of children's riddles and rhymes based on linguistic creativity and polysemy, as do English-speaking children. This can be seen by comparing German collections of children's humour (e.g. Helmers 1971) with English-language ones (e.g. Opie and Opie 1959/1967, Turner 1969). The German children's joke centres far more around situations than on linguistic aspects such as polysemy.[3] Most of the children's verbal humour referred to by Helmers appears to be based on a reaction to linguistic errors made by the informant or by someone else – i.e. a prescriptive attitude to language. The stereotypical linguistic riddles on which many English speakers have been brought up – such as 'When is an X not an X?' or 'Knock, knock, who's there?'[4] – have no equivalent in German. (One exception is the pattern: 'What is the difference between an X and a Y?' which is common to both cultures.) Perhaps the best source of verbal humour in German are bilingual puns, which are the province of an older, more elitist group. It may be that the *general* tendency towards, or away from verbal humour is one that is developed early in life.

6.4 The German address system

Although the German system of pronouns of address is generally perceived as a *du* (singular) + *ihr* (plural) [informal]/*Sie* [formal] dichotomy (e.g. by Brown and Gilman 1960), there are actually seven modes of address in use:

1   *du* as the informal pronoun of address in the singular.
2   *ihr* as the informal pronoun of address in the plural.
3   *ihr* as the plural pronoun of address for a group of two or more people, of whom at least one is addressed as *du* and at least one is addressed as *Sie*, e.g. *Kommt ihr vor oder nach dem Essen?* (Are you coming before or after dinner?) Addressed, for example, to a friend and his wife.
4   *ihr* as a marked plural pronoun of address for a group of two or more people addressed as *Sie*, e.g. *Wieviel Bücher habt ihr in der Bibliothek?* (How many books are there in your library?)

---

[3] This is borne out in Baulch's (1979) comparison of jokes told by German and Australian schoolchildren. However, there are local differences, e.g. some ad hoc rhyming in Bavaria and ritual insults in Saarland mining areas (personal communication, Wolfgang Klein).
[4] e.g. Q: When is a tree not a tree?
  A: When it is a lava*tory*.

  Q: Knock knock, who's there?
  A: Mike . . .
  Q: Mike who?
  A: *My Keys* are locked in your car and I can't get into mine.

(stressing that the speaker is referring to the speech partner's institution and not to his personal library).

5   *Sie* as plural pronoun of address for a group of two or more people, of whom at least one is addressed as *du* and at least one as *Sie*, e.g. *Ich möchte Sie nicht zu lange aufhalten.* (I don't want to keep you too long.) This is intended to be polite, and the utterance is oriented to the speech partner(s) with whom one is ordinarily on *Sie* terms.

6   *Sie* as the formal pronoun of address in the singular.

7   *Sie* as the formal pronoun of address in the plural.

The rarest pattern is 5, and 2 and 3 are much more common than 4 and 5.

In the past, the use of *du* has been a manifestation of a fairly closed system of relationships. English *friend* corresponds to both German *Freund(in)* (friend) and *Bekannte(r)* (acquaintance), but there are fairly strict boundaries between these. *Freundschaft* (friendship) is a rather exclusive mutually binding relationship, particularly when it involves people of opposite sexes. *Du* relations have been more common among people of the same sex than between the sexes.[5]

The 'traditional' pattern of pronoun selection is as follows:

1   *Sie* is the unmarked pronoun of address; *du* is marked as the pronoun of solidarity (Brown and Gilman 1960).

2   Members of a family address each other as *du*.

3   *Du* is used to children under the age of 15.

4   Young children tend to call everyone *du*. (Bates (1976: 283) points out that Italian children acquire the polite form between the ages of 3 and 4. The situation among German monolinguals may be the same.)

5   *Du* is employed in prayer.

6   People may, as a sign of friendship, *decide* (i.e. make a verbal agreement) to use *du*. Sometimes this is associated with a ritual drink (*Brüderschaft trinken*). The use of *du* is then reciprocal.

7   Older people (especially those of higher status) may asymmetrically address younger people (especially those of lower status),

---

[5]   *Du* is also used generically, i.e. instead of *man*, where no specific person is addressed, e.g. Wenn *du* einsam bist (if you are lonely). It is also employed in advertising to establish 'direct' interaction, e.g. Leidest *du* an Kopfschmerzen? (Do you suffer from headaches?)

i.e. the older person uses *du*, the younger one *Sie* (this is what Brown and Gilman term the 'power semantic'). As Ervin-Tripp (1971: 20) explains, a senior person can dispense the younger one from this by suggesting a symmetrical informal mode of address. For instance, parents-in-law would do this to comply with rule 2 (above).

Du has also become traditional in parts of the labour movement and in some political parties as well as on the shop floor.

The *Sie* partner in a gathering of people on *du* terms will show up as an outsider. *Siezen* is instrumental as a technique in excluding someone from a group (*jemanden schneiden*). The boundaries between 'business' and 'private' sectors being vaguer than in English-speaking countries, selective *du* relationships may cause 'diplomatic' problems in the work domain. They may give the impression of favouritism. The influence of alcohol will frequently mean the withdrawal of normal *Sie* relationships. In a drinking situation, *du* relations may be initiated, which have effect only for the particular occasion.

The past decade or so has seen a marked change in the rules for *du* and *Sie*, particularly among the younger generation, who are using *du* more widely than did previous generations. According to a survey conducted at the University of Mannheim in April 1981 (*Spiegel* 1981: 34), 84.5% of citizens up to the age of 24 prefer people to enter into a *du* relationship faster; the same applies to 59.1% of the 25–49 age group. Nowhere is the change in rules more conspicuous than in universities and other tertiary institutions – a result of the anti-authoritarian upheavals which commenced in 1967. As Bayer (1979) has shown, there are two competing interpretations of address systems – one based on an unmarked pronoun for formality vs. a marked one for intimacy, the other based on an unmarked pronoun for solidarity vs. a marked one for social distance. Before the late 60s, German students addressed each other and their lecturers as *Sie*, which was the unmarked pronoun of respect and formality as citizens and 'bearers of social roles'. *Du* was used only among 'special friends'. As from the late 60s, students, protesting against traditional social values, adopted a general *du* as the unmarked pronoun for communication among themselves (regardless of sex). *Sie* became a marked form of social distance. Some university staff (especially younger and sub-professorial staff) adopted the reciprocal *du* for communication among themselves and with students. Those that did not were seen as upholding social distance rather than maintaining an atmosphere of mutual respect, due to confusion between the two competing interpretations. Since the 'student revolt', status marked situations (e.g. seminars, congresses, committee meetings) no longer need to bring about a temporary withdrawal of the *du* relationship, leading to a public exhibition of social relations (especially among the younger generation). Teachers who had been members of the student movement introduced *du* communication between teachers and their secondary school pupils.

Apart from common work, *common ideology* is a feature promoting *duzen*. Not only – as previously – membership of the same party (especially the Social Democratic and Communist Parties), club or student group, but also similarly radical or progressive political and social views will automatically start a *du* relationship (the 'solidarity semantic' as discussed by Brown and Gilman 1960). The decision to employ *du* may be governed by environment and/or dress. *Du* is more likely to occur as a spontaneous form of address in the *Mensa* (student cafeteria) of a university than on a tram, and between two young people with long hair, beards and scruffy clothes or between two people wearing the uniform of railway conductors than between people with no such common 'externals'.

The traditional 'co-occurrence' rules for forms of address are:

du +   first name

$$Sie + \begin{Bmatrix} Herr \\ Frau \\ Fräulein^6 \end{Bmatrix} + \begin{Bmatrix} \text{surname} \\ \text{title} \\ \text{title – surname} \end{Bmatrix}$$

In addition, there is the less usual:

Sie +   first name

where the 'first name' part is non-reciprocal. This occurs sometimes when the younger partner turns 15 (and therefore has to be addressed as *Sie*) but has been addressed by the first name by the much older interlocutor over a long period of time. Another use of *Sie + first name* is in TV or radio interviews with popular sportsmen or entertainers. There are at least two other co-occurrence possibilities:

---

[6] *Fräulein* is being replaced by *Frau*, see below, 8.5.

    du +   no name
    du +   name of occupation.

The first of these co-occurrences stems from the fact that group membership, common job or institution, and common ideology are *du*-promoting factors, and some latter-day 'Duzbrüder' (people on *du* terms, e.g. students) do not know each other's names. The second co-occurrence (e.g. 'Du, *Schlosser*, komm mal her!' 'Hey, locksmith, come here, will you?'), promoted by a common work situation (and a somewhat 'playful' disposition) has been overheard frequently among groups of tradesmen. Both these combinations are associated with an only partial fulfilment of the criteria for either *du* or *Sie* address.

Over the past five years or so, there has been a slight reversion to the earlier rules of address. Students in most universities still address each other as *du*, but tendencies among young people towards an unmarked *du* appear to have stopped. It is far less usual than say in 1972–3, for university staff and students to *duz* each other.[7] *Du* relations between teachers and their secondary school classes are now again quite rare. This relaxation of the new rules, like the reduced general pressure for orthographical reform (4.1.1) and the subsiding of the 'language barriers in education' debate (4.3) are reflections of a change of course (*Tendenzwende*) towards social and political conservatism in the Federal Republic in recent years. Such linguistic manifestations require careful diachronic study.

It should be noted that the use of rules of address varies nationally and regionally, with *du* traditionally being used more in South Germany, Austria and Switzerland than in North Germany, and more in rural areas than in urban ones. In some universities (e.g. Free University of (West) Berlin, Bremen, Frankfurt, Marburg), radicalism has led to a wider application of *du*.

In the GDR there has been little change in the rules of address in recent years. *Du* is used between students and, *on the whole*, between party members (except between the sexes where there is a large age difference) but generally, the more traditional rules persist (personal communication, Manfred Richter). The system of address in the GDR would need to be the object of detailed study.

---

[7] This comment is based on participant observation and discussions with West German colleagues, in 1972–3 and 1978.

6.5 Brief summary

German expository discourse tends to be less linear and less formally organized than its English equivalent, something that could be attributed to the differing role and rules of essay-writing within the education systems. There are some parallels in the structure of expository discourse and meetings. As in English, turns in German are relatively short.

Comparing routine formulae in German and English, we find rules showing similarity in form but differences in communicative intention, similarity in communicative intention but differences in form, and ones that are present in one language and absent in the other. German attaches more importance to standardized routines marking the beginning or end of interaction. However, there are few set formulae to provide the next step, since one then has to establish one's identity. Small talk is less usual in the Germanies than in English-speaking countries. Germans appear to perform requests and complaints with a greater degree of directness, and upgraders are more frequently employed in German than in English. Many communication rules have regional currency, leading to communication breakdown within the Federal Republic. Proxemic patterns and degree of verbality also vary regionally.

Germans, but not Austrians, tend to take a more prescriptive (and less creative) attitude to language than do English speakers. Hence, verbal humour and verbal irony are rare in everyday speech and usually restricted to creative writing and cabaret in the Germanies. German children play less with language than do their English-speaking counterparts.

The 'traditional' system of address in the Federal Republic has been modified considerably over the past decade. This is particularly so in the universities, where students have replaced a system based on formality (unmarked) vs. intimacy (marked) by one based on solidarity (unmarked) vs. social distance (marked). *Du* is now used in a generalized way between students, and, where lecturers did not adopt this pattern, this was often (mis)interpreted as an indication of social distance. Common work and common ideology promote *duzen*. *Siezen* is sometimes an instrument of exclusion. The use of *du* may be stimulated by the outward appearance of the speech partner. '*Sie* + first name' is employed non-reciprocally, for instance by older people addressing younger interlocutors whom they knew as children. '*Du* + no name' and '*du* + name of occupation' are promoted by solidarity semantics. Over the past five years or so, there has been a slight relaxation of the new rules. This, like other sociolinguistic phenomena, appears to reflect a pendulum swing to conservatism. The situation in other German-language countries needs to be studied in detail.

6.6 Further reading

The area of this chapter that has been studied most is the address system. Apart from Brown and Gilman's (1960) seminal paper, I recommend Bayer (1979), which covers a subsequent period but a narrower field of investigation.

7

Linguistic markers of political theory and practice

The language of political groups and parties is another area which requires far more research. A problem in this type of study is the fluid political situation. This chapter was completed before the FDP's withdrawal from the coalition with the SPD and the formation of the CDU/CSU–FDP coalition (October 1982). It will be interesting to see what changes take place, for instance, in the kind of language used by the FDP to explain its foreign policy. Far-left and far-right parties and political lobby groups come and go, amalgamate and split, and it is difficult to keep track of their language usage.

7.1 The German language and political polarization

German is a language which has been polarized by political attitudes. Between 1933 and 1945 it was the language of a racist, fascist state; it is now the language of both a socialist East Bloc country and a capitalist Western European one. Transitions have been rapid. They have involved purging the language of the immediate past, at the lexical, pragmatic and, to a slight extent, the syntactic level, within a process of 'de-Nazification'. *Bodentreue* (loyalty to the land you belong to), *charakterlich* (of moral character, i.e. in keeping with Nazi morals), *Endlösung* (final solution, i.e. genocide of the Jews), *entartet* (degenerate, applied to the arts, i.e. not approved by the Nazis), *reinrassig* (racially pure), and *mit deutschem Gruß* (with a German greeting – closing routine in letters) are all examples from that section of the lexicon which is now taboo outside neo-Fascist circles.[1] *Fremdarbeiter* (foreign worker) reminiscent of the forced

---

[1] The stylists Klemperer (1947) and Sternberger (1945) played an important role in shaping people's consciousness as to the language planning that had taken place during the Third Reich.

labour of the Nazi period has been replaced by *Gastarbeiter* (guest worker). *Fremdarbeiter* is now used only in Switzerland.

An instance of the political polarization of German in the Federal Republic today is the word given to the barring of people holding 'extremist' political views of the right, and especially the left, from public office (e.g. as academics, schoolteachers, hospital doctors, railwaymen, postal clerks). The term officially given to the legislation is *Radikalenerlaß* (declaration on radicals), and this is the word used by the middle-of-the-road newspapers. Conservatives refer to it as the *Extremistenbeschluß* (resolution on extremists), and left-wingers as *Berufsverbot* (prohibition from following your calling or occupation), which is an effect of the legislation. Each group expresses, through its term, its views on the legislation and its practice. It is therefore impossible to refer to them without revealing your attitude. The strength of people's opposition to left-wing terrorism was indicated by whether they referred to the *Baader-Meinhof-Gruppe* (group) or the *Baader-Meinhof-Bande* (band of gangsters or robbers). Similarly, it is impossible for West Germans to refer to their country and to the political entity on their eastern boundary without indicating their views on international politics. Is there a *Deutschland* or are there only a *Bundesrepublik* and a *DDR*? And, in either case, how do you refer to the Federal Republic? The official designations are *Bundesrepublik Deutschland* or *BR Deutschland*, while the left-wing term *BRD*, which conceals the word *Deutschland*, parallels *DDR* and is, in fact, commonly used in the GDR, is not approved by the West German Government (*Spiegel* 1978a; Carstensen 1978: 5). However, *Deutschland* is frequently employed in everyday speech and writing and in newspapers to refer to the Federal Republic, and *Bundesrepublik Deutschland* is often abbreviated to *Bundesrepublik*. Another unofficial term *Westdeutschland* is employed much less than its English equivalent, except in West Berlin. It plays down the present political situation. As to the GDR, the official designation is *DDR* or *Deutsche Demokratische Republik*. There are a number of right-wing terms current in the Federal Republic: e.g. '*DDR*' (in quotation marks), which implies a denial of the sovereign and 'democratic' status due to the absence of western-type elections, and *der andere Teil Deutschlands* (the other part of Germany), which implies national unity. *Mitteldeutschland* (Central Germany) – which leaves *Ostdeutschland* (East Germany) free for the former German provinces east of the Oder and the Neiße – is now practically obsolete except in refugee organizations. And yet, since the Federal Republic is west, the GDR is east for all West Germans, by implication, in sentences such as: 'Bei uns ist es so, (drüben) im Osten dagegen . . .' (This is how things are here, (over) in the east, however . . .) The spoken equivalent of the inverted commas around *DDR, die sogenannte DDR* (the so-called GDR) is dated and reminiscent of the 50s and early 60s. It should be noted that all major political parties in the Federal Republic and the GDR have the word *Deutschland* in their title.

7.2 The language of the 'mainstream parties'

7.2.1 Federal Republic

The political parties in the Federal Republic are keenly aware of the role of language in their relationship to the electorate. It is in the interests of each party to create a terminology and a register that appeals to the people and encourages them to think, and see issues, in a way advantageous to it. The development of a suitable usage is crucial to the wooing of voters at election time, as this characterizes the image each party projects.[2]

As Dieckmann (1964) has demonstrated, political language circulates around catchwords. Each party produces slogans that reduce the multiplicity of alternatives to a *Für mich – gegen mich* (for me – against me) (Dieckmann 1964: 46). Klaus (1971: 56–76), writing from a GDR perspective, shows the importance of 'complex symbols' (*aggregierte Symbole*) – general symbols embracing diverse denotative and connotative components which may solicit a favourable attitude towards one's own viewpoint and an unfavourable one towards that of one's opponents.

In the 1980 election, each of the main parties had an overall slogan:

Christlich-demokratische Union Christlich-soziale Union[3]	(CDU/CSU; conservative) *Für Frieden und Freiheit* (For peace and freedom)

---

[2] I am not dealing with the personalities of the parties, who have played a dominant role in election campaigns.

[3] The CSU is the Bavarian sister-party of the CDU.

133

Freie Demokratische Partei (FDP; liberal) *Unser Land soll auch morgen liberal sein* (Our country shall be liberal tomorrow too)

Sozialdemokratische Partei Deutschlands (SPD; social democrat/pre-1981 (British) labour) *Sicherheit für Deutschland* (Security for Germany)

All parties use both *Frieden* (peace) and *Sicherheit* (security) as catchwords, but the semantic features of these complex symbols vary vastly. The following discussion is based on an operational study of policy statements and election propaganda of the political parties during the 1972, 1976 and 1980 federal elections. The collection, Inter Nationes (1980), was useful as it presents the parties' own policy description on a large number of issues.[4]

Frieden, in the discourse of the SPD, is frequently associated with *Entspannung* (détente) and (to a lesser extent) with *Kompromiß* (compromise), *Verständigung* (communication), *Gleichberechtigung* (equality), *Gleichgewicht* (balance) and *Unabhängigkeit* (independence) (especially in references to the Third World). The word is often collocated, by the SPD, with *Sicherheit* or compounded with *-sicherung* (securing). The SPD emphasizes the securing of peace as its achievement through successful and tolerant negotiations with the GDR (and other East Bloc nations) (*Ostpolitik*). In the CDU/CSU's policy and election publications, *Frieden* is associated closely with *Freiheit* and *Sicherheit*. *Sicherheit*, in CDU/CSU discourse, involves military defence against potential outside aggression, and internal (police) protection against terrorism and radicals (*Ruhe und Ordnung*, law and order). It is stressed that a strong army is 'ein unentbehrliches Instrument der Friedenssicherung' (an indispensable instrument for securing peace) (Wörner 1972: 34, for example). The CDU/CSU meaning of *Freiheit* was developed in the political culture of the Federal Republic to express [western/capitalist] as opposed to [eastern/communist], e.g. the following statement by Schröder (1972: 5) of the CDU:

. . . daß die Deutschen in der Bundesrepublik in Freiheit, die Deutschen in der DDR in Unfreiheit leben und nach Freiheit streben. (. . . that the

---

[4] Many of the ideas were developed in Clyne (1979), based on the 1972 West German election campaign, and have been updated by more recent material. At the time of each election (1972, 1976, 1980) the SPD–FDP coalition was in government, and the CDU/CSU formed the opposition.

Germans in the Federal Republic live in freedom while the Germans in the GDR live in bondage and strive for freedom.)

The CDU/CSU 1980 alternative slogan, *Frieden in Freiheit* (Peace in freedom), presupposes that the coalition is offering 'Frieden *ohne* Freiheit' (peace without freedom), or 'Frieden um jeden Preis' (peace at any price) – intended to be derogatory – as verbalized by Biedenkopf of the CDU (1980: 33). This kind of alternative follows the one expressed in the opposition's 1976 slogan, *Freiheit statt Sozialismus* (Freedom instead of socialism) or *Freiheit ohne Sozialismus* (Freedom without socialism). Geißler (1980: 23) of the CDU declared: 'Nicht Krieg oder Frieden ist das Thema, sondern Frieden und Freiheit.' (Not war or peace is the topic, but peace and freedom.) The SPD, on the other hand, develops associations from Freiheit to *Gerechtigkeit* (justice), *Chancengleichheit* (equality of opportunity) and *Solidarität der Gesellschaft* (solidarity of society).

The FDP, which presents itself as the party of the centre, uses language in a way which lies somewhere between the usage of the two larger parties. As the party which has provided the foreign minister since 1969, the FDP developed complex symbols very similar to those of their former coalition partner, the SPD, for foreign policy (e.g. *Frieden*), but intermediate ones for domestic policy. While the CDU/CSU stress *Ruhe und Ordnung* most, and the SPD least, as a basis for *Sicherheit*, the FDP's literature occupies a middle position. On both social and economic matters, the FDP and CDU/CSU describe their policies as *freiheitlich* (free) and stress the rights of individual citizens. There is a feature [+collective] running through the SPD discourse and one [−collective] permeating that of the CDU/CSU, with the FDP compromising on [±collective]. While the SPD stresses *Solidarität, Chancengleichheit, Gleichberechtigung,* and the CDU *Selbstverantwortung* (responsibility for yourself), *Mitverantwortung* (joint responsibility) and *verantwortliche Selbsthilfe* (responsible self-help) through *Leistung* (achievement), the FDP especially emphasizes *Mitbestimmung* (participation, co-determination). The SPD's unit of cohesion, *Gesellschaft* (the international enlightenment term, 'society') is countered by the CDU/CSU's *Gemeinschaft* (the German romantic notion of the organic 'community') (Dieckmann 1964: 140ff). This relates well to the CDU/CSU's preoccupation with family structure. *Soziale Marktwirtschaft* (social market economy) is a concept claimed by both the FDP and the CDU/CSU, in opposition to the *sozialdemokratische Wirtschaftspolitik* (Social Democrat economic policy). Both the CDU/CSU and the FDP regard as part of *Freiheit* the minimizing of the powers of the state. The 1980 CSU/CDU candidate for the chancellorship, Franz-Josef Strauß (1980: 29) offered voters 'Freiheit statt Dirigismus' (Freedom instead of planned economy, the latter in a pejorative sense). *Vorsicht* (caution) and *Vernunft* (commensense) are part of the shared vocabulary of the CDU/CSU and the FDP, which has tried to portray itself as the liberal conscience of the coalition government. The FDP, more than any other party, has set out to woo the sophisticated and established middle class voter, and its literature contains frequent reference to *Mitte* (centre), *Mittelstand* (middle class), *mittelständisch* (middle class–adjective), *Mittelstandspolitik* (middle class politics), and *Mittelstandskonzept*. (*Stand* is the pre-Industrial Revolution term used euphemistically, as compared with the leftist *Klasse*.) Both the CDU/CSU and the FDP avoid mention of class struggle, and the CDU/CSU often accuse the SPD of inciting the division of the nation on class lines.

While the SPD and the FDP have referred to the *beide deutsche Staaten* (two German states) or specifically to the GDR and the Federal Republic, the CDU/CSU try, where possible, to use the terms *Deutschland, deutsche Nation* and *Einheit der nationalen Kultur* (unity of national culture) to maintain nostalgia for reunification. They (especially Strauß 1980) do not shy away from the emotive word *Vaterland* (as in 'des freien Teiles unseres geteilten Vaterlandes', the free part of our divided fatherland; Strauß 1980: 4), which is reminiscent of National Socialist propaganda.[5] There is frequent repetition, in CDU/CSU foreign policy statements, of restoring *Würde* (dignity) and *nationales Selbstbestimmungsrecht* (national self-determination) to the entire *deutsches Volk*.

To return to the SPD, FDP and CDU/CSU meanings of *Frieden*, the main difference lies in the varying position of some features in the

---

[5] *Vaterland* is also used extensively in the GDR, usually collocated with *sozialistisch*. Because of the GDR's interpretation of recent German history (complete break with the Germany of 1933–45, therefore rejection of responsibility for it), it has been able to redevelop patriotism, nationalism and a pride in 'Germanness' which, in the Federal Republic, are a province of the right. *Nationaler Erbe* (national heritage) has been part of GDR vocabulary since the early 1950s, when German historical traditions were reinstated.

hierarchy, when we regard the sequencing of features hierarchically; based on emphasis in party literature.

SPD and FDP	CDU/CSU
+ positive	+ positive
− war	− war
+ détente towards the east	+ alliances with the west
+ desire and ability to compromise	+ tranquillity/law and order
+ alliances with the west	+ rearmament
+ tranquillity/law and order	− danger
− danger	+ self-confidence
+ rearmament	+ détente towards the east

Conjoined with *Sicherheit* and *Freiheit*, we get for the CDU/CSU:

> + positive
> − war
> + alliances with the west
> + tranquillity/law and order
> − danger
> + caution
> + protection
> + free enterprise
> − state interventions
> + western parliamentary democracy
> + détente towards the east

All the main parties stress the importance of world development. The CDU/CSU refer to the recipients of such aid mainly as *Entwicklungsländer* (developing countries), and the FDP and SPD term them *Dritte Welt* (Third World).[6]

The CDU/CSU allude to *technisch-wissenschaftlicher Fortschritt* (scientific and technical progress) in a positive way, while the FDP refers to it less frequently and with both positive and negative connotations, and the SPD appears to avoid mention of it. The

---

6 Generally in West German texts on international relations there is a tendency to add an antithesis between North and South ('haves' and 'have-nots') to that between East and West, following the Brandt Report.

CDU/CSU see its protection of the individual as including the rights of 'das ungeborene Leben' (the unborn life) (Geißler 1980: 23), this being part and parcel of its basis in the 'christliches Sittengesetz' (Christian moral law) (Strauß 1980).

As differences between the language use of the parties are mainly at the contextual semantic level, it would not be appropriate to talk of different varieties of German used by different parties. Propaganda directed at particular groups often uses a register characteristic of them. For instance, electioneering literature (especially that of the SPD) intended for average young people is in a register marked by colloquial vocabulary, elliptic sentences and more anglicisms. The more educated are addressed with political puns, some making use of transference from English. Alliteration often occurs in political slogans and advertisements, e.g. *St*oppt *St*rauß (SPD, 1980); *V*or-fahrt *f*ür *V*ernunft (give way to commonsense) (FDP, 1972); *W*ache *W*ähler *w*ählen *W*illy (alert voters vote Willy), *W*illy *w*illi' (I want Willy) (SPD, 1972).

7.2.2 Austria

For historical reasons, it is impossible to assume a one-to-one correspondence between the main Austrian parties and their West German counterparts:

> Österreichische Volkspartei (ÖVP) – CDU/CSU
> Freiheitliche Partei Österreichs (FPÖ) – FDP
> Sozialistische Partei Österreichs (SPÖ) – SPD

On some issues, the SPÖ and ÖVP have a large measure of convergence, while the FPÖ (the SPÖ's smaller coalition partner) is to the right of the ÖVP. Kadan and Pelinka (1979) show that, on many questions, including democracy, society, religion, and the Austrian nation, there is considerable ideological uniformity among the three parties. It should be pointed out that while, in the Federal Republic, German nationalism is of dubious value as a vote-catcher, with its reminiscences of the Third Reich, Austrian nationalism in Austria is something positive, clearly distinguished from German nationalism. After all, during the Nazi period, Austria was compulsorily part of Germany, and the myth of Austria as a victim of Nazi aggression is one that Austrians like to propagate.

Each of the main parties had a prewar forerunner – the SPÖ's predecessor was the Socialist Party, the ÖVP's the Christian-Social Party, while the forerunners of the FPO were the German Nationalists (*Großdeutsche*) of the First Republic. (The term *freiheitlich* is also employed as the political self-designation of ultra right wing newspapers in the Federal Republic, the *National-Zeitung* and *Deutscher Anzeiger*, as well as the NPD; see below, 7.4.1.) The parties' pre-history is reflected in their platforms, although they all present themselves as parties of the people. The following discussion is based on an operational study of the constitution and policy platforms, topic by topic, and on some of the recent election campaign literature of the three main parties.

The same political catchwords that were described in 7.2.1 recur in Austria. For instance, all three parties allude to *Freiheit*. The common features of this complex symbol are [human dignity], [self-determination] and [social responsibility]. The SPÖ, which tends to use this symbol together with *Gleichheit* and *Gerechtigkeit*, stresses [+ social and material preconditions] and [– privileges]. For the ÖVP *Freiheit* has the features [+ own decision], [+ power to act], [– welfare state] and [+ social and material preconditions]. The FPÖ, for whom the concept of *Freiheit* is absolutely central, constructs the complex symbol with the features [+ self-chosen development], [+ responsibility], [+ order], [+ authority], [+ diversity] and [– uniformity]. This makes the FPÖ's concept of *Freiheit* vastly different from that of the SPÖ. To the SPÖ, *Gerechtigkeit* entails *Gleichheit*, while for both the ÖVP and the FPÖ it entails [– uniforming measures]. This is especially apparent in their conflicting attitudes to comprehensive schooling.

The SPÖ's *Solidarität*:
$$\begin{bmatrix} + \text{ mutual responsibility} \\ + \text{ mutual consideration} \\ + \text{ pluralism} \\ - \text{ suppression} \\ - \text{ exploitation} \\ + \text{ conflict resolution} \end{bmatrix}$$

139

has a close equivalent in the ÖVP's *Partnerschaft*:

$$\begin{bmatrix} + \text{ mutual responsibility} \\ + \text{ mutual consideration} \\ + \text{ pluralism} \\ + \text{ conflict resolution} \end{bmatrix}$$

It seems that these notions partially contradict the FPÖ's 'Leistungsgesellschaft ohne Beschränkung' (performance-oriented society without limits) (Kadan and Pelinka 1979: 49), which is rejected outright by the SPÖ. Unlike the distinction between *Gemeinschaft* and *Gesellschaft* in the Federal Republic (see 7.2.1), the terms are used more or less interchangeably by all the main Austrian parties. *Partizipation* is accepted by them all as [+ taking part in societal decisions], [+ responsibility] and [+ tolerance], the FPÖ employing *Mitbestimmung* particularly often. As is apparent from the above, the SPÖ's social policy can be generally marked [+ collective], the ÖVP's [± collective], and the FPÖ's [− collective], in contrast to the situation outlined for the Federal Republic.

Each of the three mainstream Austrian parties purports to be a party of the centre. The SPÖ and the ÖVP both try to project themselves as offering a 'golden medium' between the conflicting world systems of capitalism and communism. At the same time, they parallel this with the idea of Austria itself being a 'golden medium' between the extremes in Eastern and Western Europe. Each of the parties claims to present Austria (on behalf of itself, the party), and the world (on behalf of Austria), with a package comprising the features:

$$\begin{bmatrix} + \text{ democracy} \\ + \text{ openness} \\ + \text{ new consciousness} \\ + \text{ détente} \\ + \text{ moderation} \\ + \text{ freedom} \\ + \text{ peace} \\ + \text{ wholesomeness} \end{bmatrix}$$

In this the SPÖ has been most effective through its success in office in the fields of economics and international politics. For a decade, Austrian electors accepted the SPÖ's claim of sole ability to offer

Sicherheit und eine gute Zukunft (security and a good future). In much of the election propaganda, the then chancellor, Kreisky, the SPÖ and *Österreich* are collocated or associated, visually through colours, in order to be equated in people's minds (Borbé 1977: 75). Kreisky and the SPÖ have played up Austrian nationalism (a revival of Austria's past glory, even with reference to the Habsburgs) and Austria's role in the world (especially in the 1979 election campaign). Kreisky emphasized the policy of *Aktive Neutralität* (active neutrality), which distinguishes Austria from a traditional (passively) neutral state like Switzerland. The policy was challenged by the ÖVP in April 1980, in the controversy over Tito's 'successor' as leader of the non-aligned group of nations, on the grounds that active neutrality made Austria a non-aligned rather than a neutral country. Certainly Kreisky's independent pronouncements (e.g. on the Middle East, Iran and Poland in 1980) have given Austrians generally a new kind of collective self-confidence.

The FPÖ alone, while upholding international principles, still maintains a declaration of allegiance to the *deutsche Volks- und Kulturgemeinschaft* (German ethnic and cultural community), though it too stresses its support of a neutral Austria.

7.3 Die Grünen in the Federal Republic [7]

This party, which has gained representation in West German federal and state parliaments in recent years, is the parliamentary offspring of various extraparliamentary movements: conservation, anti-nuclear, peace and disarmament, feminist, human rights, world development, Christian activist, workers' independence – many of them new left, some quite conservative. This coalition of interests is reflected in the issues they propagate and the language they use. Die Grünen see all traditional parties as long-term failures and claim to offer an alternative to both capitalism and communism.

As is foreshadowed in the name of the party, a key-word in the vocabulary of the Die Grünen is *ökologisch* (ecological), which comprises the features:

---

[7] Based on their policy platform and 1980 election campaign literature.

141

$$\begin{bmatrix} - \text{ wastage} \\ - \text{ destruction} \\ - \text{ violence} \\ + \text{ health} \\ + \text{ wholesomeness} \\ - \text{ nuclear} \\ + \text{ equality} \end{bmatrix}$$

The word is employed in many areas, including the environment, medicine, and social relations. The antithesis of *Ökologie* is *unverzügelter Verbrauch* (unrestrained consumption) (e.g. *Energie-, Arzneimittel-, Nikotinverbrauch* – consumption of energy, medication, nicotine), *Verschwendung* (wastage) and *Wachstum* (growth) (and including *technischer Fortschritt*), which are given negative connotations, connected with destruction. The answer provided by Die Grünen is *Schutz* (protection), including: *Gesundheits-, Lebens-, Menschen-, Mütter-, Natur-, Tierschutz*, and, most particularly, *Umweltschutz* (protection of health, lives, people, mothers, nature, animals, the environment). *Menschenschutz* (protection of the people) can be promoted by counteracting *Belastung* (stress) at the physical, physiological and mental levels (often brought about by overwork).

Reference to 'nuclear' energy and power use compounds with *Atom* – and the adjective *atomar* (see below, 7.8.2). A great deal of emphasis is placed on energy policy, hence the frequent use of compounds with *Energie*, e.g. *-konsum, -politik, -wachstum* (energy consumption, policy, growth).

Die Grünen deny the existence of real freedom and democracy in the Federal Republic (*Abbau demokratischer Rechte* – erosion of democratic rights) since the conviction of the individual is not respected, and majority decisions are binding on minorities. To this somewhat utopian party of 'cultural pessimism', *Freiheit* consists of the features:

$$
\left[
\begin{array}{l}
- \text{ compulsion} \\
+ \text{ self-determination} \\
+ \text{ participation} \\
+ \text{ opportunities for the individual} \\
- \text{ suppression} \\
+ \text{ full information} \\
- \text{ bureaucratization} \\
- \text{ centralization} \\
+ \text{ local initiatives} \\
- \text{ atomic energy/pollution} \\
+ \text{ 'Back to Nature'} \\
- \text{ environmental threats} \\
- \text{ privileges} \\
+ \text{ solidarity} \\
+ \text{ right to work in one's profession} \\
+ \text{ right to demonstrate}
\end{array}
\right]
$$

Demokratie is understood as direct, grassroots democracy (rather than a completely representational system).

Central Europe (East and West) is seen as an open and independent cultural region where there should be freedom of movement. The developing nations are referred to exclusively as *die Dritte Welt*. *Frieden* is considered to entail:

$$
\left[
\begin{array}{l}
+ \text{ total disarmament} \\
- \text{ violence} \\
+ \text{ détente} \\
+ \text{ solidarity with Third World countries} \\
- \text{ military service}
\end{array}
\right]
$$

7.4 Fringe parties and political groups

7.4.1 The far right in the Federal Republic

The nearest political successor to the National Socialists in the Federal Republic today is the Nationaldemokratische Partei Deutschlands (NPD), which enjoyed flashes of momentary success in state elections in the late 60s, but now has no parliamentarians and only 8000 members on its books. The election propaganda of this party, its weekly newspaper, *Deutsche Nachrichten*, another weekly,

Deutscher Anzeiger, and the longer-established weekly newspaper, *National-Zeitung* (formerly *Soldatenzeitung*; present circulation about 10,000) give some insights into the language usage of the 'far right'.

There are few indications in these publications of residual 'Nazi language' (the language of the National Socialist régime as described by Berning 1964, Seidel and Seidel-Slotty 1961), and it seems that, to a large extent, the new right has developed its own usage. Because of the limited support for ultra-right groups, the function of their publications is, of course, vastly different from those of the Third Reich. *Volk* is still employed to refer to the German people, and not to the populus (e.g. the 'Hetzkampagne gegen *das deutsche Volk*' (smear campaign against the German people) of which Britain, France and the United States are accused) (*National-Zeitung*, 7 February 1978). Like the CSU (see above, 7.2.1), the *National-Zeitung* uses the word *Deutschland* to refer to both German states as one unit, and there is frequent reference to the *Teilung des Vaterlandes* (division of the fatherland). The GDR specifically is referred to as *Mitteldeutschland* (see 7.1). Members of the political left, including students, are termed *Gangster, Nihilisten* (and *Anarcho-Nihilisten*), *Revoluzzer* (derogatory term for radicals), *Rote Verfassungsfeinde* (red enemies of the constitution), *Roter Mob, Terroristen, Staatsfeinde* (enemies of the state), *Subversive* (subversives), and *Ultra-Linke* (ultra-left). Both SPD members and Communists are referred to ironically as *Genossen* (comrades). Compounds with *Terror* were coined to describe both the SPD/FDP coalition and the far left (e.g. *Terrorherrschaft* (rule of terror), *Terrororganisation, Terrorsystem*). There is a polarization of friend- and foe-words, e.g. *Sieg* (victory; the 'Germanic' noun with its associations of *Sieg Heil!*) is used only for a right-wing and German success, while a left-wing or foreign one (e.g. for Euro-Communists) is referred to as *Triumph*. *Feind* (enemy) tends to be applied to left-wing dissidents in the Federal Republic, *Gegner* (opponent) to dissidents in the Soviet Union and other East European countries. Pacifists are termed *Wehrfeinde* (enemies of the army) and *Soldatenfeinde* (enemies of soldiers), internationalists *Deutsch(en)feinde* (enemies of Germans).

As in National Socialist propaganda, Jews and Communists are referred to in collocation: e.g. *Jüdische und kommunistische Organisationen*. In far-right newspapers, there is a recurring discussion

144

of *Deutsche Würde* (German dignity) and argumentation against the *Verzicht* (renunciation, sacrifice) of this, particularly in the framework of '*Verrat an Vertriebenen*' (betrayal of those expelled). They often add inverted commas when using left-wing terms ironically, e.g. '*fortschrittlich*', '*fortschrittliche Kräfte*' (progressive forces), '*NPD-Schlägerkolonien*' (NPD rowdy colonies).

There are also 23 ultra-right-wing groups in the Federal Republic, with a total of 2500 members. To my knowledge, no research has been done on their use of language.

7.4.2 The far left in the Federal Republic

There have been several opposing and competing communist groups in the Federal Republic in recent years, some of which have now folded up. The groups are of little significance today, but a study of them tells us something about language and politics in the Federal Republic in the immediate past. Each of the groups has its own newspaper. The language usage in the newspapers is indicative of both their ideology and their audience (*Spiegel* 1980, Schlomann 1980). This can be illustrated from the following examples from 1977–80.

The Deutsche Kommunistische Partei (DKP), the first of the communist parties to be established in the Federal Republic after the banning of the old Kommunistische Partei Deutschlands (KPD), is more traditionally communist and 'moderate', and supports the Soviet Union and the GDR. It is the only communist party in the Federal Republic with a daily newspaper, *Unsere Zeit* (daily circulation: 30,000; 60,000 on Fridays).[8] This newspaper uses a general vocabulary with some traditional communist terms and attempts to appeal to the 'ordinary man and woman'. Words like *Angestellte* (employees), *Arbeitgeber* (employers) and *Unternehmer* (entrepreneurs) are employed freely. There is a disproportionately large number of colloquialisms (in general columns) for a daily newspaper other than a news-pictorial like *Bild*, e.g. *den Hebel ansetzen* (to apply the lever); *das schlägt dem Faß den Boden aus* (that's the last straw!); *von der Inflation aufgefressen werden* (to be eaten up by inflation). As in GDR newspapers, capitalists are treated with some disdain, e.g.

---

[8] Personal communication, Herbert Dege (*Unsere Zeit*).

Bosse (bosses), *Konzernherren* (tycoons), *Millionäre*. Terms like *Demagogie* are also used. Lexical transfers from English tend to be directed at the youth, e.g. *Festival, live, Rockpop, Show, Songgruppen.*

The Kommunistische Partei Deutschlands (KPD), a Maoist party which emerged in the early 1970s, received the most votes of any communist party on the state lists in the 1976 federal elections. This party was both anti-Soviet and anti-Peking, its main supporters being 'veterans' of the student movement (see 7.5) (*Spiegel* 1980). Its official organ, the weekly *Rote Fahne* (circulation 5000 in 1980), used both traditional Marxist-Leninist catchwords and new left clichés. Its language would probably not be accessible to the general reader. Some examples: *Ausbeutertätigkeit* (exploitation activities), *Klassenherrschaft der Ausbeuter* (class domination by the exploiters), *Reformisten und Revisionisten* (reformers and revisionists), *Gefangener der bürgerlichen Legalität* (prisoner of bourgeois legality), *Unterdrückungsapparat* (suppression apparatus), *Verbrechersyndikat* (syndicate of criminals), *kapitalistische Rationalisierung* (capitalist rationalization), *Klassenbewußtsein* (class consciousness). *Profit* is, predictably, used in a negative sense. *Volk* is used widely, but only with the meaning 'populus, masses'. Lexical transfers from English are restricted to a western, capitalist context, e.g. *Bosse* (for capitalists – in a very negative sense), *Hearings in Washington, Image, Swimming-pools.*

The Kommunistische Partei Deutschlands – Marxist-Leninist (KPD/ML) had about 600 members in 1980 and may best be described as Maoist. Both anti-Soviet and anti-Peking, it has acclaimed Albania as 'Vaterland aller Werktätigen' (fatherland of all working people) (*Spiegel* 1980). Its monthly newspaper *Roter Morgen* applied the terms *Revisionisten* (revisionists) and *revisionistisch* to the DKP. The paper had a strongly anti-trade union line and referred to both capitalists and union leaders as *Bosse*, although the latter are also called *Bonzen* (big shots; originally a term for Buddhist priests, also used by the trade unions in the past). Capitalists are also derogatorily called *Herren* (lords), while workers are termed both *Arbeiter* (workers) and *Kollegen* (colleagues, the old SPD term of solidarity).

The Kommunistischer Bund Westdeutschlands (membership about 2500 in 1980) was pro-China, anti-Soviet, pro-Arab, and supported independence movements in all Third World nations. The KBW was in favour of conservation in the capitalist and Eastern European countries but did not favour it for China and the Third World. Its weekly, *Kommunistische Volkszeitung*, abounded with economic and political *Fachsprache*, political metaphors and other stylistic devices, and compounds of left-wing clichés. It is perhaps a good example of how radical intellectuals have failed to develop a language usage that would enable them to communicate with workers (the *Volk*), e.g. *imperialistischer Handels-*, *Währungs-*, *Finanzkrieg* (imperialist trade, currency, financial war), *Waren-* und *Kapitalexportoffensive* (goods and capital export offensives); *militärische Wellenbrecher* (military breakwaters), *Schlachtschiff der Expansion* (battleship of expansion); *Lohnsklaven* (wage slaves), *Schuldknechtschaft* (debt serfdom), *Plünderpolitik* (plunder policy), *Chefplünderer* (chief plunderer = minister of finance). They also use such metaphors as: *Bourgeoisieschreiberlinge* (bourgeois pen-pushers), *Ford-Köln-Kapitalisten*, *Automobil-*, *Chemie-*, *Versandhauskapitalisten* (car, chemistry, mail order store capitalists). Marx's term *Bourgeoisie* is used in many compounds, being preferred to *Bürgertum*. Like the far right, the *Kommunistische Volkszeitung* designated its opponents as *Gangster*. *Imperialismus* and *imperialistisch* (western, capitalist) were contrasted with the *sozialimperialistische Supermacht* (i.e. the USSR).

Arbeiterkampf, the bi-monthly of the Kommunistischer Bund, a small Maoist group, has attracted a much larger readership (in 1977: 24,500; in 1980: 9200) from non-aligned left-wingers because of the general social and political issues it discusses and its comprehensible style. The paper could be described as anti-SPD, KPD and KPD/ML, anti-Trotzkyist, anti-Soviet and anti-Peking, expressly anti-fascist, and committed to conservation all over the world, the Arab cause, and the freeing of political prisoners. There is very little vocabulary that one could not find in a regular daily newspaper. Occasionally the police were referred to as *Bullen* (the anti-establishment term for them). *Arbeiterkampf* has made frequent use of irony, for instance through inverted commas, e.g. '*realer Sozialismus*' for the self-styled policy in the Soviet Union and the GDR.

7.4.3 The Kommunistische Partei Österreichs (KPÖ)[9]

The KPÖ, which was one of the foundation parties of the Second Austrian Republic, uses *kapitalistisch* and *staatsmonopolistisch* (state-monopolistic) to describe the economic policies of *all* the other parties and *Sozialismus* for itself, and sees itself as the guardian of the interests of the *Arbeiterklasse* (working class) and the *werktätige Bevölkerungsschichten* (working sections of the population). It supports *aktive Neutralität*, and its use of *Frieden* embraces the features:

$$
\begin{bmatrix}
- \text{'western imperialism'} \\
- \text{'soviet imperialism'} \\
+ \text{class struggle} \\
+ \text{détente} \\
+ \text{national independence} \\
+ \text{social reform}
\end{bmatrix}
$$

7.5 The language of student activism[10]

The student revolt in the Federal Republic, to which a number of sociolinguistic developments can be attributed,[11] was sparked off by discontent with an anachronistic power structure in the universities and with the parliamentary situation. At the time, the two large political blocks, CDU/CSU and SPD, formed the coalition government, the parliamentary opposition (the FDP) was small and ineffective, emergency legislation was passed, giving governments very extensive powers in crisis situations, and the NPD enjoyed considerable success. Other factors, such as distrust of liberalism, enhanced by a relative lack of democratic tradition in Germany and an unusually wide generation gulf due to the events of the Third Reich, the international new left student movement, and a reaction

---

[9] These remarks are based on party platforms.

[10] This section is based on thousands of student pamphlets and newspapers distributed at universities in the Federal Republic between 1967 and 1978, mainly from the Free University of Berlin and the universities of Bonn, Stuttgart and Tübingen. For more general contemporary information on the student movement, see e.g. Bergmann *et al* (1968), Schönbohm *et al* (1968).

[11] For example, changes in the system of address (6.4), pressure for orthographical reform (4.1.1), and dialect resurgence and the debate on language barriers in education (3.4; 4.3).

against the conservative press also contributed to what became the 'Apo' (*Außerparlamentarische Opposition*, Extra-parliamentary opposition).

The main student body of the time, the Sozialistische Deutsche Studentenschaft (SDS), which was expelled from the SPD in 1961, was in the vanguard of the Apo. The linguistic manifestations of their political aims and attitudes may be discerned through the collocations and lexical choices in their pamphlets. Four main catchwords of the SDS were *Demokratie* (and *demokratisch*), *Emanzipation*, *Kritik* (and *kritisch*) and *Politisierung* (and *politisiert*) (Democracy/ democratic, emancipation, criticism/critical, politicization/politicized). Another was *antiautoritär* (anti-authoritarian). *Demokratie* and *demokratisch* referred to both the state and the university, and entailed participation in decision-making. The emergency legislation was described as *Abbau der Demokratie*. *Emanzipation* too was employed for the university and general political scenes, e.g. *Emanzipation der Studenten* (emancipation of students), *Emanzipation der Menschen von Unterdrückung, Mangel und Manipulation* (emancipation of people from suppression, want, and manipulation). *Kritisch* was generally used to mean critical of traditional values and of the Establishment, e.g. *kritische Intelligenz*, *kritische Stellungnahme* (critical position), *kritische Studentenschaft* (critical student body), *kritische Wissenschaft* (critical learning), *kritische Universität* (the 'alternative university' set up by students and left-wing staff at the Free University of Berlin, after the Berlin demonstration in June 1967 at which a student was shot dead by police). *Politisiert* is an adjacent member of the same lexical field, and *politisierte Wissenschaft* (politicized learning) was contrasted with *bürgerliche Wissenschaft* (bourgeois learning). The word *Universität* (also termed *Klassenuniversität*) was collocated with *elitär* (élitist), *feudal*, and *vernunftfeindlich* (hostile to reason). The behaviour of the police at the June 1967 demonstration in Berlin was described as a *Massaker*, *Pogrom*, and *Polizeiterror*. Lectures were referred to as, among other things, *Säkular-Predigten* (secular sermons). In contrast to the democratic aims of the student movement, the language use was largely abstract and in-group, strongly influenced by the political philosophy of the Frankfurt School (members of the influential Institute of Social Research in Frankfurt, led by Adorno and Horkheimer).

As the West German student movement was part of an international one, there were numerous transfers from English, e.g. *Teach-in, Go-in, Sit-in* (with stress on the final syllable), and *direkte Aktion*. Some of the traditional communist terms used gave the protesting students common vocabulary with the GDR, e.g. *aktivistisch/Aktivismus, dialektisch, Genosse, Kollektiv, Neuerer, revolutionär* (see Ch. 2).

The politicians and newspapers on the right, and the Establishment in general, described the students as *Rowdies*, and their actions as *Gewaltaktionen* (tactics of violence), *Störung* (disturbance), *Störaktionen* (disturbance tactics), *terroristische Akte*, and *Beseitigung der parlamentarischen Demokratie* (elimination of parliamentary democracy).

In the early 70s, the SDS dissolved and was replaced by a number of left-wing student organizations, most of them corresponding to existing Marxist, Maoist, and Trotzkyist groups (see 7.4.2). Right and centre political organizations have (re)appeared on the campus, with considerable support, e.g. Ring Christlich-Demokratischer Studenten (RCDS), Liberaler Hochschulbund (LHB), Sozialliberaler Hochschulbund (SLH). There is also the nihilist group, the Spontis. In the meantime, a number of important political reforms were achieved within universities (e.g. the establishment of a *Mittelbau*, 'sub-professorial' academic staff; *Drittelparität* – university committees being composed of equal representations from professors, *Mittelbau* and students; relaxation of compulsory *Habilitation* – a second doctorate as a prerequisite for chairs). Many of these have since been retracted. The SPD/FDP coalition, although unpopular with the far left, was not as repulsive to it as were CDU/FDP or CDU/SPD coalitions.

Most of the student pamphlets in recent years have dealt with individual general and university political issues. *Demokratisch* and *kritisch* are still key-words, but not as common as in the days of a uniform programme. All the left-wing groups use *Bewegung* (movement) and *Kampf* (struggle, standing for *revolutionärer Kampf* in local politics, and *Freiheitskampf* when referring to the Third World) in a positive sense. The Kommunistische Studentengruppen employ *Politik*, and of course *Staatsmonopolkapitalismus*, in a negative sense, and *Veranstaltungen* (functions) to mean *Demonstrationen*. *Teach-ins* are still the order of the day. The Kommunistischer Studentenbund ML uses the strongest language and many political clichés like

150

Kapitalistenklasse, Interessen der Bourgeoisie, Studentenfunktionäre, Terroristenhysterie. It is this organization that has often boycotted university committees to which its candidates have been elected. In comparison, the Marxistischer Studentenbund (Spartakisten) employs a very 'moderate' language to appeal to the 'average student', who is far less politicized today than in the late 60s. At the other end of the spectrum is the Ring freiheitlicher Studenten, which designates itself as *freiheitlich* and *anti-kommunistisch* and all left-wingers as *Rote Rechtssprecher* (red administrators of justice) and *Bonzen* (see above, 7.4.2), whom they describe as *eine Gefahr* (a danger), promoting *Terror*. It refers to the *DDR* in inverted commas. The RCDS, too, stresses the vocabulary of law and order (e.g. *Gewalt* and *Terrorismus* applied to left-wing students).

Each group tends to treat the language usage and frame of reference of its political opponents ironically (e.g. the SPD as *Reformpartei* and the *Radikalenerlaß* (otherwise often in inverted commas) in the *Marxistische Studentenzeitung*).

7.6 Youth protest in Zürich, 1980

Although the student movement of the late 60s and early 70s attempted to establish itself as the champion of the working class and to defend the interests of both workers and students, there was little effective communication between the two. The same may be said for the Zürich youth protests of 1980, despite the fact that student bodies supported them, and students (including former 1968-ers) joined in their demonstrations. (*Tagesanzeiger*, 14 June 1980: p. 17).

The young people, mainly workers and apprentices, protesting against the lack of provision for, and later the closure of, an autonomous alternative youth centre, did not have a common ideology. Among other things, they, like the student movement of the late 60s and early 70s (which was very insignificant in Switzerland), were protesting against materialism and a coalition government of the main political parties, with no parliamentary opposition. In Switzerland, the latter is perpetuated by a convention that the government comprises representatives of the biggest parties in parliament in accordance with their number of parliamentarians (cf. the 'Grand Coalition' in the Federal Republic in 1967–8; above 7.5). Like anti-establishment groups generally, the Zürich youth movement uses a strong, colloquial and 'vulgar' register in public situations, e.g. *beschissen* (rotten), *Geldscheißer* (filthy rich), *Scheißgesellschaft* (filthy society), *Sauwut* (hell of a rage), *total unpolitische Sau* (completely unpolitical swine). They lack econonic and political *Fachsprache* and the articulateness of the student movement in the Federal Republic. A universal *du* form of address appears to be employed also among fellow-protesters in Zürich. These remarks also apply largely to the language of youth and house squatters in the Federal Republic, who may be seen, in the same way, as 'cultural pessimists'.[12]

7.7 The language of protest in the GDR

It is difficult to identify a distinctive language usage of protesters in the GDR. Quite apart from the 'underground' nature of protest there, it generally takes place within the general political context and works with 'official' concepts and terms.

What characterizes critical interaction in the GDR is irony and semantic shift, especially in the lexical fields of politics and economics. Such words as *Freunde* (friends; officially referring to the Soviet Union and other Warsaw Pact nations, but also the term of address among members of the Freie Deutsche Jugend), *Genossen* (comrades; a term of address among members of the SED), *Befreiung* (liberation, e.g. the arrival of Warsaw Pact troops in Czechoslovakia in August 1968), and *Fabrikbesitzer* (factory owners; referring to the workers) are used ironically in such a way that supporters of official policy cannot object but critics understand the negative or ironical connotations. The much-used GDR political cliché *dank aufopfernder Arbeit* (thanks to self-sacrificing work), for example, is parodied in Günther Kunert's poem *Verkündigung des Wetters* (Proclamation of the weather) to refer to clouds:

> Dank aufopfernder Arbeit der Wolken
> Regnet es.
> (*Thanks to the self-sacrificing work* of the clouds
> It is raining.)

[12] There are, of course, specific terms which are part of the language of house-occupiers, for example. *Befreites Gebiet* (freed region) for the area around occupied houses and *Straßenläufer* (street runners) for those looking for potential vacant houses to occupy, are but two instances.

Poems of Reiner Kunze make ironical use of *Arbeiter-und-Bauern-Macht* (power of workers and peasants), *Feinde der Arbeiterklasse* (enemies of the working class), *Ordnungswidrigkeiten* (summary offences), *staatliche Organe* (organs of the state), and many other GDR political expressions. Jürgen Fuchs also parodies frequent genitives and combinations thereof (e.g. in *Gedächtnisprotokolle*, Minutes of the memory). The ironical use of *Freunde* is apparent in Stefan Heym's *Collin* (1979: 236–7):

. . . die Panzer der sowjetischen *Freunde* waren in Budapest eingerollt, schon das zweite Mal, und nun wurde scharf geschossen, *sozialistische Armee* gegen *sozialistische Armee*. (. . . the tanks of the Soviet *friends* had moved into Budapest for the second time, and now there was heavy shooting, *Socialist army* against *Socialist army*.)

It can also be found in Erich Loest's *Es geht seinen Gang* (It goes its course) (1978: 221):

Ich musterte mit den fachmännischen Blicken des Reservisten die Gruben, die *Freunde* oder meine Nachfolger bei der NVA ausgewühlt hatten, auf daß ihre Fahrzeuge in der kritischen Wertung ihrer Vorgesetzten einen angenommenen Atomschlag überstanden, und dachte: Warum sollt ihr's besser haben als ich! (I examined with the expert glances of a reservist, the pits which *friends* or my successors in the National People's Army had dug up, so that their vehicles could, by the critical assessment of their superiors, survive a hypothetical atomic attack and I thought: Why should you be better off than I!)

Ironical use of *Freunde, Genossen, revolutionär* and *Frieden* occur, for instance, in the protest song of the ex-GDR socialist song-writer Wolf Biermann, e.g.

Aber ich singe auch Krieg in diesem
dreimal verfluchten mörderischen *Frieden*
der ein *Frieden* ist vom Friedhoffrieden
der ein *Frieden* ist hinter dem Drahtverhau
der ein Frieden ist hinter dem Knüppel.
      (Wolf Biermann, *Gesang für meine Genossen*)
  (But I also sing war in this
thrice cursed murderous *peace*
which is a *peace* of the cemetery peace
which is a *peace* behind the barbed wire entanglement
which is a *peace* behind the truncheon.)

Traces of GDR Standard German with ironical overtones are also present in the works of other East German writers who have defected or been deported or expelled to the Federal Republic. Many such writers have settled in West Berlin, which offers them a sort of 'intermediate existence' between the 'two worlds'. It should be noted that the writings of GDR and ex-GDR authors have enjoyed great success in the Federal Republic in recent years. Paradoxically this is also due to their (often wrong) interpretation by the naive public as not being obsessed with political ideology like their West German counterparts, resulting partly from sympathy with their *Zivilcourage*, and partly from left-wing solidarity with the GDR (Leslie Bodi, personal communication).

The most marked departure from all this is probably Ulrich Plenzdorf, especially in his *Die neuen Leiden des jungen W.* (The New Sufferings of Young W.), published in both Rostock (GDR) and Frankfurt (Federal Republic) in 1973. This novel, based both on Goethe's *Die Leiden des jungen Werthers* and Salinger's *Catcher in the Rye* represents a questioning of the prevailing value system in the GDR (Brettschneider 1972: 134). Plenzdorf creates a youth dissenter type (Edgar W.) with a 'new look' language usage, one which has had an important effect on the way in which many young people in the GDR speak and behave. It is flippant and brash, e.g. Das *poppt* nicht mehr (It doesn't turn you on any more), *stank* mich fast gar nicht *an* (It did not bother me at all); or ironical, e.g. echte Musik – nicht *Händel*sohn-*Bach*oldy (Real music – not *Handel*son-*Bach*oldy); and abounds with English lexical transfers from the pop (and drug) scene, e.g. (*Blue*) *Jeans, Hasch, Happening, Mike, Recorder, Show, Song, Sound, Speech*. In fact, *Jeans* became a symbol of the protest. Apart from very established GDR words like *Brigade* and *Brigadier*, this book and others by Plenzdorf are devoid of the more usual GDR vocabulary (see Ch. 2).

'In-groups' of critics will also employ a large number of lexical transfers from English, but not with the derogatory meanings generally current in the GDR (see 5.3.5).

7.8 Issues and lobbies, especially in the Federal Republic

In the German-language countries, as elsewhere, groups dedicated to particular causes will develop their own 'in-group' use of language to express their ideology. In addition, those groups that are anti-establishment, anti-authoritarian, left-wing, will often employ a register of protest that includes lexemes that may be generally considered 'vulgar' or aggressive, ones that are metaphors from the anal and sexual sphere.

Over the past decade, people with a common cause in the Federal Republic have been organizing themselves into *Bürgerinitiativen* (citizens' action groups). Initially, these groups were formed mainly at the local level and concerned themselves with local issues, such as a protest against the construction of an *Autobahn*, or an initiative to start a parent-controlled kindergarten. More recently, there has been some national co-ordination, and people involved in social action and 'alternative thinking' on different subjects have started interacting. A monthly magazine *Bürger-Initiative* was established in 1977. A local issue of national significance has been the proposed construction of a new runway at Frankfurt Airport.

Generally, in the language usage of the citizens' groups, *Bürger* (including collocations and compounds: *Mitbürger* (fellow citizens), *engagierte Bürger* (committed citizens), *Bürgeraktionen, -aktivitäten*) is always employed in a positive sense and *Behörde* (authorities) and *Bürokratie* are always used negatively. Governments and politicians are treated with some scorn, e.g. *Hohes Haus* (Parliament) as opposed to *Untertanen* (subjects; Bürger).[13] Actions of the *Bürger* are universally described as *gewaltfrei* (non-violent) and *friedlich* (peaceful), those of governments are collocated or identified with *Gewalt* (violence) and *Schlacht* (battle).[14] On the whole, protest groups have moved away from the political clichés of the 1968-ers towards 'middle-of-the-road' usage. This also applies to the leading protest magazine *Alternative*.

7.8.1 Feminism

German feminist groups do not appear to have devoted as much attention to the desexing of the language as a major part of their programme as have their English-speaking counterparts (but cf. 8.5).

[13] It has to be taken into account that German *Bürger* can mean 'middle class' and 'burgeois' as well as 'citizen', and that any of the meanings may carry connotations of the others.
[14] cf. Die Grünen, above 7.3.

This is obvious from a perusal of German-language feminist magazines, such as *Emma, Courage,* and *Frauen und Film* (the latter being devoted to feminist cinema). Recently feminist linguists in the Federal Republic have agitated for non-sexist modes of address and occupational terminology, and references to the sexes in an unbiased form (Guentherodt 1979, Hellinger 1980, Pusch, Trömel-Plötz, Hellinger and Guentherodt 1981; see 8.5). In feminist circles, *man* (one pronoun) has been replaced by *frau* or *man/frau.* This substitution also occurs in a letter to *Emma* from a male reader (*Emma* Nr. 4, 1980: 63). What also stands out in feminist newspapers and leaflets is the following:

(i)   recurring slogans, similar to those of other protest groups, e.g. *Emanzipation, Frauenemanzipation* (women's lib) (always in a positive sense), *Abbau der Herrschaft* (abolition of domination), *Abbau des Sexismus* (abolition of sexism), *Unterdrükkung der Frauen* (suppression of women), *Diskriminierung der Frauen* (discrimination against women), *grundlegende Herrschaftsstrukturen des Patriarchats* (basic patriarchal domination structures);

(ii) the generalized use of *du* and *ihr,* even in formal situations, and irrespective of whether the interactants were previously known to each other, obviously as a symbol of solidarity (cf. 6.4);

(iii) strong or 'vulgar' use of language, for instance in appeals and letters to the editor, to depart from the submissive image of women (cf. Lakoff 1975: Part II), e.g. *Scheiße* (crap), *beschissen* (rotten);

(iv) *Frauen* and *Männer* are polarized, e.g. *Frauenprogramm, Männerwelt* (the world of men, like the world of science). (Also, *Frauen und Film,* like some other alternative publications, uses minisculization throughout, even for names and titles, and at the beginning of sentences.)

7.8.2 The language of the nuclear energy debate

Perhaps the most important protest movement today is that which is opposed to war. An anti-nuclear lobby has been in existence for some years and there is considerable overlap between its objectives and those of the peace movement. At the time of writing, it was too early to come to any conclusions on the language of the peace movement. As Dahl (1977) has pointed out, the protagonists of nuclear energy in the German-language countries and elsewhere (in the Federal Republic, this includes virtually all politicians of the traditional parties) have created a terminology which plays down the dangers, and influences thinking on this subject. Even the word *Kernkraft* (nuclear power) is really a euphemism for *Atomkraft* (atomic power), which bears associations with *Atombombe*, while *Kern* (core, kernel, nucleus) is something wholesome and usually stable. The [+war] feature of *Atom* is counteracted by the collocations of *Kernkraft* with *friedlich*, embracing the feature [−war]. Nuclear accidents are designated as *Störfälle* (temporary disruptions), not *Unfälle* (accidents). Waste disposal areas are referred to as *Entsorgungsparks.* Parks are associated with recreation, relaxation, areas kept in a natural state for the public benefit, and *entsorgen* (taking away one's worries) is the answer to all problems of this modern age. *Tanks*, the name given to the steel containers of nuclear waste, ascribes to such containers an image of safety and enclosure which is not justified in reality. *Wiederaufarbeitung* (literally, reprocessing) implies a recycling that is only marginally possible.

Moreover, Dahl shows that, on some issues, through a vague academic register, the nuclear energy supporters have given the impression of understating a case when they are, in fact, being deliberately non-committal, e.g. Es besteht *kaum* Zweifel (There is *hardly* any doubt); Lösung*selemente* (elements of solution); *noch* unbewältigte Probleme (problems not *yet* overcome).[15]

The *Bürgerinitiativen* and other groups opposing nuclear energy avoid the above euphemisms and tend to use *Atom* and not *Kern*, as in the compounds *Atom*kraftwerk (*AKW*), *Atom*energie, *Atom*reaktion, *Atom*technologie. Occasionally *nuklear* is substituted. This, being both a lexical transfer and a part of *Fachsprache*, is more neutral and used by both the pro- and anti-nuclear lobbies. (*Atom*)*mülldeponie* (atomic waste deposit area) is employed by the opponents of nuclear power in place of *Entsorgungspark*, and *Wiederaufbereitung* (re-preparation) for *Wiederaufarbeitung*. Anxieties are generated through expressions such as *radiochemische*

---

[15] In GDR newspapers, the dangers of nuclear waste are reported only with regard to the western world (e.g. nuclear accidents). However, the same pro-nuclear vocabulary is used for plants in the east and west.

Küche (radio-chemical kitchen) (possible analogy with *Teufelsküche*, the devil of a mess; literally, the devil's kitchen).

7.8.3 The language of right-wing *Bürgerinitiativen*: 'Volksbegehren gegen Kooperative Schulen' ('Referendum against Co-operative Schools') as an example

In the first months of 1978, a campaign was conducted in the state of North Rhine-Westphalia against the introduction of a modified type of comprehensive school known as the *Kooperative Schule*, which has ten- and 11-year-olds, in the 5th and 6th Grades (*Orientierungsstufe*), and the three kinds of secondary schools – *Hauptschule, Realschule*, and *Gymnasium* – as departments of a single-campus institution, with shared resources of all kinds. The highly successful campaign, run by a citizens' action group 'Bürgeraktion Volksbegehren gegen Kooperative Schulen in Nordrhein-Westfalen' in co-operation with the CDU and the Roman Catholic Church, culminated in a petition. Linguistic devices were used in three main lines of attack:

(i)   Through expressions like *völlig ungesichertes Experiment* (completely unsafe experiment), *Schul-Wirrwarr* (school chaos) and *Auflösung des bewährten Systems* (dissolution of the time-tested system), the view was evoked that the existing (élitist) system was stable and completely satisfactory, and that the new system was confused and not thought-out.

(ii) There was a continual implication that the *Kooperative Schule* was only devised because it was cheaper than the traditional types of schools. This was cleverly reinforced through the abbreviation of *Kooperative Schule* to *Koop-Schule, Koop* being a chain of supermarkets owned by the DGB (German Council of Trade Unions) which offers goods (in the view of some, of inferior quality) at low prices.

(iii) There was also an implication that the *Kooperative Schule* was a Socialist plot by the SPD/FDP coalition, which would lead to a socialist system like that of the GDR, e.g. through frequent references to this being a first step towards, or preparation for the *Sozialistische Einheitsschule*. The *Einheitsschule* is a GDR term for its 10-year comprehensive school. Apart from the negative connotations intended by the use of *sozialistisch*, there is a linguistic association with the *Sozialistische Einheitspartei*, the result of the forced merger, in the GDR, of the SPD and the KPD.[16]

7.9 Brief summary

German is a language polarized by political attitudes, as is illustrated by words like *Berufsverbot* and the designations of the two German states. Each of the major political parties in the Federal Republic and Austria has developed its own set of complex symbols and collocations according to its ideology and the image it wishes to transmit. Differences in historical tradition and present political context have greatly contributed to the existing variations in political language. Some catchwords common to two or more parties have developed different semantic features. This is shown through a study of the language policy statements and election propaganda.

The 'fringe parties', too, have developed their own usage which, in many cases, is based on a friend–foe dichotomy at the lexicosemantic level. Some of the communist groups have employed a mixture of traditional Marxist terminology and clichés of the new left, which would be difficult for the average German speaker to comprehend. This contrasts, for instance, with the language of the Zürich youth protest movement (1980). Die Grünen have evolved a vocabulary centred around *ökologisch* (ecology), *Freiheit* (freedom) and *Schutz* (protection).

Student groups and citizens' action groups similarly develop a language usage in keeping with their objectives, as do the feminist movements of the German-language regions, who have so far not appeared to be taking the 'desexing of language' as seriously as their counterparts in English-speaking countries.

The protagonists of nuclear energy in the Federal Republic have devised a euphemistic vocabulary which plays down the dangers. Anti-nuclear groups have therefore invented their own terms for the same processes. On the whole, most protest groups have moved away

---

[16] On the last day of voting, the *Tagesschau* (news) on TV interviewed a number of people leaving the polling booths after signing the petition who could not explain what a *Kooperative Schule* was. Some of them declared that they had voted to prevent conditions from developing as they had in the GDR.

from the political clichés of the late 1960s and early 1970s to a more 'middle-of-the-road' usage.

In the GDR, opposition tends to be expressed within the general political context and works within the official concepts and terms. However, such words are often employed ironically. The novelist Plenzdorf has created a 'new look' youth protest register which is flippant, colloquial, ironical and introduces lexical transfers from English.

7.10 Note

This chapter is based almost entirely on primary sources. However, Dieckmann (1964) is a good introduction to German language and politics.

8

Some other new developments

8.1 Sentence and word formation

Several writers have commented on syntactic developments in modern German. Eggers (1963, 1969) reports a trend towards shorter, less complex sentences, reflecting more universal (rather than elitist) access to the written language and a consequential colloquial influence on written German. Moser (1967) observes tendencies towards differentiation, systematization, abstraction, and especially economy, resulting from the urgent pressures of modern life. Lengthy compounds (e.g. *Hochleistungsultrakurzwellengeradeausempfänger*, high capacity very high frequency straight-circuit receiver – from the field of electronics) are the result of the need for differentiation and precision. The zero (uninflected) form of the noun demonstrates a tendency towards systematization. (For instance, *Wort* can now be dative (cf. older form *Worte*) as well as nominative and accusative.) On the other hand, the tendency to choose a Subjunctive II form instead of Subjunctive I if the latter is identical in form to the indicative is an example of a trend towards clarity.

Economy of comprehension can be facilitated by nominalizing the main predicate of a subordinate clause, which allows it to be moved forward and thus heard earlier. (This is accompanied by a semantically empty or near-empty verb occupying the syntactic position of the original predicate.) This moving forward of the main predicate is characteristic of the bureaucratic register, e.g. 'Wir bitten Sie, *die Abholung* des Fernsprechbuches am 12. Dezember von 15 bis 17 Uhr, Wilhelmstraße 20, Zimmer 5, vorzunehmen' (rather than 'Wir bitten Sie, . . . *abzuholen*') (Moser 1967: 25). ('To undertake the collection' instead of 'to collect'. *Abholung* (collection) is placed well before *abholen* (to collect) would be.)

Adjectives formed with the increasingly productive *-mäßig* and *-weise* suffixes are examples of both abstraction and economy, e.g. alkohol*mäßig* (alcoholwise), lebensmittel*mäßig* (grocerywise), witterungs*maßig* (weatherwise), wohnungs*mäßig* (housingwise); gerücht*weise* (as rumour has it, rumourwise), gesprächs*weise* (in conversation, conversationwise), instinkt*weise* (instinctively, instinctwise). It has been argued that the latter formation has found its way from German into American English – and through it into British and Australian English (Eichhoff 1976, Taylor 1978).

It is to the tendency towards economy that the large number of compound nouns can be attributed – words that are prominent in the media and especially in newspaper headlines, e.g. *Christdemokrat* (< *Christlicher Demokrat*, Christian Democrat), *Kleinkrieg* (< *kleiner Krieg*, mini-war), *Linkspolitiker* (< *linksgerichteter Politiker*, left (-wing) politician); and potentially 'ambiguous' compounds, such as *Europa-Unterhändler* (Europe negotiator), *Extremistenbeschluß* (extremists resolution), *Kanzler-Memorandum* (chancellor memorandum), and *Madrid-Botschafter* (Madrid ambassador). For instance, a lexeme such as *Polenreise* can be interpreted as: Reise *des* Polen (journey of the Pole), Reise *der* Polen (journey of the Poles), Reise *nach* Polen (journey to Poland), Reise *in* Polen (journey in Poland), or Reise *durch* Polen (journey through Poland) (Clyne 1968a). Such words, which are not new, but used especially frequently today, are disambiguated through the context (except in newspaper headlines, where they contribute to people's curiosity).

8.1.1 Abbreviations

Another result of a desire for economy is the large number of acronyms and abbreviations. Moser (1967: 23) estimated that there were 90,000 abbreviations and acronyms in use in the Federal Republic at the time. Some of these are common to all German-language countries, e.g. *Bus* (for *Omnibus* or *Autobus*), *UB* for *Universitätsbibliothek* (university library), *D-Zug* for *Durchgangszug* (express). Others are specific to a particular country, as illustrated below.

Federal Republic:

Apo (*Außerparlamentarische Opposition*, extra-parliamentary opposition), BAT (*Bundesangestelltentarif*, federal framework for wage

162

scales and conditions of contract), BGB (*Bürgerliches Gesetzbuch,* civil law statute book), DGB (*Deutscher Gewerkschaftsbund,* German Council of Trade Unions), DKP (*Deutsche Kommunistische Partei*), Mofa (*Motorfahrrad,* motor-bike), ZDF (Zweites Deutsches Fernsehen, second national German TV channel).

GDR:
DAM (*Deutsches Amt für Meßwesen der DDR,* German Office of Measures, GDR), DAW (*Deutsche Akademie der Wissenschaften,* German Academy of Sciences), FDJ (*Freie Deutsche Jugend,* Free German Youth), LPG (*Landwirtschaftliche Produktionsgenossenschaft,* collective farm), VEB (*Volkseigener Betrieb,* publicly owned company), ZK der SED (*Zentralkomitee der Sozialistischen Einheitspartei*).

Austria:
AHS (*Allgemeinbildende höhere Schule,* high school), ASVG (*das allgemeine Sozialversicherungsgesetz,* general social insurance legislation), AA (Austrian Airlines), DDSG (*Donaudampfschiffahrtsgesellschaft,* Danube Steamship Company), FPÖ (*Freiheitliche Partei Österreichs*).

Switzerland:
BIGA (*Bundesamt für Industrie, Gewerbe und Arbeit,* Federal Office of Industry, Trades and Employment), CVP (*Christlich-Demokratische Volkspartei*), SBB (*Schweizerische Bundesbahnen,* Swiss Federal Railways), SRG (*Schweizer Radio- und Fernsehgesellschaft,* Swiss Radio and TV Corporation), ZGB (*Zivilgesetzbuch,* civil law statute book).

Some abbreviations are part of the in-group sociolect of a particular occupation, party, club or society, town or community, firm or factory. In such cases, abbreviations can contribute to economy, group identification, and communication barriers. According to Moser (1967), abbreviations of initial letters occur most in German, while Russian and English go in more for acronyms (e.g. QANTAS – Queensland and Northern Territory Air Service).

8.2 Changes in professional terminology

The upgrading of some occupations has necessitated new terminology. At the same time, automation and other technological advancements have led to new jobs, which have had to be named, and a general 'democratization' or 'humanization' has given rise to new euphemisms.

Of the 33 occupations created in the Federal Republic between 1961 and 1965, eleven are referred to by compounds with -*techniker* (Oksaar 1976: 46). In fact, most recent occupational terms are compounds, e.g. *Bekleidungsfabrikationstechniker* (clothing manufacture technician), *Automateneinrichter* (slot machine setter), *Verkaufstrainer* (sales trainer). An exception is *Pharmakant* (person qualified in the production of medicines) which was introduced in 1979 (Carstensen 1980a: 21). Many relatively new occupational terms have been transferred from English, e.g. *Designer, Layouter, Public-Relations-Manager, Sales-Promoter*. Sometimes a status difference or a greater degree of specialization distinguishes a new transferred term from its earlier German equivalent, e.g. *Stewardeß/Flugbegleiterin* (flight companion), *Logopädin/Sprecherzieherin* (speech therapist), *Moderator/Gesprächsleiter* (conversation leader) (Oksaar 1976: 91).[1]

On the other hand, some low-status occupations are often referred to by euphemisms in advertisements and in job descriptions, e.g. *Raumpflegerin* (room nurse) for *Putzfrau* (cleaning lady); *Auszubildende*(r) (trainee) for *Lehrling* (apprentice), *Verwaltungsassistent* (administrative assistant) for *Hausmeister* (caretaker). It is doubtful whether such terms would be used in general conversation, except ironically. Another example of a euphemism is *Mitarbeiter* (co-worker), which is not a neologism, for a subordinate.

8.3 New concepts – new developments – new words

New developments in politics, technology, and working and living conditions entail lexical renewal, so that a study of new German vocabulary can tell us something about social change in the German-language countries. Such lexical change can be seen as a pointer to developments that may also be occurring in other languages. As mentioned in other sections of this book, it is difficult to capture developments as they take place and to keep one's remarks up-to-date due to rapid changes. Also, some innovations are only of a very temporary nature and it is not always possible to assess how widespread they are.

---

[1] The linguistic consequences of the opening-up of new occupations to women are discussed under 8.5.

8.3.1 Politics (see also Chapter 7)

Within the Federal Republic, political events are often reflected in neologisms. Since about 1977, the population has been considerably preoccupied with the threat of terrorism. This has given rise to words like *Sympathisant* (and its abbreviation *Sympi*) (person who conspires with terrorists), *konspirative Wohnung* (dwelling used as a hideout by terrorists and their conspirators), *Lauschangriff* (bugging attack), *Lauschaktion* (bugging tactics), and *Lauschoperation* (bugging operation), as well as *Terrorszene*, *Terroristenszene* and *Sympathisantenszene* (Carstensen 1978).

The increased political contact between the Federal Republic and the GDR is discussed by means of the compound adjectives *deutsch-deutsch* and *gesamtdeutsch* (total German). The arrival of ethnic Germans from Poland under an agreement between Poland and the Federal Republic added the category of *Aussiedler* (transferee) to that lexical field which also includes *Flüchtling* (refugee) and *Vertriebener* (expellee). While the CDU/CSU opposition insisted that the *Aussiedler* were really *Vertriebene*, the coalition government instituted the term *Transfer* as the accompanying word for their migration as opposed to *Vertreibung* (Carstensen 1978: 3). Like many other countries, the Federal Republic has integrated a small number of Indo-Chinese refugees. They go by the name of *Bootsmenschen*, a lexical transfer from English, or *Bootsflüchtlinge*.

8.3.2 Life-style

Departure from the traditional life-styles in at least the western German-language countries is also reflected in lexical renewal. Carstensen (1980a) records several derivatives from the English *jog*, e.g. *Jogger*, *joggen* (or *joggern*), *Jogging-Suit* (which is replacing *Trainingsanzug*, track-suit), and *Joggingfieber* (jogging fever). Jogging has become part of the continuing preoccupation with *Fitneß*.

Especially in the realm of entertainment and among the younger generation, *freak* has been integrated, e.g. *freaken*, *an/ausfreaken* (to freak on/out), *freaky*, *Jesus-Freaks*, *Tanz-Freaks* (dance freaks). *Alternativ* is employed widely as an adjective or as the first part of a compound noun, e.g. *Alternative Energien*, *Lebensweise* (life-style), *Verlage* (publishers), (*Wahl*)*liste* (voting ticket), *Alternativ-Urlaub* (alternative holidays), *-architektur*, *-bewegung* (movement), *-frisur* (hairdo), *-gruppen*, *Alternativler* (alternative people).

Alternative life-styles may include changes in diet, as is mirrored in the categories of *biologisch*, *biologisch-organisch* and *biologisch-dynamisch*, for organic vegetable-growing and food, drink and clothing production, and compounds such as: *Bio-Auflauf* (bio soufflé), *Bio-Brot* (bio bread), *Bio-Gemüsesaft* (bio vegetable juice), *Bio-Pizza*, *Bio-Quark* (bio cottage cheese), *Bio-Wein* (see *Tagesanzeiger-Magazin* 1980). The *bio*-craze, especially in the Federal Republic and Switzerland, is part of an international trend but also reflects a long-standing preoccupation with a healthy life-style in German-language countries.

Concern about work pressure has led to a reaction against the *Wirtschaftswunder* (economic miracle), and the German vocabulary (especially in the Federal Republic) has been enriched by words with such negative meanings as *Leistungsdruck* (rat race), *Streß*, *Arbeitsstreß* (work stress), and *Schulstreß* (school stress), *Frust* (frustration) and *Managerkrankheit* (manager sickness). The co-operation of English and German morphology in this lexical field will be obvious. Pragmatic formulae for work avoidance, complaints about overwork, and buck-passing have been evolved, e.g.:

Da bin ich *überfragt* (in reply to a request).
(There you've got me stumped; *überfragen*, to ask too much.)
Wir sind hier so *überfordert*.
(We are so overworked here.)

A routine of apology that frees the speaker/writer of responsibility is:

Wir bitten um Verständnis (dafür, daß . . .)
(We ask for your understanding . . .)

This routine, like the others mentioned above, sometimes violates the old code of devotion to duty (*Pflichtbewußtsein*). It is employed not only where 'understanding' might naturally be forthcoming, e.g.:

Vom 23.12. bis zum 6.1. geschlossen.
Wir bitten um Verständnis.
(Closed from 23.12 to 6.1. We ask for your understanding.)

But also in cases where the cause of the problem is obscured, e.g.:

Benutzen des Fahrstuhls verboten.
Wir bitten um Verständnis.
(Use of lift prohibited. We ask for your understanding.)

Expressed in another way, an authoritative routine is combined with a new 'democratic' request formula.

8.4 Generation gap

The gulf between the parents' and young people's generations has been marked in Germany throughout the postwar period. Rejection of the 'older generation' is part of the development of the teenager's identity. A peer group register excludes 'older' people. According to Henne (1980: 376), fifteen- to sixteen-year-old West Germans avoid traditional greetings in communication among themselves. They choose expressions like: *Hallo friends*; *Hi, wie sieht's aus?* (Hi, how are things?; literally, how does it look?); *na du Bär* (oh you bear); *hey Freaks*. There is also a deliberate clustering of interjections, such as *naja*, *hm*, or *äh*, and other markers of caution and understatement, even in written forms of communication, such as letters to youth and pop magazines, e.g. 'Zum schluß noch billige anbiederung meiner-seits – ihr habt euch – ähm – ganz proper entwickelt' (Finally a bit of cheap crawling from me – you've turned out to be – um – terrific) (Henne 1980: 379–80).

Teenagers and people in their early twenties are able to adapt American teenage slang into their German youth register. Many of the parents' generation are still limited in their knowledge of English (see Chapter 5), apart from not understanding the 'in-group' language. The state school acts as an 'informal distributor' of this type of German, which has its origins largely in pop and drug culture, and guarantees at least its widespread comprehensibility among young people. Using questionnaires based on words to be found in the young people's magazine, *Bravo*, Walter (1978) shows that English-influenced youth register is understood fairly uniformly among a group of 14–15-year-olds – regardless of sex, type of school attended, contact with teenage magazines, and discotheque atten-dance. Only 43% felt that English transfers provided a more precise expression and 15% that they were indispensable for communication.

On the other hand, 91% admitted uncertainty as to meanings and 64% experienced pronunciation difficulties (this applied least to those at *Gymnasien*). In some cases, the youth register spreads from children to parents, who, however, tend to use it only in communication with the children (personal communication, Broder Carstensen). Some such expressions are used by many sections of the population, being propagated by journals such as *Titanic* (personal communication, Wolfgang Klein).

Some examples of the register: *high sein* (to be happy), *er tickt nicht richtig* (he's off his rocker), *groovy*, *psycho*, *poppig*, *super*, *urst* (from *ur-*, original, prime) (all adjectives expressing approval), *es törnt mich (nicht) an* (it turns (doesn't turn) me on), *cool*, *crazy*, '*rumfreaken* (to loaf, muck about; literally, to freak around), *stehen* auf . . . (to like . . .), *Bock haben auf* (to feel like; literally, to have a buck (he-goat) on . . .), *sich aufspulen* (to film; literally, to wind (yourself) up). According to Oschlies (1981), *urig*, *urst*, *kernig* (pithy) and *fetzig* (ragged) are all adjectives expressing approval in GDR youth register, which is not unlike its counterpart in the Federal Republic. Youth register, its spread to other sections of the population, and the agents of distribution are topics requiring more attention.

8.5 Language and sex

According to Lakoff (1975: 4), there are two means by which language usage discriminates against women – firstly in the way they are taught to use language, and secondly in the way they are treated by language usage. In this section, I shall concentrate on the former. Trömel-Plötz (1978a) has suggested that women have a greater tendency than men to use diminutives and euphemisms and a lesser tendency to employ swear-words, 'vulgarisms', and certain interjections. They are reported to use more 'weak expressions' such as: vielleicht (perhaps), scheinbar (apparently), e.g.:

> *Es scheint, daß. . . .* (It seems that. . . .)
> *Ist das nicht so?* (Isn't that the case?)
> *. . . . nicht wahr?* (isn't it?, hasn't she?, doesn't he?, etc.);

expressions of caution and apology, e.g.:

> *Ich bin eben nur eine Hausfrau.* (Well, I'm only a housewife.)
> *Das ist nur so eine Idee von mir.* (That's just an idea of mine.)

and objective formulations with *man* (one) rather than *ich*. The reader is referred also to 7.8.1, which discusses attempts by women's lobbies to change their language usage. Viereck (1980, *et al* 1975; see above, 5.7) has shown that, in Austria, men understand more transfers from English, especially in the fields of politics and economics, than do women. This may be indicative of the continuing sex roles in that country.

Guentherodt (1979) contends that German lends itself less to the equality of the sexes than does English. To begin with, German has grammatical genders with marked articles, so that names of occupations have to be either masculine or feminine. In English, the main problem is pronominalization, which entails distinguishing the sex. Apart from the question of occupational terms, the German pronouns *man* (one; literally, man), *jeder* (everyone) and *jedermann* (everyone; literally, every man), *niemand* (nobody), and *wer* (who) are grammatically masculine although they can relate to either sex. Inapt examples of masculine pronouns referring to women cited by Trömel-Plötz (1978a: 53) including the following:

> *Man* erlebt *seine* Schwangerschaft und Geburt jedesmal anders. (*One* experiences *one's* (masculine pronoun) pregnancy and birth differently every time.)
> *Jemand* spricht über *seine* Entbindung bei Leboyer. (*Someone* is talking about *his* delivery by the Leboyer method.)
> *Wer* hat *seinen* Lippenstift im Bad gelassen? (*Who* left *his* lipstick in the bathroom?)

Das Kind (child) takes *es* and *sein* as pronouns, regardless of its sex and, strictly speaking, so does *das Mädchen* (girl)! The use of *man* as an indefinite pronoun for women is particularly inappropriate. There is no way of 'neutralizing' *man* or *jemand*, since *eine Frau* would unduly emphasize the femininity.

It was only in July 1977 that the Federal Republic repealed a law (Paragraph 1356) which declared that women were entitled to work only insofar as this was compatible with their duties in marriage and family (Guentherodt 1979: 121). In accordance with the European Community's commitment to equality of work opportunity, the names of numerous occupations have been given female equivalents. Similar developments have been taking place in the GDR, Austria and Switzerland.

To form female equivalents of masculine occupational terms, four main transformational rules are traditionally employed. We can establish a hierarchy of such rules according to how gender-neutral they make the occupation.

(i)   N→N + in
      (-*in* added to a traditional agent noun), e.g. Archivar*in* (archivist), Minister*in* (minister of state), Notar*in* (notary), Pastor*in*, Professor*in*, Programmierer*in* (computer programmer), Redakteur*in* (editor), Tankwart*in* (petrol pump attendant) (but also *Ä*rzt*in* (doctor), Autor*in* (author), K*ö*ch*in* (cook), which are more traditional).

(ii) N-mann→N-frau
      e.g. *Kauffrau* (businesswoman), *Bürokauffrau*[2] (member of office staff).

(iii) N→weiblich(er/e) + N
      (the adjectival designation *weiblich* (female) is added) e.g. *weiblicher* Soldat (female soldier), *weibliche* Lehrkräfte (female teachers).

(iv) N-mann→N-männin
      (-mann changed to -*männin*, female man) e.g. Amtmänn*in* (senior clerk), Fachmänn*in* (expert), and compounds thereof, designations resisted by women's liberationists.

'Neutralized' terms like *Schutzmensch* (policeperson), *Fachmensch* (expert) or *Schutzperson*, *Fachperson* (cf. Chairperson) have never caught on in German-language countries; they sound ridiculous despite the long history of plurals such as *Feuerwehrleute* (firemen; literally, firepeople), and *Schutzleute* (policemen; literally, policepeople) for *Feuerwehrmann* and *Schutzmann*.

Because of the gender-marked article in German the solution of adopting a 'less sexist' term like *camera operator* or *office assistant* instead of *cameraman* or *office boy* is less effective than in English. However, the change, e.g. from *Bootsteuermann* (coxswain; literally, boat-steersman) to *Bootsteuerer* (literally, boat-steerer) and from *Pumpenmann* (pump man) to *Pumpenwärter* (pump attendant) (Guentherodt 1979) has facilitated a feminine formation (*Bootsteuererin*, *Pumpenwärterin*) according to transformation (i), above. The change of terms from *Steuerfachmann* (taxation expert) and

---

[2] Both official designations as from 1979.

Kunstfachmann (art specialist) to the adjectival nouns *Steuersach-verständiger* (taxation expert) and *Kunstsachverständiger* (art special-ist) respectively has also led to ready feminization (*Steuersachver-ständige*, etc.). In advertisements, the use of both *männlich* and *weiblich* indicate a non-discriminatory employment policy (e.g. *männliche und weibliche Angestellte*, male and female employees). Even so, the meaning of the masculine- and feminine-gender words may be quite different. As Guentherodt (1979: 121) points out, *Sekretär* is usually a high position in a party or other association, while *Sekretärin* is an office job, synonymous with *Stenotypistin* – sometimes elevated in status through the addition of another morpheme, e.g. *Chefsekretärin* (chief secretary), *Verwaltungssekre-tärin* (administrative secretary). In a survey conducted by Hellinger (1980) among 497 schoolchildren, 28% of girls (average age 15 years) are continuing to use the masculine occupation term to apply to their preferred (and second preference) occupations. Another study by Hellinger (1980) shows that male and female informants attribute sex stereotypes to male and female occupational designations.

Whereas the transformation rules discussed above make it possible to convert purely male occupations into dual-sex ones, they are not frequently applied in reverse. Designations for purely female occup-ations generally include a morpheme derived from an identifiably female word, e.g. Kranken*schwester* (nurse; literally, sister for the sick), Bar*dame* (barmaid; literally, barlady), Reinmache*frau* (clean-ing lady). However, male equivalents, *männliche Reinmachefrau* (male cleaning lady), *männliche Bardame* (male barmaid; literally, male barlady), *männliche Krankenschwester* (male nurse), or, for that matter, *Krankenbruder* (brother for the sick), *Barherr* (literally, bar gentleman), are not possible. An example of a traditionally female occupation that has been opened up to males is kindergarten teaching. The old *Kindergärtnerin* (kindergarten teacher – female) has been partly replaced by *Erzieherin/Erzieher* (educator). Similarly, *Krankenpfleger/Krankenpflegerin* (nurse) have replaced *Kran-kenschwester* (nursing sister), without any change in status. In a parliamentary debate in 1978 on the designation of male midwives, the SPD preferred *Geburtshelfer* (birth helper) while the CDU/CSU wanted to stick to *Hebamme (männlich)* (midwife (male)) (Carstensen 1979a: 21).

Some occupations still lack a 'neutral' or female equivalent, despite the existence of a morphological device to form a female designation, e.g. *Dirigent* (musical conductor), *Lehrling* (apprentice), *Tischler* (carpenter). This can be attributed to sex discrimination. In October 1981, 48 firms in the Zürich region declared their preparedness to consider females for apprenticeships in areas usually restricted to males. 30 of them expressed the occupations in a feminine equivalent. The areas in which the majority of the firms did not do so were the electrical and metal trades, the others being building, graphic, laboratory, and woodwork (*Tagesanzeiger* 24 October 1981: p. 23). *Der Spiegel* (1978b) discusses the absence of female members of the armed forces in the Federal Republic and compares the situation with other countries. It uses some unusual feminine terms such as *Soldatin* (soldier), *Matrosin* (sailor), *Pilotin, Fliegerin* (aviator), *Rekrutin* (recruit). More common designations are *weiblicher Soldat, weiblicher Matrose, weiblicher Rekrut* and *weiblicher Pilot*. In a language with grammatical genders and gender-marked articles, a language without a suffix that is

$$
\begin{bmatrix}
+ \text{ human} \\
\pm \text{ masculine} \\
\pm \text{ feminine}
\end{bmatrix}
$$

equivalent to English *person*, the best that can be achieved to avoid discrimination between the sexes is a male and a female equivalent for each (occupational and other appropriate) category without having to resort to the *-männin* derivative.

However, this creates the problem of focusing on sex rather than occupation, and can lead to further discrimination. Pusch (1980) recommends that male *and* female genders be assigned to the unmarked occupational term, with a neuter gender employed where the identity of the referent is not clear, and the plural form taking *-s*, e.g. der Lehrer, die Lehrer, das Lehrer, die Lehrers. As she herself admits, that *das* form could result in a 'dehumanization' of the referent.

Since 1970 in Austria and since 1972 in the Federal Republic of Germany, the general form of address for adult women (married or otherwise) has been *Frau* (+ surname) (previously reserved for married women), something which feminists have demanded for a long time.[3] This avoids the need for an unmarked female form of address equivalent to *Ms*, which is politically marked.

8.6 Brief summary

There are many other ways in which language change in German is mirroring social changes. Shorter and less complex sentences reflect universal (rather than élitist) access to the written language. Nominalization of the verb, morphological tendencies towards economy and abstraction, and the increased use of compounds and abbreviations are in keeping with the time constraints of modern life. Neologisms meet and reflect the demands of new developments in technology and politics as well as changes in living and working conditions and in the occupation structure. Young people have developed a register of their own.

Grammatical genders and the absence of feminine equivalents of indefinite and interrogative pronouns impede the development of equality of the sexes in the German language. The entry of women into more professions has increased the productivity of four traditional transformation rules which form female equivalents. The equivalents range from sex-specific and equal, to sexist and unequal. These rules do not usually work in reverse (i.e. feminine → masculine). Nor are the male and female professional counterparts necessarily of equal status. A neutral suffix equivalent to English *-person* is not used. *Frau* (+ surname) has become the general form of address for all adult women in Austria and the Federal Republic of Germany.

8.7 Further reading

The reader is referred to the *Sprache der Gegenwart* series published by Schwann, Düsseldorf. These books contain the results of research on contemporary spoken and written German undertaken by the Institut für deutsche Sprache, Mannheim, or discussed at its annual conferences. Each year, Carstensen publishes an article in *Sprachdienst* on the words that were introduced into, or became popular in

---

[3] This has also been proposed for female public servants by the head of the Swiss civil service and discussed with women's organizations (Keller 1978: 9).

German in the previous year (*Die Wörter des Jahres . . .*). Women's language has developed into a popular problem for discussion in articles and conference papers. *Beiheft* 3 of the *Osnabrücker Beiträge zur Sprachtheorie* (1979), for instance, is devoted to the papers of a German symposium on the subject.

Closing remarks

It is hoped that the preceding eight chapters might offer some stimulus to reflection about and perhaps investigation of the German language in social context. It should be noted that language both mirrors and influences social change and that there are some elements of the German language which can only be understood as traditional or historical and not as contemporary societal indicators. The German language is both a unifier and a separator of people. It reflects both cultural cohesion and socioeconomic and political division, as I have tried to show throughout this monograph.

The study of the German language in social context reflects an antithesis between national and international communication; different national and political entities with varying social structures, political systems and international alignments; identification at larger and smaller levels; political polarization; communication barriers; and changing social and communicative patterns subject to virulent discussion (especially in the Federal Republic).

For the picture to be complete, much more sociolinguistic research will need to be undertaken, particularly in Austria and Switzerland, on issues other than dialectology. Innumerable projects are awaiting graduate students. Even small-scale research assignments can activate a better understanding of the relation between language, culture and society in the countries that are the object of the study, as well as a better consciousness of how language functions in society.

Glossary of linguistic terms used

Basilect The variety of lowest prestige or most deviant from the standard on the pidgin or creole continuum (cf. *mesolect*).

Cloze test Test involving a continuous text from which words have been deleted and which informants are required to complete.

Code-switching Switching from one language to another, often due to sociolinguistic variables (such as interlocutor, domain, type of interaction).

Collocation A particular combination of words.

Complex symbol Word that functions as a general symbol, encompassing diverse components which may solicit an attitude on the part of the hearer or reader.

Contrastive analysis Contrasting the phonology, grammar, and/or semantics of two languages; often involves emphasizing the differences rather than the similarities; used as a basis for teaching materials to combat interference, *one* of the sources of errors in second language acquisition.

Conversation opener Routine used formulaically to open a conversation.

Co-occurrence rules Rules about which routines can be used with which other ones.

Copula An overt connecting link between subject and complement (e.g. *is* in *He is an old man*).

Creole (Usually) a pidgin which has developed into a mother tongue.

Deficit hypothesis The hypothesis that some language varieties are cognitively inferior to others (see also *restricted* and *elaborated* codes).

Descriptive approach Describing a language as it is used (cf. *prescriptive*).

Dialect A local or regional variety of a language.

Difference hypothesis The hypothesis that no language variety is cognitively inferior or less logical than another.

Diglossia A language situation in which two different languages or varieties are functionally complementary, one (H, the 'high' variety) being used for written and more formal spoken purposes, the other (L, the 'low' variety) for ordinary interaction (cf. *triglossia*). Adjective: diglossic.

Discourse Connected speech (including writing) extending beyond a single sentence.

176

Domain Institutionalized context, sphere of activity, totality of interaction (e.g. family, work, school).

Downgrader Modal particle or other means used to play down the impact of an utterance.

Elaborated code More complex strategies of verbal planning identified by Bernstein with middle class varieties (cf. *restricted code*).

Elliptic sentence Sentence from which have been deleted parts generally considered to be essential for it to be grammatical and well-formed.

Embedding Putting one clause (the embedded or lower clause) inside another (the matrix or higher one) so that the lower clause functions as part of the higher clause (e.g. subordination).

Fachsprache The special (technical) language of a particular field, e.g. sociology, chemistry.

Feature The smallest element constituting larger ones such as phonemes, morphemes and sememes. Features are of a binary nature: + or − indicates if a segment belongs to a particular class of elements or not, e.g. [−voice] voiceless, [+male].

Foreigner talk Modified (often reduced) variety used to people with less than full competence in a language, or generally to people identified as foreigners.

Grapheme Minimum unit of the writing system, or of the relation between the sound and writing systems, of a language.

Graphic interference Interference in the spoken language caused by the written language.

Graphotactic Referring to the rules for combining graphemes in a particular language.

Internationalism Word or expression used in many (or most) languages, e.g. atom, radio, radium.

Koine Levelled ('compromise') language variety which spreads as a common form for inter-dialectal communication.

L1 First language.

Lexeme Word. Adjective: lexical.

Lexical field Area of vocabulary, indicating which words belong together semantically.

Lexicon Vocabulary of a language.

Lexicosemantic Lexical and semantic at the same time (i.e. referring to both the form and meaning of words).

Loan-creation Word created in a language as an equivalent to one existing in another language (e.g. *Bahnsteig* (platform) for *perron*).

Loan-meaning Semantic transfer in which a meaning is taken over from a word in one language to a similar sounding or meaning word in the other language.

Loan-rendition Semantic transfer in which one element is transferred from another language, the other element created.

Loan-translation Semantic transfer in which each morpheme is translated from one language to the other.

'*Loanword*' Word transferred from one language to another; here referred to as 'lexical transfer'.

Macrosociolinguistic Concerned with broad aspects of the relation between language and society (e.g. *language use*) rather than the sociolinguistic variables (e.g. rounding of vowels) distinguishing between varieties.

Marked Displaying a particular distinctive feature (cf. *unmarked*).

Mesolect The variety between that of highest (acrolect) and lowest (basilect) prestige or between the least and most deviant from the standard on the pidgin or creole continuum (cf. *basilect*).

Modality markers Markers strengthening or weakening the force of an utterance, e.g. absolutely, terribly, indeed, bloody, you must understand that (strengthening); perhaps, a bit, would you mind if. . . .? (weakening).

Morpheme The smallest significant unit of grammatical form that conveys a meaning.

Morphology The system of word structure or word formation in a language.

Neologism A new word.

Phoneme One of the set of speech units that distinguish one utterance or word from another.

Phonology (here) The sound system of a language. Adjective: phonological.

Phonotactic Referring to the rules for combining phonemes in a particular language.

Pidgin Reduced (simplified) variety which arises for restricted communication functions between speakers of different L1s but which is no-one's L1.

Polysemy Term used when a word has two or more meanings.

Pragmatic(s) (Pertaining to) that area of linguistics concerned with the communicative function, intention and effects of utterances.

Prescriptive approach Laying down how a language *ought* to be used (cf. *descriptive*).

Pseudo-transfer New lexeme that appears to be a transfer from another language but is not; often the result of compounding of morphemes from that language.

Register A (stylistic) variety of a language chosen according to particular situational circumstances.

Restricted code Less complex strategies of verbal planning identified by Bernstein with lower class varieties (cf. *elaborated code*).

Semantic(s) (Pertaining to) the meaning aspect of language.

Semantic features Components into which the meaning of a word can be broken up.

Sociolect Social variety of a language.

Sprachkultur (language cultivation) That aspect of language planning concerning normative questions such as correctness and efficiency of particular forms.

Sprechbund Societies sharing sets of non-grammatical (communication) rules.

Substratum The effects of a previously-spoken language in an area or speech community on the language now spoken.

Syntax The part of grammar concerning rules for the arrangement of words in sentences, constructions, and for relations between sentences.

Transfer An instance of transference.

Transference The adoption of a rule or element from another language (lexical – word transferred; semantic – meaning transferred; syntactic – grammatical rule transferred).

Triglossia A language situation in which three different languages or varieties are functionally complementary (cf. *diglossia*). Adjective: triglossic.

Turn-taking The parts played by individual participants in verbal interaction.

Umgangssprache ('colloquial language') In some German writings, the varieties between local dialect and standard language; unclear concept which defies definition.

Unmarked Not displaying a particular distinctive feature (cf. *marked*).

Upgrader Modal particle or other means used to intensify the impact of an utterance.

Variation The use of different varieties, the selection of which is determined by such variables as who are the interlocutors, their role relationship, where they are, their topics, domains and interaction.

Variety A national, regional or social variant of a language which can be distinguished at the national, regional or social level by grammatical, phonological and/or lexical features.

Bibliography

Abbreviations of journals used below

DS	*Deutsche Sprache*
IJSL	*International Journal of Sociology of Language*
LB	*Linguistische Berichte*
LiLi	*Zeitschrift für Literaturwissenschaft und Linguistik*
OBST	*Osnabrücker Beiträge zur Sprachtheorie*
ZDL	*Zeitschrift für Dialektologie und Linguistik*
ZGL	*Zeitschrift für germanistische Linguistik*
ZMF	*Zeitschrift für Mundartforschung*

List of newspapers used in corpus or referred to in text (see also bibliography)

Arbeiterkampf. Hamburg.
Arbeiterzeitung. Vienna.
Bild-Zeitung. Cologne/Esslingen/Frankfurt a.M.
BZ-Am Abend. East Berlin.
Der Morgen. East Berlin.
Die Presse. Vienna.
Die Welt. Hamburg.
Die Zeit. Hamburg.
Frankfurter Allgemeine. Frankfurt a.M.
Kommunistische Volkszeitung. Stuttgart.
National-Zeitung. East Berlin.
National-Zeitung. Munich.
Neue Kronen-Zeitung. Vienna.
Neue Zeit. East Berlin.
Neue Zürcher Zeitung. Zürich.
Neues Deutschland. East Berlin.
Roter Morgen. Dortmund.
Salzburger Nachrichten. Salzburg.
Süddeutsche Zeitung. Munich.
Tagesanzeiger. Zürich.

Unsere Zeit. Neuss.

Wiener Morgen-Kurier. Vienna.

Allensbach. 1981 Mundart wird hoffähig. *allensbacher berichte* 14. Allensbach.

Althaus, H.P., H. Henne and H.E. Wiegand (eds.). 1980 *Lexikon der germanistischen Linguistik.* Tübingen (2nd edition).

Ammon, U. 1972 *Dialekt, soziale Ungleichheit und Schule.* Weinheim.

1973a *Probleme der Soziolinguistik.* Tübingen.

1973b *Dialekt und Einheitssprache in ihrer sozialen Verflechtung.* Weinheim.

1975 Die Schwierigkeiten der Dialektsprecher in der Grundschule und das Bewußtsein davon bei den Lehrern. In H. Halbfas *et al* (eds.), *Sprache, Umgang und Erziehung.* Stuttgart; 87–115.

1979 Regionaldialekte und Einheitssprache in der Bundesrepublik Deutschland. *IJSL* 21; 25–40.

Appel, K.O. (ed.). 1976 *Sprachpragmatik und Philosophie.* Frankfurt a.M.

Arbeitskreis für Rechtschreiben der ständige Konferenz der Kultusminister. 1959 *Empfehlungen.* Mannheim.

Arndt, W.W. 1970 Non-random assignment of loanwords: German noun gender. *Word* 26; 1973; 244–54.

Augst, G. (ed.). 1974 *Deutsche Rechtschreibung mangelhaft? Materialien und Meinungen zur Rechtschreibreform.* Heidelberg.

1980 Internationales Kolloquium 'Die Zukunft der deutschen Rechtschreibung'. *DS* 3; 281–7.

Bach, A. 1956 *Geschichte der deutschen Sprache.* Heidelberg (5th edition).

Barkowski, H., U. Harnisch and S. Kumm. 1976 Sprachhandlungstheorie Deutsch für Ausländer. *LB* 45; 103–10.

Bartholomes, H. 1956 *Tausend Worte Sowjetdeutsch.* Göteborg.

Bates, E. 1976 *Language and context: the acquisition of pragmatics.* New York.

Bauer, G. 1973 Einige Grundsätze im Kampf um die vereinfachte Rechtschreibung. *LB* 45; 42–54.

Baulch, H. 1979 An investigation of the language and the subject matter of the jokes of North German and Australian children. B.A. (Hons.) thesis, Monash University.

Bausch, K.H. 1979 *Modalität des Konjunktivgebrauchs in der gesprochenen deutschen Standardsprache.* Munich.

Bausinger, H. 1967 *Deutsch für Deutsche.* Frankfurt a.M.

Bayer, K. 1979 Die Anredepronomina Du and Sie. *DS* 3; 212–19.

Becker, K. 1948 *Der Sprachbund.* Leipzig.

1956 *Sieben Sprachbriefe zur Gegenwart.* Halle.

Bergmann, U., R. Dutschke, W. Lefèvre. 1968 *Rebellion der Studenten oder Die Neue Opposition.* Reinbek.

Berning, C. 1964 *Vom 'Abstimmungsnachweis' zum 'Zuchtwart'. Vokabular zum Nationalsozialismus.* Berlin.

Bibliography

Bernstein, B.B. 1962 Social class, linguistic codes and grammatical elements. *Language and Speech* 5; 31–46.

1970 Der Unfug mit der 'Kompensatorischen Erziehung'. *betrifft: erziehung* 9; 15–19.

Berschin, H. 1978 Ein Geisterreich wie Utopia? In *Der Spiegel* 32, 50; 11 December 1978; 68–74.

Bertaux, P. 1982 Quelques remarques sur les termes d'adresse en français et en allemand. *Contrastes* 4–5; 7–28.

Besch, W. 1975 Bericht über das Forschungsprojekt 'Sprachvariation und Sprachwandel in gesprochener Sprache'. *DS* 2; 173–84.

Besch, W. and K. Mattheier. 1977 Bericht über das Forschungsprojekt 'Sprachvariation und Sprachwandel in gesprochener Sprache'. In H.U. Bielefeld, E. Hess-Lüttich and A. Lund (eds.), *Soziolinguistik und Empirie*. Wiesbaden; 30–58.

Besch, W., H. Löffler and H.H. Reich. 1977 *Dialekt/Hochsprache-Kontrastiv* (series). Düsseldorf.

Besch, W., U. Knopp, W. Putschke and H.E. Wiegand (eds.). 1982–3 *Dialektologie: ein Handbuch zur deutschen und allgemeinen Dialektforschung.* 2 vols. Berlin.

Betz, W. 1949 *Deutsch und Lateinisch.* Bonn.

1960 Der zweigeteilte Duden. *Der Deutschunterricht* 12, 5; 82–98.

1980 Die Opfer und die Täter – Rechtextremismus in der Bundesrepublik. *Aus Politik und Zeitgeschichte. Beilage zu Parlament.* 1327/80; 5 July 1980; 29–45.

Bichel, U. 1973 *Problem und Begriff der Umgangssprache in der germanistischen Forschung.* Tübingen.

1980 Umgangssprache. In Althaus, Henne and Wiegand (1980); 379–83.

Biedenkopf, K. 1980 Rede vor dem 28. Bundesparteitag der CDU. *Union in Deutschland* 19; 30–36.

Biermann, W. 1972 *Für meine Genossen.* Berlin.

Bliesener, T. 1980 Erzählen unerwünscht. Erzählversuche von Patienten in der Visite. In K. Ehlich (ed.), *Erzählen im Alltag.* Frankfurt a.M.; 143–78.

Bloomfield, L. 1933 *Language.* New York.

Bluhme, H. 1980 Zur funktionalen konkurrenz von ostfälisch, nordniedersächsisch und hochdeutsch im südlichen Niedersachsen. *ZGL*8; 314–27.

Bodemann, Y.M. and R. Ostow. 1975 Lingua franca und Pseudo-pidgin in der Bundesrepublik: Fremdarbeiter und Einheimische im Sprachzusammenhang. *LiLi* 5, 18; 122–46.

Bodi, L. 1980 Österreichische Literatur – Deutsche Literatur. Zur Frage von Literatur und nationaler Identität. *Akten des VI. Internationalen Germanisten-Kongresses.* Basel; 486–92.

Boesch, B. (ed.). 1957 *Die Aussprache des Hochdeutschen in der Schweiz.* Zürich.

1968 Sprachpflege in der Schweiz. In H. Moser *et al* (eds.), *Sprachnorm, Sprachpflege, Sprachkritik.* Düsseldorf; 222–35.

Böhm, S. *et al.* 1972 Rundfunknachrichten. Sozio- und psycholinguistische Aspekte. In Rucktäschel (1972); 153–94.

Borbé, T. 1977 Text und Bild bei Wahlplakaten. *Wiener Linguistische Gazette* 15; 69–78.

Braun, P. 1979 *Tendenzen in der deutschen Gegenwartssprache.* Urban-Taschenbücher, Stuttgart.

1981 Untersuchung zu deutsch-deutschen Wörterbüchern. *Muttersprache* 91; 157–68.

Brekle, H.E. 1972 *Semantik: eine Einführung in die sprachwissenschaftliche Bedeutungslehre.* Munich.

Brettschneider, W. 1972 *Zwischen literarischer Autonomie und Staatsdienst: die Literatur in der DDR.* Berlin.

Brown, R. and A. Gilman. 1960 The pronouns of power and solidarity. In T.A. Sebeok (ed.), *Style in Language.* Cambridge, Mass.; 253–76.

Bruch, R. 1953 *Grundlegung einer Geschichte des Luxemburgischen.* Luxembourg.

Bruderer, H. 1973 Kommt die Kleinschreibung? *LB* 24; 87–102.

Buch, H.C. (ed.). 1978 *Deutschland, das Kind mit den zwei Köpfen (= Tintenfisch 15).* Berlin.

Bücherl, R.F.J. 1982 Regularitäten bei Dialektveränderung und Dialektvariation. *ZDL* 49; 1–27.

Bungarten, T. (ed.). 1981 *Wissenschaftssprache.* Munich.

Burger, A. 1979 Die Konkurrenz englischer und französischer Fremdwörter in der modernen deutschen Pressesprache. In P. Braun (ed.), *Fremdwort-Diskussion.* Munich; 246–72.

Carstensen, B. 1965 *Englische Einflüsse in der deutschen Sprache nach 1945.* Heidelberg.

1967 Amerikanische Einflüsse auf die deutsche Sprache. In B. Carstensen and H. Galinsky (1967); 11–32.

1971 *Spiegel-Wörter, Spiegel-Worte. Zur Sprache eines Nachrichtenmagazins.* Munich.

1978 Wörter des Jahres 1977. *Der Sprachdienst* 22; 1–8.

1979a Wörter des Jahres 1978. *Der Sprachdienst* 23; 17–24.

1979b Evidente und latente Einflüsse auf das Deutsche. In P. Braun (ed.), *Fremdwort-Diskussion.* Munich; 90–4.

1980a Wörter des Jahres 1979. *Der Sprachdienst* 24; 17–22.

1980b Semantische Scheinentlehnungen des Deutschen aus dem Englischen. In Viereck (1980a); 77–100.

1980c Das Genus englischer Fremd- und Lehnwörter im Deutschen. In Viereck (1980a); 37–75.

1982 Wörter des Jahres 1981. *Der Sprachdienst* **26**, 1/2; 1–16.

Carstensen, B. and H. Galinsky. 1967 *Amerikanismen der deutschen Gegenwartssprache: Entlehnungsvorgänge und ihre stilistischen Aspekte.* Heidelberg.

Charleston, B.H. 1959 The English linguistic invasion of Switzerland. *English Studies* 40; 271–82.

Bibliography

Christ, H. *et al.* 1974 *Hessische Rahmenrichtlinien Deutsch. Analyse und Dokumentation eines bildungspolitischen Konflikts.* Düsseldorf.

Christophory, J. 1974 *Mir schwätze lëtzebuergisch.* Luxembourg.

Clahsen, H., J. Meisel and M. Pienemann. 1983 *Deutsch als Zweitsprache: der Spracherwerb ausländischer Arbeiter.* Tübingen.

Clyne, M.G. 1968a Ökonomie, Mehrdeutigkeit und Vagheit bei Komposita in der deutschen Gegenwartssprache. *Muttersprache* 78; 122–6.
1968b Zum Pidgin-Deutsch der Gastarbeiter. *ZMF* 34; 130–9.
1973 Kommunikation und kommunikationsbarriere bei englischen entlehnungen im heutigen deutsch. *ZGL* 1; 163–77.
1975 German and English working pidgins. In *Papers in Pidgin and Creole Linguistics* (= *Pacific Linguistics* A, 57). Canberra; 135–50.
1977a The speech of foreign workers in Germany (review article). *Language in Society* 6; 268–74.
1977b Multilingualism and pidginization in Australian industry. *Ethnic Studies* 1, 2; 40–55.
1977c European multinational companies in Australia and the exportation of languages. *ITL* 37; 83–91.
1979 Communicative competence in contact. *ITL* 43; 17–37.
1980 Writing, testing and culture. *The Secondary Teacher* 11; 13–16.
1981 Culture and discourse structure. *Journal of Pragmatics* 5, 1; 61–6.

Clyne, M.G. and S.I. Manton. 1979 Routines for conducting meetings in Australia: an inter-ethnic study. *Ethnic Studies* 3, 1; 25–34.

Collinson, W.E. 1953 *The German Language Today.* London.

Cooper, R.L. 1969 Two contextualised measures of degree in bilingualism. *Modern Language Journal* 53, 3; 172–8.

Cordes, G. 1963 Zur Terminologie des Begriffs 'Umgangssprache'. In W. Simon, W. Bachofen, W. Dittmar (eds.) *Festgabe für Ulrich Pretzel*; 338–54.

Coulmas, F. 1979 On the sociolinguistic relevance of routine formulae. *Journal of Pragmatics* 3; 239–66.

Coulthard, M.C. 1969 A discussion of restricted and elaborated codes. *Educational Review* 22, 1; 38–50.

Dahl, E.S. 1974 Interferenz und Alternanz – zwei Typen der Sprachschichtenmischung in der Deutschen Demokratischen Republik. In G. Ising (ed.) *Aktuelle Probleme der sprachlichen Kommunikation: soziolinguistische Studien zur sprachlichen Situation in der Deutschen Demokratischen Republik.* Berlin; 9–36.

Dahl, J. 1977 Kommt Zeit, Kommt Unrat. *Schneidewege* 7; 39–62.

Dahrendorf, R. 1979 *Lebenschancen. Anläufe zur sozialen und politischen Theorie.* Frankfurt a.M.

Dalcher, P. 1966 Der Einfluß des Englischen auf die Umgangssprache der deutschen Schweiz. *Schweizerdeutsches Wörterbuch Bericht des Jahr 1966.* Zürich; 11–12.

Debus, F. 1962 Zwischen Mundart und Hochsprache. *ZMF* 29; 1–43.

Deprez, K. and G. de Schutter. 1980 Honderd Antwerpenaars en honderd

Rotterdammers over dertien Nederlandse taalvariëteiten: Een attitude – onderzoek. *Leuvense Bijdragen* 69; 167–256.

Dieckmann, W. 1964 *Information oder Überredung?* Marburg.

Dieth, E. 1938 *Schwyzertütschi Dialäktschrift.* Zürich.

Dittmar, N. 1973 *Soziolinguistik: exemplarische und kritische Darstellung ihrer Theorie, Empirie und Anwendung.* Frankfurt a.M.

1978 Ordering adult learners according to language abilities. In Dittmar *et al* (1978); 119–54.

1979 Fremdsprachenerwerb im sozialen Kontext: das Erlernen von Modalverben. *LiLi* 33; 84–103.

Dittmar, N. and B. Schlieben-Lange. 1981 Stadtsprache. In K.H. Bausch (ed.), *Mehrsprachigkeit in der Stadtregion* (= *Sprache der Gegenwart* 56). Düsseldorf; 9–86.

Dittmar, N., H. Haberland, T. Skuttnabb-Kangas and U. Teleman (eds.). 1978 *Papers from the 1st Scandinavian-German Symposium on the Language of Immigrant Workers and their Children.* Roskilde.

Dittmar, N., B. Schlieben-Lange and P. Schlobinski. 1981 Teilkommentierte Bibliographie zur Soziolinguistik von Stadtsprachen. In Bausch (ed.) (1981), op. cit.; 391–423.

Dobaj, M. 1980 Anglizismen in der Rundfunkwerbung und von Verständnis von Werbeanglizismen beim Branchenpersonal. In Viereck (1980a); 101–7.

Donath, J. 1977 Überlegungen zur semantischen Norm zentraler Termini in der materiellen Produktion. In Hartung (1977a); 247–79.

1980 Zum Einfluß der Kommunikationssituation auf die sprachliche Variation im Produktionsbetrieb. In *Linguistische Studien. Reihe F. Arbeitsberichte* **72**, 1; 28–35.

Dresden, A. 1978 Emigranten im eigenen Land. In Buch (1978); 7–13.

Dressler, W. and R. Wodak. 1982a Soziolinguistische Überlegungen zum 'Österreichischen Wörterbuch'. In M. Dardano, W. Dressler and G. Held (eds.), *Parallela* (= *Akten des 2. österreichischen–italienischen Linguistentreffens*). Tübingen; 247–60.

1982b Sociophonological methods in the study of sociolinguistic variation in Viennese German. *Language in Society* 11; 339–70.

Drosdowski, G. and H. Henne. 1980 Tendenzen der deutschen Gegenwartssprache. In Althaus, Henne and Wiegand (eds.); 619–52.

Duden. 1952 *Rechtschreibung.* Mannheim.

1954 *Rechtschreibung.* Mannheim.

1959 *Grammatik.* Mannheim.

1972 *Rechtschreibung.* Leipzig.

1973 *Rechtschreibung.* Mannheim.

1976 *Das große Wörterbuch der deutschen Sprache.* 6 vols. Mannheim.

Ebner, J. 1969 *Wie sagt man in Österreich?* Mannheim.

Eggers, H. 1963 Contemporary German: a sociological point of view. *Te Reo* 6; 1–8.

1969 Deutsche Gegenwartssprache im Wandel der Gesellschaft. In H.

Moser *et al* (eds.), *Sprache – Gegenwart und Geschichte.* Düsseldorf; 9–29.

Ehlich, K. and J. Rehbein. 1972 Zur Konstitution pragmatischer Einheiten in einer Institution: das Speiserestaurant. In D. Wunderlich (ed.), *Linguistische Pragmatik.* Frankfurt a.M.; 209–54.

1977 Wissen, Kommunikatives Handeln und die Schule. In Goeppert (1977); 36–113.

1980 Sprache in Institutionen. In Althaus, Henne and Wiegand (eds.) (1980); 338–45.

Eichhoff, J. 1976 Bibliography of German Dialect spoken in the United States and Canada, and problems of German-English language contact, especially in North America 1968–1976 with pre-1968 supplements. *Monatshefte* 68; 196–208.

1977–8 *Wortatlas der deutschen Umgangssprachen.* Marburg.

1980 Zu einigen im 20. Jahrhundert entstandenen geographischen Unterschieden des Wortgebrauchs in der deutschen Sprache. In R. Hildebrant and H. Friebertshäusen, *Sprache und Brauchtum. Bernhard Martin zum 90. Geburtstag.* Marburg; 154–78.

Eichholz, R. 1975 Geschrieben wie gesprochen. Mundart wiederentdeckt. *Wirkendes Wort* 25; 377–83.

Engel, U. 1961 Die Auslösung der Mundart. *Muttersprache* 7; 129–35.

1962 Schwäbische Mundart und Umgangssprache. *Muttersprache* 72; 257–61.

Ervin-Tripp, S.M. 1971 Sociolinguistics. In J.A. Fishman (ed.), *Advances in the Sociology of Language.* The Hague; 15–92.

Faulseit, D. 1965 Von Fremdwörtern und anderen Unarten des Zeitungsdeutsches. *Sprachpflege* 14; 98–100.

1971 Vom Sinn und Unsinn des Fremdwortgebrauchs. Überlegungen nach dem VIII. Parteitag der SED. *Sprachpflege* 20; 241–3.

Fenske, H. 1973 *Schweizerische und österreichische Besonderheiten in deutschen Wörterbuchern* (=Institut für deutschen Sprache *Forschungsberichte* 10). Mannheim.

Ferguson, C.A. 1959 Diglossia. *Word* 15; 325–44.

Filipović, R. 1974 A contribution to the methods of studying anglicisms in European languages. *Studia Romanica et Anglica Zagrabiensia* 37; 135–48.

Fink, H. 1970 *Amerikanismen im Wortschatz der deutschen Tagespresse, dargestellt am Beispiel dreier überregionaler Zeitungen (Süddeutsche Zeitung, Frankfurter Allgemeine Zeitung, Die Welt)* (= *Mainzer Amerikanische Beiträge* 11).

1975 'Know-How' und 'Hifi-Pionier'. Zum Verständnis englischer Ausdrücke in der deutschen Werbesprache. *Muttersprache* 85; 186–203.

1977 'Texaslook' und 'party-bluse': assoziative effekte von englischem im deutschen. *Wirkendes Wort* 27; 394–402.

1980 Zur Aussprache von Angloamerikanischem im Deutschen. In Viereck (1980a); 109–83.

Fishman, J.A. 1965 Who speaks what language to whom and when? *Linguistique* 2; 67–88.

1967 Bilingualism with and without diglossia; diglossia with and without bilingualism. *Journal of Social Issues* **23**, 2; 29–38.

1972 The sociology of language. In J.A. Fishman (ed.), *Advances in the Sociology of Language*. The Hague 1972; 217–404.

Fishman, J.A. and E. Lueder. 1972 What has the sociology of language to say to the teacher? In C.A. Cazden, V. John and D. Hymes (eds.), *Functions of Language in the classroom*. New York; 67–83.

Fishman, J.A., R.L. Cooper and A.W. Conrad. 1977 *The Spread of English*. Rowley, Mass.

Flader, D. 1978 Die psychoanalytische Therapie als Gegenstand sprachwissenschaftlicher Forschung. *Studium Linguistik* 5; 37–51.

Fónagy, I. 1963 *Die Metaphern in der Phonetik*. The Hague.

Fox, J.A. 1977 Implications of the jargon/pidgin dichotomy for social and linguistic analysis of the Gastarbeiter Pidgin German speech community. In C. Molony, H. Zobl, W. Stölting (eds.), *Deutsch im Kontakt mit anderen Sprachen*. Kronberg; 40–6.

Fuchs, J. 1977 *Gedächtnisprotokolle* (roro aktuell 480). Hamburg.

Galinsky, H. 1977 Amerikanisch-englische und gesamtenglische Interferenzen in dem Deutschen und anderen Sprachen der Gegenwart. In H. Kolb and H. Lauffer (eds.), *Sprachliche Interferenz. Festschrift für Werner Betz*. Tübingen; 463–517.

1980 American English post 1960. Neologisms in contemporary German: reception-lag variables as a neglected aspect of linguistic interference. In Viereck (1980a); 213–35.

Garbe, B. 1978 *Die deutsche Rechtschreibung und ihre Reform. 1722–1974* (=*Germanistische Linguistik* 10). Tübingen.

Geerts, G., J. Nootens and J. Vandenbroeck. 1977 Opinies van Vlamingen over Dialekt en Standaardtaal. *Taal en Tongval* 29; 98–141.

Geißler, H. 1980 *Unser Grundsatz-Programm=ein Dokument geistiger Erneuerung*. (Rede auf dem 26. Bundesparteitag der CDU, 23–25. Oktober 1978, Ludwigshafen) Cologne.

Gilbert, G.G. 1978 Review of Klein (ed.) *Sprache ausländischer Arbeiter*. In *Language* 54; 983–7.

Gilbert, G.G. and M. Orlović. 1975 *Pidgin – German spoken by foreign workers in West Germany: the definite article*. Paper presented at the International Congress on Pidgins and Creoles, Honolulu.

Giles, H. 1977 Social psychology and applied linguistics: toward an integrative approach. *ITL* 35; 27–42.

Glattauer, W. 1978 *Strukturelle Lautgeographie der Mundarten im Südöstlichen Niederösterreich und in den angrenzenden Gebieten des Burgenlandes und der Steiermark* (=*Schriften zur deutschen Sprache in Österreich*). Vienna.

Gloy, K. 1974 *Sprachnormen: Probleme ihre Analyse und Legitimation*. Konstanz.

Bibliography

1978 Ökologische Aspekte der Dialekt-Verwendung. Ein Beitrag zur neuen Dialektwelle. In U. Ammon *et al* (eds.), *Grundlagen einer dialektorientierten Sprachdidaktik: theoretische empirische Beiträge in einem vernachlässigten Schulproblem.* Weinheim; 73–91.

1980 Behördliche Sprachregelungen gegen und für eine sprachliche Gleichbehandlung von Frauen und Männern. *LB* 69; 22–36.

Goeppert, H.C. (ed.). 1977 *Sprachverhalten im Unterricht.* Munich.

Graf, R. 1977 *Der Konjunktiv in gesprochener Sprache.* Tübingen.

Grebe, P. 1968 Sprachnorm und Sprachwirklichkeit. In Moser (1968); 28–44.

Gregor, B. 1983 *Genuszuordnung.* Tübingen.

Greiner, U. 1982 Gezielte Flucht. *Die Zeit.* 17 December 1982. 50; 17–18.

Grimm, J. and W. 1854–1961 *Deutsches Wörterbuch.* 16 vols. Leipzig.

Grimminger, R. 1972 Kaum aufklärender Konsum. In Rucktäschel (1972); 15–68.

Guentherodt, I. 1979 Berufsbezeichnungen für Frauen. Problematik der deutschen Sprachen im Vergleich mit Beispielen aus dem Englischen und Französischen. In *OBST,* Beihefte 3; 120–32.

Guggenberger, G. 1979 Die Kulturrevolution der Bürgerinitiativen. *Frankfurter Allgemeine Zeitung,* 29 September 1979; 1.

Gustafsson, L. 1978 *Die Allemande.* In Buch (1978); 73–81.

Gutfleisch, I. and B.-O. Rieck. 1981 Immigrant workers (Gastarbeiter) in West Germany: teaching programmes for adults and children. In J. Megarry, S. Nisbet and E. Hoyle (eds.), *Education of Minorities.* London; 341–58.

Hain, M. 1951 *Sprichwort und Volkssprache.* Gießen.

Halliday, M.A.K. 1978 *Language as a social semiotic: the social interpretation of language and meaning.* Baltimore.

Hammarberg, B. and Λ. Viberg. 1977 The place-holder constraint, language typology and the teaching of Swedish to immigrants. *Studia Linguistica* **31**, 2; 106–63.

Hard, G. 1966 *Zur Mundartgeographie.* Düsseldorf.

Hartung, W. and H. Schönfeld (eds.). 1981 *Kommunikation und Sprachvariation.* Berlin.

Hartung, W. *et al* (eds.). 1974 *Sprachliche Kommunikation und Gesellschaft.* Berlin.

(eds.) 1977a *Normen in der Sprachlichen Kommunikation.* Berlin.

1977b Zum Inhalt des Normbegriffs in der Linguistik. In Hartung (1977a); 9–69.

Hasselberg, J. 1972 Die Abhängigkeit des Schülererfolgs vom Einfluß des Dialekts. *Muttersprache* 82; 201–23.

1976a *Dialekt-Hochsprache Kontrastiv: Hessisch.* Düsseldorf.

1976b *Dialekt- und Bildungschancen.* Weinheim.

1981 Mundart als Schulproblem. In R. Schanze (ed.), *Sprache in Hessen.* Gießen; 29–55.

Haugen, E. 1966 *Language conflict and language planning: the case of modern Norwegian.* Cambridge.

Heidelberger Forschungsprojekt. 1975 *Sprache und Kommunikation ausländischer Arbeiter*. Kronberg.

1976 *Untersuchung zur Erlernung des Deutschen durch ausländische Arbeiter*. Heidelberg.

1978 *Zur Erlernung des Deutschen durch ausländische Arbeiter: Wortstellung und ausgewählte lexikalisch-semantische Aspekte*. (Mimeo) Frankfurt a.M.

Hein, V. and P. 1980 Dialekt und Hochsprache im Deutschunterricht. *LB* 65; 37–50.

Heller, K. 1966 *Das Fremdwort*. Leipzig.

Hellinger, M. 1980 Zum Gebrauch weiblicher Berufsbezeichnungen im Deutschen – Variabilität als Ausdruck außersprachlicher Machtstrukturen. *LB* 69; 37–58.

Hellmann, M. 1973 Wortschatzdifferenzen und Verständigungsprobleme. Frage bei der Erforschung der sprachlichen Situation in Ost und West. In M. Hellmann (ed.), *Zum öffentlichen Sprachgebrauch in der Bundesrepublik Deutschland und in der DDR*. Düsseldorf; 126–45.

1978 Sprache zwischen Ost und West – Überlegungen zur Wortschatzdifferenzierung zwischen BRD und DDR und ihren Folgen. In W. Kühlwein and G. Radden (eds.), *Sprache und Kultur: Studien zu Diglossie, Gastarbeiterproblematik und Kultureller Integration*. Tübingen 1978; 15–54.

Helmers, H. 1971 *Sprache und Humor des Kindes*. Stuttgart.

Henne, H. 1980 Jugendsprache und Jugendgespräche. In P. Schröder and H. Steger (eds.) *Dialogforschung* (= *Jahrbuch 1980 des Instituts für deutsche Sprache*). Düsseldorf; 370–84.

Herrmann-Winter, R. 1974 Auswirkungen der sozialistischen Produktionsweise in der Landwirtschaft auf der sprachlichen Kommunikation in den Nordbezirken der Deutschen Demokratischen Republik. In Ising (1974b); 135–90.

1977 Soziolinguistische Aspekte empirischer Erhebungen zum sprachlichen Varianz. In Hartung (1977a); 209–46.

1979 *Studien zur gesprochenen Sprache im Norden der DDR*.

Heuwagen, M. 1974 *Die Verbreitung des Dialekts in der Bundesrepublik Deutschland*. Staatsexamenarbeit (unpublished). Bonn.

Heym, E. 1979 *Collin*. Gütersloh.

Hoffmann, F. 1969 *Das Luxemburgische im Unterricht*. Luxembourg.

1979 *Sprachen in Luxemburg*. Wiesbaden and Luxembourg.

1981 *Zwischenland*. Hildesheim.

Hoffmann, L. 1980 Zur Pragmatik von Erzählformen vor Gericht. In K. Ehlich (ed.), *Erzählen vom Alltag*. Frankfurt a.M.; 28–63.

Hofmann, E. 1963 Sprachsoziologische Untersuchung über den Einfluß der Stadtsprache auf mundartsprechende Arbeiter. *Marburger Universitätsbund*; 201–81.

Hoppenkamps, H. 1977 *Information oder Manipulation? Untersuchungen zur Zeitungsberichterstattung über eine Debatte des Deutschen Bundestages*. Tübingen.

Hornung, M. 1968 Sprachpflege in Österreich. In Moser (1968); 215–19.

House, J. 1979 Interaktionsnormen in deutschen und englischen Alltagsdialogen. *LB* 59; 76–90.

House, J. and G. Kasper. 1981 Politeness markers in English and German. In F. Coulmas (ed.) *Conventional Routine*. The Hague; 157–86.

Hughes, E.C. 1972 The linguistic division of labour in industrial and urban societies. In J.A. Fishman (ed.), *Advances in the Sociology of Language* Vol. 2. The Hague; 296–309.

Humboldt, W. 1830–5 *Über die Verschiedenheit des menschlichen Sprachbaues und ihren Einfluß auf die geistige Entwicklung des Menschengeschlechtes*. Berlin.

Hutterer, C.J. 1978 Der Standarddialekt von Graz in Vergangenheit und Gegenwart. In W. Steinbock (ed.), *850 Jahre Graz*; 323–54.

Hyltenstam, K. 1977 Implicational patterns in interlanguage syntax variation. *Language Learning* 27; 383–411.

Hymes, D. 1974 *Foundations in Sociolinguistics: an ethnographic approach*. Philadelphia.

Inter Nationes. 1979 Erster 'Sprachatlas' wurde fertiggestellt. *Bildung und Wissenschaft*. **10**, 11:135.

1980 *Prozeduren Programme Profile: die Bundesrepublik Deutschland wählt am 5. October 1980 den Deutschen Bundestag*. Mainz.

Ising, G. 1974a Struktur und Funktion der Sprache in der gesamtgesellschaftlichen Entwicklung. In Ising (1974b); 9–35.

(ed.) 1974b *Aktuelle Probleme der sprachlichen Kommunikation. Soziolinguistische Studien zur sprachlichen Situation in der Deutschen Demokratischen Republik*. Berlin.

(ed.) 1977 *Sprachkultur – warum – wozu?* Berlin.

Jaene, H.D. 1981 Das gedachte Dach. Zwei Staatsbürgerschaften – eine deutsche Nation? *Die Zeit* 8; 20 February 1981; 5.

Jäger, K.H. 1982 Sprachliches Handeln von Schülern. *Deutsche Sprache* **2**, 82; 156–92.

Jäger, S. 1972 Sprachbarrieren und kompensatorische Erziehung: ein bürgerliches Trauerspiel. *LB* 19; 80–99.

1978 *'Warum weint die Giraffe?'* Kronberg.

Jakob, N. 1981 Sprachplanung in einer komplexen Diglossiesituation. *Language Problems and Language Planning* 5; 153–71.

Jespersen, O. 1922 *Language: its Nature, Development and Origin*. London.

Jungk, R. 1977 *Der Atom-Staat*. Munich.

Kachru, B.B. 1981 American English and other Englishes. In C.A. Ferguson and S.B. Heath (eds.), *Language in the U.S.A.* Cambridge 1981; 21–43.

Kadan, A. and A. Pelinka. 1979 *Die Grundsatzprogramme der österreichischen Parteien*. St Pölten.

Kaiser, S. 1969–70 *Die Besonderheiten der deutschen Schriftsprache in der Schweiz* (2 vols.). Mannheim.

Kalverkämpfer, H. 1979 Die Frauen und die Sprache: eine Erwiderung auf S. Trömel-Plötz 'Linguistik und Frauensprache'. *LB* 62; 55–71.

Keller, R.E. 1961 *German Dialects.* Manchester.

1973 Diglossia in German-speaking Switzerland. *Manchester Library Bulletin.* **56**, 1.

1978 *The German Language.* London.

Keller, T. 1976 *The city dialect of Regensburg.* Hamburg.

Klann, G. 1975 *Aspekte und Probleme der linguistischen Analyse schichtenspezifischen Sprachgebrauchs.* Berlin.

1978 Sprache in der Psychoanalyse. *Stadium Linguistik* 5; 52–66.

Klappenbach, G. and W. Steinitz. 1976 *Wörterbuch der deutschen Gegenwartssprache.* Berlin.

Klaus, G. 1971 *Sprache der Politik.* Berlin.

Klein, W, and N. Dittmar. 1979 *Developing Grammars.* Berlin.

Klein, W. and D. Wunderlich (eds.). 1971 *Aspekte der Soziolinguistik.* Frankfurt a.M.

Kleinschmidt, G. 1972 Sprachvermögen und sozialer Status. In *Sprache–Brücke und Hindernis.* Munich; 99–110.

Klemperer, V. 1947 *LTI: Notizbuch eines Philologen.* Berlin.

Klieme, R.B. 1976 *Untersuchungen zum Verhältnis von Gesellschaftsformation, Nation und Sprache und seiner Behandlung in der Sprachwissenschaft der DDR* (dissertation). Berlin.

Kloss, H. 1978 *Die Entwicklung neuer germanischer Kultursprachen seit 1800* (2nd edition). Düsseldorf.

Koller, W. 1978 Angloamerikanismen in der DDR-Zeitungssprache. *DS* 4; 306–23.

König, W. (ed.). 1978 *dtv-Atlas zur deutschen Sprache.* 2nd edition. Munich.

Konrád, G. and I. Szélenyi. 1978 *Die Intelligenz auf dem Weg zur Klassen-Macht.* Frankfurt a.M.

Korlén, G. 1962 Zur Entwicklung der deutschen Sprache diesseits und jenseits des eisenen Vorhangs. *Sprache im technischen Zeitalter* 4; 259–80.

1964 *Das Aueler Protokoll – Deutsche Sprache im Spannungsfeld zwischen West und Ost.* Düsseldorf.

1973 Rezension zu: Duden Rechtschreibung der deutschen Sprache und der Fremdwörter, 17. Auflage, Mannheim. *Muttersprache* 67; 272–5.

Kristensson, G. 1977 *Angloamerikanische Einflüsse in DDR-Zeitungstexten.* Stockholm.

Kufner, H.L. 1961 *Strukturelle Grammatik der Münchener Stadtmundart.* Munich.

Kühn, P. 1980 Deutsche Sprache in der Schweiz. In Althaus, Henne and Wiegand (eds.) (1980); 531–6.

Kunert, G. 1966 *Verkündigung des Wetters: Gedichte.* Munich.

Kunze, K. 1978 *Die wunderbaren Jahre. Lyrik, Prosa, Dokumente* (ed. K. Corino). Frankfurt a.M.

Küpper, H. 1977 Die deutsche Schülersprache. *Wirkendes Wort* 27; 318–30.

Labov, W. 1966 *The social stratification of English in New York City.* Washington.

Bibliography

1969 the logic of non-standard English. *Georgetown Monographs on Language and Linguistics* 22; 1–22, 26–31.

1970 The study of language in its social context. In J.A. Fishman (ed.), *Advances in the Sociology of Language.* Vol. 1. The Hague 1971; 447–72.

1972 *Sociolinguistic Patterns.* Philadelphia.

Lakoff, R. 1975 *Language and Woman's Place.* New York.

Lattey, E.M. and B.D. Müller. 1976 Temporary language acquisition: migrant workers' speech in Germany. *Proceedings of the 4th International Congress of Applied Linguistics.* Stuttgart. 213–27.

Latzel, S. 1975 Perfekt und Präteritum in der deutschen Zeitungssprache. *Muttersprache* 85; 38–49.

Lehmann, H. 1972 *Russisch–deutsche Lehnbeziehung im Wortschatz offizieller Wirtschaftstexte der DDR (bis 1968).* Düsseldorf.

Lehrplan für die Primärschulen im Fürstentum Liechtenstein. n.d.

Leodolter, R. 1975 *Das Sprachverhalten von Angeklagten vor Gericht.* Kronberg.

Leopold, W.F. 1968 The decline of dialects. In J.A. Fishman (ed.), *Readings in the Sociology of Language.* The Hague; 340–64.

Lerchner, G. 1974 Zur Spezifik der Gebrauchsweise der deutschen Sprache in der DDR und ihrer gesellschaftlichen Determination. *Deutsch als Fremdsprache* 1; 259–65.

Lettau, R. 1978 Deutschland als Ausland. In Buch (1978); 116–22.

Lippert, H. 1978 Sprachliche Mittel in der Kommunikation im Bereich der Medizin. In Mentrup (1978); 84–99.

Loest, E. 1978 *Es geht seinen Gang oder Mühen in unserer Ebene.* Stuttgart.

Ludwig, K.D. 1977 Sportsprache und Sprachkultur. In Ising (ed.) (1977); 49–90.

Mackensen, L. 1952 *Deutsches Wörterbuch.* Laupheim.

Magenau, D. 1964 *Die Besonderheiten der deutschen Schriftsprache in Luxembourg und in den deutschsprachigen Teilen Belgiens.* Mannheim.

Maroldt, E. 1979 Anpassung des Letzebuergischen an das Industriezeitalter. Außersprachliche Faktoren des Sprachwandels und der Sprachtreue. *Dialektologie Heute: Festschrift für Hélène Palgen.* Luxembourg.

Mattheier, K.J. 1980 *Pragmatik und Soziologie der Dialekte.* Heidelberg.

Meisel, J. 1975 Ausländerdeutsch und Deutsch ausländischer Arbeiter: zur möglichen Entstehung eines Pidgin in der BRD. *LiLi* 5, 18; 9–53.

1977 The language of foreign workers in Germany. In C. Molony, H. Zobl and W. Stölting (eds.), *Deutsch im Kontakt mit anderen Sprachen.* Kronberg; 184–212.

Mentrup, W. 1978 *Fachsprache und Gemeinsprache.* Düsseldorf.

1979 *Die gemäßigte Kleinschreibung: Diskussion einiger Vorschläge zu ihrer Regelung und Folgerungen.* Mannheim.

1980 Deutsche Sprache in Österreich. In Althaus, Henne and Wiegand (eds.) (1980); 527–31.

Meyers Lexikon. 1973 Leipzig.

Meyer-Ingwersen, J., R. Neumann and M. Kummer. 1977 *Zur Sprachentwick-klung türkischer Schüler in der Bundesrepublik*. Kronberg.

Mitchell, A.G. and A. Delbridge. 1965 *The speech of Australian adolescents*. Sydney.

Mittelberg, E. 1967 *Wortschatz und Syntax ber Bild-Zeitung*. Marburg.

Morain, G. 1979 The Cultoon. *Canadian Modern Language Review* **35**, 4; 676–96.

Moser, H. 1961a *Deutsche Sprachgeschichte*. Stuttgart (4th edition).
1961b Umgangssprache: Überlegungen zu ihren Formen und ihrer Stellung. *ZMF* 19; 215–32.
1961c *Sprachliche Folgen der politischen Teilung Deutschlands* (= *Wirkendes Wort*, 3. Beiheft) Düsseldorf.
1962 *Sprachliche Folgen der politischen Teilung Deutschlands* (= *Wirkendes Wort*, 3. Beiheft). Düsseldorf.
1964 Sprachprobleme bei der Bundeswehr. *Muttersprache* 74; 129–33.
1967 Wohin steuert das heutige Deutsch? In H. Moser (ed.), *Satz und Wort im heutigen Deutsch* (= *Sprache der Gegenwart* 1).
(ed.). 1968 *Sprachnorm, Sprachpflege, Sprachkritik*. Düsseldorf.
(ed.). 1972 Sprachbarriere als linguistisches und soziales Problem. In Rucktäschel (1972); 195–222.
(ed.). 1979 *Studien zu Raum- und Sozialformen der deutschen Sprache in Geschichte und Gegenwart*. Berlin.
1980 Sprachnorm und Sprachentwicklung: zur Rolle sprachökonomischer Tendenzen in der heutigen deutschen Standardsprache. In *Meyers Enzyklopädisches Lexikon*. Mannheim; 333–7.

Moulton, W.G. 1962 What standard for diglossia? The case of German Switzerland. *Georgetown University Monograph Series on Language and Linguistics* 15; 133–44.

Mühlhäusler, P. 1981 Foreigner Talk: Tok Masta in New Guinea. *IJSL* 28; 93–114.

Müller-Marzohl, A. 1961 Das schweizerische Wortgut im Jubiläumsduden. *Sprachspiegel* **17**, 4; 97–113.

Nerius, D. 1975 *Untersuchungen zu einer Reform der deutschen Orthographie*. Berlin.

Nerius, D. and J. Scharnhorst. 1977 Sprachwissenschaftliche Grundlagen einer Reform der deutschen Rechtschreibung. In Ising (1977); 156–94.

Neske, F. and I. 1972 *Wörterbuch englischer und amerikanischer Ausdrücke in der deutschen Sprache*. Munich.

Neuland, E. 1975 *Sprachbarrieren oder Klassensprache? Untersuchungen zum Sprachverhalten im Vorschulalter*. Frankfurt a.M.

Neustupný, J. 1968 Some general aspects of 'language' problems and 'Language' policy in developing Societies. In J.A. Fishman, C.A. Ferguson and J. Das Gupta (eds.), *Language Problems of Developing Nations*. New York; 285–94.
1978 *Post-structural approaches to language: language theory in a Japanese context*. Tokyo.

Newton, G. 1979 *Einige Gedanken über Sprache und Geschäft. Dialektologie Heute: Festschrift für Hélène Palgen.* Luxembourg; 49–64.

Noelle, E. and E.P. Neumann. 1967 *Jahrbuch der öffentlichen Meinung 1965–7.* Allensbach.

1974 *Jahrbuch der öffentlichen Meinung 1965–7.* Allensbach.

Noelle-Neumann, E. 1977 *Allensbacher Jahrbuch der Demoskopie 1977.* Vienna.

Nüssler, O. 1979 Das Sprachreinigungsgesetz. P. Braun (ed.) *Fremdwort-Diskussion.* Munich; 186–9.

Oevermann, U. 1970 *Sprache und soziale Herkunft: ein Beitrag zur Analyse schichtenspezifischer Sozialisationsprozesse und ihrer Bedeutung für den Schulerfolg.* Frankfurt a.M.

Oksaar, E. 1976 *Berufsbezeichnungen im heutigen Deutsch* (= *Sprache der Gegenwart*, 25). Düsseldorf.

Opie, I. and P. 1959–67 *The lore and language of schoolchildren.* Oxford (1st and 2nd editions).

Oschlies, W. 1981 Ich glaub', mich nammt ein Rotkehlchen. *Muttersprache* 91; 185–95.

Osgood, C., G. Suci and P. Tannenbaum. 1957 *The measurement of meaning.* Urbana, Illinois.

Österreichisches Wörterbuch. 1979. Vienna

Panther, K.U. 1981 Einige typische indirekte sprachliche Handlungen im wissenschaftlichen Diskurs. In Bungarten (1981); 231–60.

Pelster, T. 1966 *Die Politische Rede im Western und Osten Deutschlands* (= *Wirkendes Wort*, 14. Beiheft). Düsseldorf.

1981 Deutsch im geteilten Deutschland. *Muttersprache* 91; 121–44.

Plenzdorf, U. 1973 *Die neuen Leiden des jungen W.* Rostock/Frankfurt a.M.

Polenz, P.v. 1954 *Die altenburgische Landschaft. Untersuchungen zur ostthüringischen Sprach- und Siedlungsgeschichte.* Tübingen.

1963 *Funktionsverben im heutigen Deutsch.* Düsseldorf.

1981 Über die Jargonisierung von Wissenschaftssprache und wider die Deagentivierung. In Bungarten (1981); 85–110.

Pomm, H.P., U. Mewes and H. Schüttler. 1974 Die Entwicklung der Rechtschreibleistung von Schulkindern unter Berücksichtigung von Reform. In Augst (1974); 59–78.

Pusch, L.F. 1980 Das Deutsche als Männersprache – Diagnose und Therapievorschläge. *LB* 69; 59–74.

Pusch, L.F., M. Hellinger, S. Trömel-Plötz and I. Guentherodt. 1980–1 Richtlinien zur Vermeidung sexistischen Sprachgebrauchs. *LB* 69; 15–21.

Radtke, I. 1978 Drei Aspekte der Dialektdiskussion. In U. Ammon (ed.), *Grundlagen einer dialektorientierten Sprachdidaktik: theoretische und empirische Beiträge zu einem vernachlässigten Schulproblem.* Weinheim; 13–32.

Reich, H.H. 1968 *Sprache der Politik.* Munich.

Reiffenstein, I. 1973 Österreichisches Deutsch. In A. Haslinger (ed.), *Deutsch heute*. Munich.
1977 Sprachebene und Sprachwandel im österreichischen Deutsch der Gegenwart. In H. Kolb and H. Lauffer (eds.), *Sprachliche Interferenz: Festschrift für Werner Betz*. Tübingen; 159–174.

Rein, K.L. and M. Scheffelmann-Meyer. 1975 Funktion und Motivation des Gebrauchs von Dialekt und Hochsprache im Bayerischen. *ZDL* **42**, 3; 257–90.

Reitmajer, V. 1975 Schlechte Chancen ohne Hochdeutsch. *Muttersprache* 85; 310–24.

Resch, G. 1974 Soziolinguistisches zur Sprache von Pendlern. *Wiener Linguistische Gazette* 7; 38–47.

Rieck, B.O. and I. Senft. 1978 Situation of foreign workers in the Federal Republic. In Dittmar *et al* (1978); 85–98.

Riemschneider, E. 1963 *Veränderungen in der deutschen Sprache in der sowjetischbesetzten Zone seit 1945 (= Wirkendes Wort*, 4. Beiheft). Düsseldorf.

Ris, R. 1979 Dialekte und Einheitssprache in der deutschen Schweiz. *IJSL* 21; 41–62.

Rittenhauer, G. 1980 Österreichische Lektoren in aller Welt tätig. *Rot Weiß Rot* **28**, 1; 22.

Rizzo-Baur, H. 1962 *Die Besonderheiten der deutschen Schriftsprache in Österreich und Südtirol*. Mannheim.

Robinson, W.P. 1965 The elaborated code in working-class language. *Language and Speech* 8; 243–52.

Roche, R. 1973 Sprachliche Beobachtung bei der Lektüre der 'Prager Volkszeitung'. In M. Hellmann, *Zum öffentlichen Sprachgebrauch in der Bundesrepublik Deutschland und in der DDR*. Düsseldorf; 293–330.

Rohrer, C. 1973 *Der Konjunktiv im gesprochenen Schweizer Hochdeutschen*. Frauenfeld.

Römer, R. 1968 *Die Sprache der Anzeigenwerbung (= Sprache der Gegenwart* 4). Düsseldorf.

Roth, K.H. 1978 *'Deutsch'. Prolegomena zur neueren Wortgeographie (= Münchner germanistische Beitrage* 18). Munich.

Rucktäschel, A. 1972 *Sprache und Gesellschaft*. Munich.

Salinger, J. 1951 *Catcher in the rye*. London.

Samuel, R.H. and J.G. Hajdu. 1969 *The German-speaking countries of Central Europe*. Sydney.

Sapir, E. 1927 *Language*. New York.

SBZ von A bis Z. 1966 Bonn.

Schegloff, E.A., G. Jefferson and H. Sacks. 1974 A simplest systematics for the organisation of turn-taking for conversation. *Language* 50; 696–735.

Schenker, W. 1978 *Sprachliche Manieren – eine sprachsoziologische Erhebung im Raum Trier und Eiffel*. Basel.

Schildt, J. 1976 *Abriß der Geschichte der deutschen Sprache*. Berlin.

Bibliography

Schiller, J.C.F. v. *Musenalmanach für 1797*. Leipzig.

Schläpfer, R. 1979 Schweizerhochdeutsch und Binnendeutsch. Zur Problematik der Abgrenzung und Berücksichtigung schweizerischen und binnendeutschen Sprachgebrauchs in einem Wörterbuch für Schweizer Schüler. In A. Löffler, K. Pestalozzi and M. Stern (eds.), *Standard und Dialekt. Festschrift für Heinz Rupp*. Bern; 151–63.

Schlieben-Lange, B. and H. Weydt. 1978 Für eine Pragmatisierung der Dialektologie. *ZGL* 63; 257–82.

Schlobinski, P. 1982 Divided city – divided language? *Sociolinguistic Newsletter* 13; 21.

Schlobinski, P. and I. Wachs. Forthcoming. Forschungsprojekt 'Stadtsprache Berlin'. Sprachsoziologische Fragestellungen in einer Großstadt. *Deutsche Sprache*.

Schlomann, F.W. 1980 Trotzkisten – Europäische Arbeiterpartei – 'Maoisten'! *Aus Politik und Zeitgeschichte: Beilage zu Parlament*. B27/80 5 July 1980; 12–28.

Schlosser, H.D. 1981 Die Verwechslung der deutschen Nationalsprache mit einer lexikalischen Teilmenge. *Muttersprache* 91; 145–56.

Schmidt, W. 1972 Thesen zu dem Thema: 'Sprache und Nation'. *Zeitschrift für Phonetik, allgemeine Sprachwissenschaft und Kommunikationsforschung* 25; 448–50.

Schoenthal, G. 1976 *Das Passiv in der deutschen Standardsprache*. Munich.

Schönbohm, W., J.B. Runge and P. Radunski. 1968 *Die herausgeforderte Demokratie*. Mainz.

Schönfeld, H. 1974 Sprachverhalten und Sozialstruktur in einem sozialistischen Dorf der Altmark. In Ising (1974b); 191–283.

1977 Zur Rolle der sprachlichen Existenzformen in der sprachlichen Kommunikation. In Hartung (1977a); 163–208.

Schönfeld, H. and J. Donath. 1978 *Sprache im sozialistischen Industriebetrieb: Untersuchungen zum Wortschatz bei sozialen Gruppen*. Berlin.

Schönfeld, H. and R. Pape. 1981 Existenzformen. In Hartung and Schönfeld (1981); 130–213.

Schröder, G. 1972 *Außenpolitik für Deutschland*. (Rede auf dem Bundesparteitag der CDU, Wiesbaden, 10 Oktober 1972.)

Schumann, J.H. 1978 *The Pidginization Process: A model of Second Language Acquisition*. Rowley, Mass.

Schwarzenbach, R. 1969 *Die Stellung der Mundart in der deutschsprachigen Schweiz*. Frauenfeld.

Seidel, E. and I. Seidel-Slotty. 1961 *Sprachwandel im Dritten Reich: eine kritische Untersuchung faschistischer Einflüsse*. Halle.

Senft, G. 1982 *Sprachliche Varietät und Variation im Sprachverhalten Kaiserslautener Metallarbeiter*. Bern.

Siebs, T. 1969 *Deutsche Aussprache*. Berlin.

Sluga, W. 1977 Sprachsituation in geschlossenen Anstalten. *Dialekt. Internationale Halbjahresschrift für Mundartdichtung* 1. Vienna; 19–39.

Snow, C.E., R. Van Eeden and P. Muysken. 1981 The interactional origins of foreigner talk: municipal employees and foreign workers. *IJSL* 28; 81–92.

Spangenberg, K. 1963 Tendenzen volkssprachlicher Entwicklung in Thüringen. In H. Rosenkranz and K. Spangenberg (eds.), *Sprachsoziologische Studien in Thüringen*. Berlin; 54–85.

Spangenberg, K. and J. Wiese. 1974 Sprachwirklichkeit und Sprachverhalten sowie deren Auswirkungen auf Leistungen auf muttersprachlichen Unterricht der Allgemeinbildenden Polytechnischen Oberschule. In Ising (1974b); 285–337.

Spender, D. 1980 *Man-made Language*. London.

Spiegel, Der. 1978a 'Wer BRD sagt, richtet Unheil an.' *Der Spiegel* **32**, 39; 13 November 1978; 36–44.

1978b Etwas anderes als sex. *Der Spiegel* **32**, 50; 11 November 1978.

1980 Wieder auf Null. *Der Spiegel* **34**, 8; 11 February 1980; 41–6.

1981 'Sagen Sie gerne du zu mir.' *Der Spiegel* **35**, 53; 28 December 1981; 34–41.

Steger, H. (ed.). 1971 Soziolinguistik. In *Sprache und Gesellschaft* (= *Sprache der Gegenwart* 13). Düsseldorf; 9–44.

Stellmacher, D. 1977 *Studien zur gesprochenen Sprache in Niedersachsen* (= *Deutsche Dialektographie*, Vol. 82). Marburg.

Sternberger, D., G. Storz and W.E. Süsskind. 1945 Aus dem Wörterbuch des Unmenschen 1945–8. In *Die Wandlung* 1957. Hamburg.

Stölting, W. 1975 Wie die Ausländer sprechen. Eine jugoslawische Familie. *LiLi* **5**, 18; 54–67.

1978 Teaching German to immigrant children. In Dittmar *et al* (1978); 99–109.

1980 *Die Zweisprachigkeit jugoslawischer Schüler in der Bundesrepublik*. Wiesbaden.

Strauß, F.J. 1980 *Mit aller Kraft für Deutschland*. (Rede vor dem CSU-Parteitag am 29. September 1979 in München.) Cologne.

Stroh, F. 1952 *Handbuch der germanischen Philologie*. Berlin.

Studer, E. 1963 Zur schweizerischen Ortographiekonferenz. *Neue Zürcher Zeitung*, 26 October 1963; 4.

Süsskind, W.E. 1968 Gedanken zur Sprachpflege. In Moser (1968); 191–203.

Tages-Anzeiger Magazin. 1980 'Bio-logisch'. T.-A. M 19; 10 May 1980; 6–14.

Tatzreiter, H. 1978 Norm und Varietät in Ortsmundarten. *ZDL* 44; 133–48.

Taylor, B. 1978 German as a source of American prestige forms entering Australian English. *Talanya* 5; 1–4.

'Thaddäus Troll' (= Bayer, H.). 1970 *Deutschland deine Schwaben*. Reinbeck bei Hamburg.

Thorne, B. and N. Henley (eds.). 1975 *Language and sex: difference and dominance*. Rowley, Mass.

Trömel-Plötz, S. 1978a Linguistik und Frauensprache. *LB* 57; 49–68.

1978b Zur Semantik psychoanalytischer Interventionen. *Studium Linguistik* 5; 52–66.

Trudgill, P. 1974 *The social differentiation of English in Norwich*. Cambridge.

Turner, I. 1969 *Cinderella dressed in Yella*. Melbourne.

Urbánova, A. 1966 Zum Einfluß des amerikanischen Englisch auf die deutsche Gegenwartssprache. *Muttersprache* 76; 91–114.

Van den Branden, L. 1956 *Het Streven naar Verheerlijking, Zuivering en Opbouw van het Nederlands in de 16de Eeuw*. Gent.

Verdoodt, A. 1968 *Zweisprachige Nachbarn*. Vienna/Stuttgart.

Viereck, W. (ed.). 1980a *Studien zum Einfluß der englischen Sprache auf das Deutsche*. Tübingen.

1980b Empirische Untersuchungen insbesondere zum Verständnis und Gebrauch von Anglizismen im Deutschen. In Viereck (1980a); 237–321.

Viereck, W. *et al.* 1975 Wie Englisch ist unsere Pressesprache? *Grazer Linguistische Studien* 2; 205–26.

Wahrig, G. 1968 *Deutsches Wörterbuch*. Gütersloh.

Walter, M. 1978 *Englische Wörter im Wortschatz deutscher Jugendlichen*. Staatsexamen thesis. University of Stuttgart.

Weigel, H. 1968 *O du mein Österreich*. Munich.

Weisgerber, L. 1962 *Grundzüge der Inhaltbezogenen Grammatik*. Düsseldorf.

Whinnom, K. 1971 Linguistic hybridization and the 'special case' of pidgins and creoles. In D.H. Hymes (ed.) *Pidginization and Creolization of Languages*. Cambridge; 91–116.

Whorf, B.L. 1956 *Language, Thought and Reality*. Cambridge, Mass.

Wodak-Leodolter, R. and W. Dressler. 1978 Phonological variation in colloquial Viennese. Michigan. *Germanic Studies* 4, 1; 30–66.

1980 Problemdarstellungen in gruppentherapeutischen Situationen. In K. Ehlich (ed.), *Erzählen im Alltag*. Frankfurt a.M.; 179–208.

Wolfsberger, H. 1967 *Mundartwandel im 20. Jahrhundert, dargestellt an Ausschnitten aus dem Sprachleben der Gemeinde Stäfa*. Frauenfeld.

Wörner, M. 1972 *Friedenspolitik in Sicherheit und Freiheit*. (Rede auf dem Bundesparteitag der CDU, Wiesbaden, 10. Oktober 1972.)

Yngve, V. 1960 A model and an hypothesis for language structure. *Proceedings of the American Philosophical Society* 104; 444–66.

Zandvoort, R.W. 1964 *English in the Netherlands: a study in linguistic infiltration*. Groningen.

Zeit, Die. 1981 Die Elbe – ein deutscher Strom, nicht Deutschlands Grenze (Günter Gaus interviewt von C.C. Kaiser, H. Rudolph und T. Sommer). *Die Zeit*, 6 February 1981; 53.

Zimmer, R. 1977 Vergleichende Betrachtungen zum deutsch–französischen Kontaktbereich in der Schweiz, im Elsaß und in Luxemburg. *ZDL* 44; 145–57.

Zoller, W. 1974 Meinungen zur Rechtschreibung und Rechtschreibreform: Ergebnisse einer Umfrage. In Augst (1974); 91–116.

Index of topics

Index of topics

Index of names

Note: f = footnote

Index of names

Index of names